Cities of America

Cities of
America

Eric Inglefield

Greenwich House

Author's acknowledgements
The author wishes to acknowledge the generous assistance provided by the various city Convention and Visitors Bureaus and other organizations in the United States in the compilation of this book.

Photographic acknowledgements
Aerial Photography Services, Inc./James F. Doane, Charlotte 48-49; J. Allan Cash Photolibrary, London 31 right, 103, 169, 200, 201; H. Armstrong Roberts Inc., Philadelphia 13, 14, 15, 21, 24, 25, 28-29, 32, 33, 35 bottom, 37, 43, 45, 46, 52-53, 54, 56, 57, 59, 66, 71, 82, 83, 87, 88, 89, 96, 99 bottom, 100, 106, 107 bottom, 110-111, 112 top, 118 right, 124, 127 top, 128, 130-131, 135 top, 139, 140-141, 143, 146-147, 152, 153, 154-155, 163, 164, 164-165 right, 168, 171 top, 174, 176, 177, 179, 186, 187, 192, 197, 198-199, 209, 211, 212, 214-215, 222, 223, 233, 237, 238, 239, 242-243, 244, 245, 250; Cincinnati Convention and Visitors Bureau 61; Bruce Coleman, London 94, 148, Colorific, London 34, 39, 63, 85 left; Greater Houston Convention and Visitors Council 97; Greater Milwaukee Convention and Visitors Bureau 136; Robert Harding Picture Library, London 16, 64-65, 92, 189, 247; Angelo Hornak, London 38, 230; The Image Bank, London and New York 31 left, 47, 85 right, 95, 99 top, 171 bottom, 194 top, 220; Indianapolis Motor Speedway Corporation, Indiana 104 top (Dave Willoughby), 104 bottom (Ron McQueeney); Eric Inglefield, London 75, 78, 80 bottom, 112, 113, 217 left, 227, 253; Kos Photos, Surrey 231 right; Louisville Convention and Visitors Bureau 125; Metropolitan Dade County Department of Tourism, Miami 133; Photo Source/Colour Library International, London 6, 8-9, 40, 90, 91, 129, 145, 149, 194 bottom, 195, 206-207, 226, 229, 251 top; Photri, Virginia 20, 26, 27, 41, 58, 68-69, 251 bottom, 252; Picturepoint, London 74; Rex Features, London 127 bottom; Tony Stone Associates, London 93, 190; Syndication International, London 119; Vision International, London and New York 115, 135 bottom, 137; Zefa, London 10, 11, 17, 18, 19, 23, 35 top, 36, 55, 72-73, 80 top, 107 top, 109, 116-117, 118 left, 121, 122, 151, 156, 157, 159, 160-161, 162, 165 right, 173, 180, 184-185, 203, 204-205, 216, 217 right, 218, 219, 224, 231 left, 232, 235, 248-249

Front cover: San Francisco, City and Bay Bridge at night (Photo Source/Colour Library International, London)
Back Cover: New York City, a street in Chinatown, Lower East Side (Photo Source/Colour Library International, London)
Endpapers: Las Vegas, Nevada (Susan Lund, Buckinghamshire)
Titlespread: New York City, view from the Empire State Building (Photo Source/Colour Library International, London)

First English edition published by
Deans International Publishing
52-54 Southwark Street, London SE1 1UA
A division of The Hamlyn Publishing Group Limited
London · New York · Sydney · Toronto

This 1984 edition published by Greenwich House
a division of Arlington House, Inc.
Distributed by Crown Publishers, Inc.

ISBN 0-517-439328

h g f e d c b a

Printed in Italy

Contents

Introduction

We will neglect our cities to our peril, for in neglecting them we neglect the nation.

John F. Kennedy, Message to the U.S. Congress, January 30, 1962.

The idea implicit in John F. Kennedy's assertion — that a nation's cities are a measure of the health of its civilization, indicating both its material prosperity and its social values — is not a new one. Many writers and thinkers over the centuries have stressed that cities must be regarded as gatherings of people rather than as clusters of buildings. As one eighteenth-century writer declared, " 'Tis the men, not the houses, that make the city." With this notion in mind, a look at American cities is particularly fascinating, since they are essentially the creations of peoples whose origins lay in other parts of the world and so reflect varying ideas about urban living held by different cultures at different times in history.

The earliest permanent communities in America, those established by Pueblo and other Indian peoples in the Southwest, were small adobe villages built predominantly in defensive locations, the best known including Mesa Verde in Colorado and Acoma in New Mexico. Although impressive to the first Spanish explorers in the region in the sixteenth century, none of these could, however, compare with the great cities built by the Aztecs and other indigenous peoples elsewhere in the Americas. The seeds of cities as we know them today in the United States were to be planted by the Spanish, French, English, Dutch, and other European colonists who established themselves in North America during the seventeenth and eighteenth centuries.

For their colonization of the Southwest and West, the Spaniards adopted a system of military garrisons (*presidios*), missions, and ranches, around which grew small villages (*pueblos*) in the characteristic adobe style of architecture. From these simple beginnings arose such great modern cities as Albuquerque, Los Angeles, San Antonio, San Diego, and San Francisco.

The French, more interested in commerce than in founding permanent settlements in their Mississippi Valley and Great Lakes territories, established fur-trading posts and military garrisons that formed the nucleus of such later cities as Chicago, Detroit, and Pittsburgh. New Orleans and St. Louis, however, were conceived from the start as key river ports servicing French trading activities and were accordingly laid out as viable communities.

The English founded their colonies along the Atlantic seaboard, where their original stockaded villages were followed by planned settlements with houses arranged around common lands and surrounded by farmland. The brick-built architecture they adopted reflected English styles of the time, elegant examples of which embellished such historic cities as Boston, Charleston (South Carolina), Hartford, Philadelphia, Providence, and Savannah, with a particularly fine collection remaining today in the colonial capital of Williamsburg, Virginia. In 1664, the English ousted the Dutch from their colony of New Netherland, which had been established along the east coast between Connecticut and Delaware. To their American settlements the Dutch, too, had brought their own distinctive style of domestic

A glorious model for statehouses across the nation, the United States Capitol, in Washington, D.C., also serves as a symbol of democracy and liberty not only for Americans but also for oppressed peoples around the world.

7

Freeways that speed traffic in and out of the central business district are a necessity for all but the smallest American cities. The huge metropolis of Houston, Texas, has such a network, although traffic congestion and resulting air pollution still present problems for the city's planners.

architecture. Among them was New Amsterdam, their most important community, which became a flourishing port at the tip of present-day Manhattan in New York.

As the European colonial powers finally lost control of their principal territories on the American mainland during the late eighteenth and early nineteenth centuries – the English in 1783, the French in 1803, and the Spanish in 1821 – the new United States embarked on a policy of westward expansion, spurred by Americans' belief that it was their "manifest destiny," and emerged as a nation spanning the entire continent from the Atlantic to the Pacific. Settlements sprouted across the virgin land as the Indians were gradually pushed out of their homelands by the inexorable advance of the pioneers, reinforced by military power.

Some of the cities that took root in the wilderness during those years – among them Des Moines, Minneapolis, and Nashville – were founded as clusters of huts huddled for protection near military forts, while others, such as Dallas and Kansas City, grew around pioneer trading posts. Rivers

were another important factor in the location of the new settlements, many of which – Cincinnati, Louisville, Memphis, and Omaha, for instance – were established as ports or crossing points along the rivers of the Mississippi Valley and the Great Plains. And in the drier Southwest, riverside sites provided water supplies for the first settlers of Austin, Las Vegas, Phoenix, and other cities. Some settlements – later becoming such cities as Atlanta, Buffalo, Chicago, and Cleveland – developed as transportation centers along the main overland and Great Lakes routes across the country. Fort Worth, like Dodge City, was one of those raw cowboy communities that blossomed along the famed cattle trails between the great ranches of Texas and the railheads of Kansas. Everywhere, the arrival of the railroads, as they pushed relentlessly through the plains and mountains of the continent in the latter half of the nineteenth century, was a spur to the growth of small communities in isolated locations; without the railroad, such cities as Miami and Las Vegas would never have grown as they did.

Not all the pioneer communities, however, survived the early years of

No longer regarded automatically as suitable for demolition, elaborately ornamented Victorian houses, built last century in cities across the whole country, are today prized by many proud owners and often beautifully restored to their original condition. In some cities, such as San Francisco, there are whole streets that are lined with such houses on their original sites, while in others, among them Houston and San Diego, houses threatened by the wrecker's ball have been rescued and relocated in museum parks.

westward expansion. The West, in particular, is littered with ghost towns that are silent reminders of those feverish days when prospectors and miners flooded into the wilderness in response to dramatic discoveries of gold, some of which either were wildly overexaggerated or soon ran out. One of the mining towns that did survive was Denver, which, like the lumber port of Seattle and the iron-making community of Birmingham, succeeded in overcoming its original reliance on a single natural resource.

Many of the towns established during the years of westward migration were planned as speculative ventures by land companies or individual businessmen and laid out in the familiar grid of identical rectangular plots and straight streets, a layout often adopted because no one knew at the time to what use the land would be put. Such cities were Cleveland, Houston, and Portland (Oregon). Others, such as Columbus (Ohio) and Indianapolis, were specifically founded as prestigious capital cities by state authorities, while Washington, D.C., was the result of the need for a planned permanent national capital when the United States came into being after the Revolution. On a site beside the Potomac River chosen by George Washington, a deliberate compromise between the ambitions of the northern and the southern states, Pierre Charles L'Enfant planned his "city of magnificent vistas," an elegant creation that later found echoes in the layouts of Buffalo and Detroit.

From the English Georgian style of architecture favored in the

eighteenth century, architects of the nineteenth century moved on to the Greek Revival style, which they found particularly appropriate for grandiose public buildings, and to the more florid Gothic style for cathedrals and churches. Later in the century, architects of the so-called Chicago school – Louis Sullivan and others – set the scene with their steel-framed commercial buildings for the emergence of the magnificent sky-scrapers that now soar above city skylines across the nation.

Throughout the nineteenth century, America's population grew by leaps and bounds as large numbers of immigrants from Europe and the Orient entered the country, attracted by the promise of new opportunities. With their skills and their labor, they made great contributions to the nation's burgeoning industries, and with their distinctive national ways of life, they enriched its cultural heritage. Yet some Americans considered their tendency to group together, like the country's existing black population, in separate ethnic enclaves within each city as Italian-Americans, Polish-Americans and so on was not conducive to the creation of a single, fully integrated nation. The sentiment that prompted President Theodore Roosevelt to declare in 1915, "There is no room in this country for hyphenated Americanism," was echoed years later by the black writer James Baldwin, who, aware of the dangers of discrimination in such ethnic divisions, was in no doubt that "a ghetto can be improved in one way only: out of existence." Despite such objections, ethnic neighborhoods remain a feature

Rather than melting pots where immigrants from other countries have intermingled to become simply Americans, many cities in the United States have distinct ethnic communities that are proud to exert their collective identity. Neighborhoods where the population is, for example, predominantly Italian, Irish, Polish, or Chinese are common and add much to the cultural heritage of American cities.

of many American cities, although now there is an evident sense of pride in ethnic roots and in the contributions that each immigrant group has made to American society.

Others who made a notable impact on the American scene were the great industrial and railroad magnates, some of them immigrants themselves, who made their fortunes as the nation awoke to its formidable economic potential. In return, men like Andrew Carnegie and John D. Rockefeller made philanthropic donations of cultural and educational institutions, parks, recreational facilities, and other bequests to the cities where they were based. But such piecemeal gestures, although welcome, were no solution to the fundamental urban problems that were beginning to appear, particularly in the older industrial centers, where overcrowding, slums, poverty, pollution, crime, and exploitation by unscrupulous political "bosses" were creating unsavory living conditions.

With the emergence of the automobile and the development of highways and public-transit systems in the twentieth century, people were able to move out of the blighted inner-city areas into pleasanter suburbs, and as they did so, the central districts decayed even further. The trend was accelerated after World War II, when many saw the attractions of moving to the Sun Belt cities of the South, Southwest and West and thus caused a rapid population explosion in such places as Albuquerque, Dallas, Houston, Phoenix, and San Diego. The overall result of these migrations was a decline in the postwar populations of many northern industrial cities, nowhere more dramatic than in Buffalo, Cleveland, and Pittsburgh.

In recent years, considerable energy has been expended in order to reverse this trend. Indeed, urban renewal has been a priority for many city governments during the last 30 years or so, the initial impetus for action coming from the federal government's Housing Acts of 1949 and 1954, which encouraged local authorities to initiate slum-clearance and rehabilitation projects. As a result, spectacular improvements have been made to decayed inner-city areas across the country, with magnificent structures designed by such leading international architects as I. M. Pei and John Portman now gracing impressive city skylines. At the same time, many historic buildings that would have been torn down have been preserved and restored for future generations, their presence amid the bolder new structures providing many cities, such as Boston, Providence, and even New York, with exciting architectural contrasts as well as cultural treasures.

As old industrial eyesores disappear, cleaner high-technology enterprises are sprouting in metropolitan areas around many cities, helping to reduce industrial pollution and congestion on the expressways into central-city areas. With the improvements being made in these inner areas and the provision of attractive housing and better public services, people are being lured back to re-create vibrant communities in the heart of many of the older cities. Decayed buildings and warehouses have been given new life by turning them into sparkling boutiques, shopping malls, and chic restaurants; traffic-free pedestrian malls are attracting shoppers into downtown districts from the suburbs; and magnificent new hotels built with splendid atriums containing shops, restaurants, and everything the visitor may need are bringing life back to the once-dead city centers. Encouragement for such developments springs partly from the realization that tourism is an important source of city revenue, and the Convention and Visitors Bureaus in most major cities are always ready to provide visitors with well-documented guides and information.

Every American city, no matter how small, has something of interest to capture the attention of the most discerning of visitors. So, following the admonition of the Greek philosopher Aristotle that "a great city is not to be confounded with a populous one," the cities in this book have been selected not because of their size, but because each has something special to contribute to America's rich and colorful urban kaleidoscope.

Albuquerque NEW MEXICO

The Duke City

Opposite, bottom: Seen from a distance, the ancient Indian village of Acoma crouches like a medieval fortress atop a 357-foot rocky butte, overlooking the desert country of New Mexico west of Albuquerque. It was through this arid territory that the sixteenth-century Spanish explorers came in a vain search for the gold they believed lay hidden in the mythical Seven Cities of Cíbola.

Below: The beautiful church of San Felipe de Neri, in Albuquerque's colorful Old Town, has been remodeled and enlarged several times since its foundation as a small adobe chapel by the first Spanish settlers in the area in the early eighteenth century.

It is perhaps appropriate to begin a tour around the great cities of the United States in that part of the country where Spanish explorers became the first Europeans to come into contact with the age-old Indian cultures of the Southwest. Tales of the fabulous riches awaiting them in the harsh, arid plateaus of this region spurred Francisco Vázquez de Coronado to set off with a small army in 1540 in search of the mythical Seven Cities of Cíbola, which they never found. But they did come across Indian villages, among them Acoma, which one member of the expedition described as "a great city in the sky . . . the strongest position ever seen in the world." Perched atop a 357-foot (109 m) rocky butte, this natural fortress remained unconquered until some 60 years later, when the Spaniards stormed it and massacred many of the inhabitants. Now almost 1,000 years old, the village is still inhabited and is a constant source of wonder to the many visitors who drive out here from the city of Albuquerque some 60 miles to the east.

Albuquerque, the largest city in New Mexico, was founded by the Spaniards, although not until 1706, when a group of colonists established a settlement among the cottonwoods on the east bank of the Rio Grande, a meandering river that often dried up completely in summer, only to become a raging torrent after thunderstorms. Here they built their church, San Felipe de Neri, with several adobe houses clustered together for protection around its small plaza. They named their little village in honor of Don Francisco Cuervo y Valdez, thirteenth duke of Alburquerque, although the first *r* in the name was later dropped.

From a trading center along the historic Chihuahua and Santa Fe trails into Mexico, Albuquerque developed into a distribution point for the military forts established in the Southwest to protect American migrants who were moving into the area after the 1850s. A separate community took root by the railroad depot built 2 miles to the east of the Old Town of Albuquerque in 1880, but it was not long before the two merged. Today, Albuquerque has a population of 320,000 and is one of America's fastest-growing cities. It spreads around the junction of Interstates 25 and 40 across the broad Rio Grande valley, especially on the eastern side, where the suburbs lap against the steep slopes of the Sandia Mountains, which rise to 10,678 feet (3,257 m) at Sandia Crest.

Over its expanse of 100 square miles, Albuquerque varies in altitude between around 4,800 feet (1,464 m) along the Rio Grande and 6,500 feet (1,983 m) along the edge of the mountains, with resulting variations in weather even from one part of the city to another. In general, however, the climate is dry, mild, and sunny, with average temperatures ranging between 48°F (9°C) in January and 90°F (32°C) in July. Tourism is consequently a major industry in Albuquerque, which offers not only sightseeing attractions, but also a wide assortment of outdoor recreational and sporting activities. As well as a health resort, Albuquerque is a university city and a center of nuclear and electronics research, with a variety of associated businesses.

The city's cultural atmosphere thus blends the nuclear age with the colorful legacy of its Indian, Spanish, and Mexican past. It is a city of Indian ceremonies and exquisite crafts, of Spanish adobe architecture and poetic place names, of Mexican food and music – a potpourri for the senses presented with all the comforts and conveniences of twentieth-century America. And adding spice to this heady mixture are countless festivals and events, such as the New Mexico State Fair in September, the Hot Air Balloon Fiesta in October, and the Fiesta Encantada and Luminaria celebrations in December.

The historic Old Town, where the city began, retains its Spanish atmosphere around the plaza of the San Felipe de Neri church, where the restored adobe buildings are occupied by thriving curio and craft shops and excellent restaurants. Indian arts and crafts are also displayed at the Indian

Albuquerque
1 *Indian Pueblo Cultural Center*
2 *Albuquerque Little Theater*
3 *Rio Grande Zoo*
4 *Albuquerque Museum*
5 *University of New Mexico*
6 *National Atomic Museum*

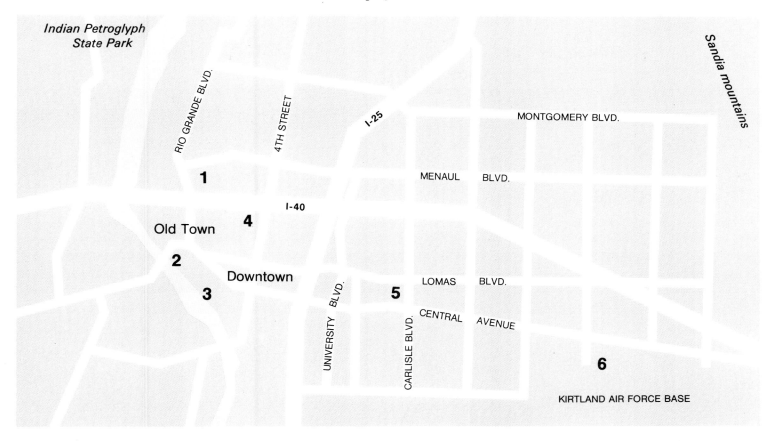

Albuquerque's Indian heritage is clearly evident in the colorful decoration, projecting beams and adobe forms used in the construction of the Theater Albuquerque.

Pueblo Cultural Center not far away, where visitors can attend dance and theater performances and films. One of the city's best theater groups stages productions at the well-known Albuquerque Little Theater a short way to the south, where a string of new parks along the river provides a pleasant setting for the Rio Grande Zoo. In the area, too, are the Albuquerque Museum, with its changing exhibits of art, science, and history, and the interesting Museum of Natural History.

To the east of the Old Town, between Lomas and Central, a loose cluster of high-rise hotels and office buildings marks the downtown district just west of Interstate 25. Among the buildings here are Albuquerque's City Hall, Civic Auditorium, Public Library, and Convention Center, and the excellent shops along Central Avenue. Albuquerque has, in addition, many fine shopping centers scattered throughout the city, with the vast Coronado and Winrock centers close together on the east side of town.

East of downtown, too, is the adobe-style University of New Mexico, whose campus contains many sports facilities and cultural institutions of interest to the visitor. Among these are Popejoy Hall, which hosts symphony concerts and performances of opera, musicals, plays, and dance; the Maxwell Museum of Anthropology, with its fine exhibits on the southwestern Indians; the fascinating Geology Museum; and the Fine Arts Center, which houses a wide-ranging collection of art. Another of the city's fine museums, the awesome National Atomic Museum, is located at the Kirtland Air Force Base in the eastern suburbs, and here you can trace the dramatic story of the atomic bomb and see a collection of nuclear weapons.

Breath-taking views overs the surrounding country await the sightseer who rides the 2.7 miles up the rugged west face of Sandia Crest on the thrilling Sandia Peak Tram, the longest cable-car ride in the United States. The forested Sandia Mountains are a recreational paradise that provides opportunities for picnicking, trail riding, hunting, and winter skiing. Evidence has been found in a cave in the slopes that people lived in the area as many as 20,000 years ago.

Around Albuquerque, there are colorful old gold-mining towns – such as Madrid, Golden, and Cerrillos – numerous Indian pueblos, Spanish missions, and such special places as the Gran Quivira National Monument, the Coronado State Monument, and Indian Petroglyph State Park – all of which reflect the rich cultural heritage of this beautiful and historic part of America.

Anchorage ALASKA

Gateway to Alaska

Anyone wishing to escape from the pressures of modern city life could do no better than to head north to America's "Last Frontier," the state of Alaska, where the city of Anchorage stands at the gateway to a breath-taking scenic wilderness that offers an astonishing choice of unusual things to do and see. Located on the state's wild southern coast, where the long Cook Inlet wraps two arms of water – the Knik and the Turnagain – around a grassy peninsula, Anchorage is surrounded by rugged snow-capped mountains, dark forests, awesome glaciers, and a coastline of deeply cut fjords, which together make up a natural paradise teeming with wildlife. Contradicting the widely held notion that Alaska is an Arctic wasteland covered in perpetual ice, the southern coastlands are warmed by the waters of the Japanese Current so that temperatures rise into the 70s (20s°C) during the short summers.

When Captain James Cook sailed into the inlet in 1778, Russian traders and missionaries already had established contact with the local Tanaina Indians, and it was from Russia that the American government purchased the territory of Alaska, now the country's largest state, for $7.2 million in

Dog sledding is a popular winter activity in the Anchorage area. The World Championship Sled Dog Race is one of the exciting events held during the Fur Rendezvous carnival every February, and is followed by the gruelling 1,049-mile Iditarod race to Nome a few weeks later.

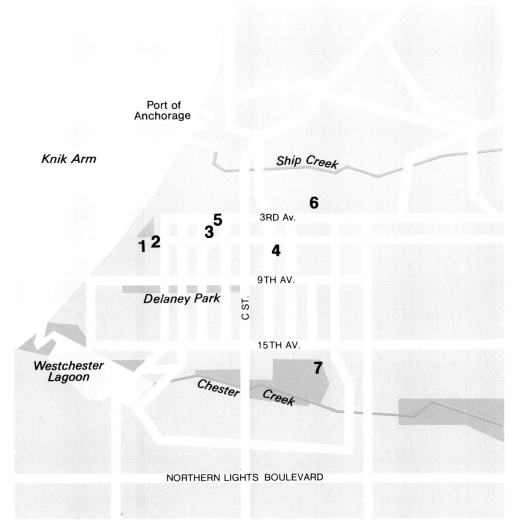

Anchorage
1 Resolution Park
2 Oscar Anderson House
3 Performing Arts Complex
4 Historical and Fine Arts Museum
5 Old Federal Building
6 Pioneer Schoolhouse
7 George M. Sullivan Sports Arena

1867. As later events proved, this was surely the best real-estate deal in history, for the state has yielded rich treasures of gold, oil, and natural gas.

Gold was first found to the south of present-day Anchorage in 1888, and mines opened up here and in the interior, culminating in the celebrated gold rush to the Canadian Klondike in 1897. When work began on a railroad from the coast to the inland community of Fairbanks in 1914, a tent city sprang up by the anchorage used by supply ships on Ship Creek, which ran into Cook Inlet. Soon wood-framed houses and two- and three-story buildings mushroomed over a well-planned grid of streets that was known simply as Anchorage, with a capital *A*. Incorporated as a city in 1920, Anchorage began to grow rapidly during World War II, when Elmendorf Airfield was built; a further surge in its prosperity came with the exploitation of oil and natural gas in the area in the late 1950s, and later with the growth of tourism. After the devastating earthquake of 1964, Anchorage made a dramatic recovery; its downtown skyline is now pierced by high-rise offices and hotels, building projects have brought new facilities to the city in recent years, and a program of tree planting and landscaping has improved its appearance. Today, around 200,000 people live in the city, which now boasts two universities.

Apart from the hypnotizing lights of the aurora borealis, the most striking impression of Anchorage for the visitor is its beautiful setting by Cook Inlet, with the mountains of the Alaska Range and 20,320-foot (6,194 m) Mount McKinley, or Denali – the highest peak in North America – towering to the north and northwest, the closer, forested slopes of the Chugach Mountains rising abruptly to the east, and the Kenai Mountains striding away to the south down the Kenai Peninsula. For a dramatic overview of this natural wonderland, you can take a "flightseeing" plane from Anchorage. You can also hike or drive over much of the area, but even more spectacular is a boat cruise past the majestic southeast coast of the Kenai Peninsula, with its deep fjords and the colossal Harding Ice Field backed by high mountains, and the magnificent Prince William Sound, with its inlets and islands, where the awesome Columbia Glacier rises from the water like a 300-foot (92 m) cliff.

A drive north from Anchorage takes you to the Indian village of Eklutna, with its unusual Indian burial ground and an old Russian Orthodox church, and through the rich vegetable-growing farmlands of the Matanuska Valley to the breath-taking scenery of Denali National Park, a rugged landscape of mountains, rivers, lakes, and forests where Mount McKinley and other high peaks soar into the clouds. On the east side of town, within a short drive, is Chugach State Park, where you can ski, hike, or, in late summer, pick a wide assortment of berries on the edge of the mountains. Other attractions close to Anchorage are the historic Crow Creek gold mine, where hopeful prospectors can still pan for gold, and Earthquake Park, which provides dramatic evidence and records of the upheaval of 1964. Farther south, there are top-rate facilities for skiing and other activities at the Alyeska Resort, and a chance to see wildlife in the Portage Valley, where the Portage Glacier presents an impressive sight across a lake filled with icebergs.

Everywhere in this natural wilderness abound wild animals and birds, including beavers, black bears, caribou, coyotes, moose, river otters, and wolves, while in the sea there are porpoises, whales, seals, and sea lions. Some of the bolder animals at times venture into the outlying parts of Anchorage, which itself boasts many interesting sights.

On the north side of town, on Ship Creek, is the port, which handles over 400 ships each year and is the biggest port in Alaska. Farther west, the statue of Captain Cook looks out over Knik Arm in Resolution Park, recalling Cook's visit in 1778. Behind the waterfront, the downtown streets are scattered with some of the city's earliest buildings, such as the restored,

wood-framed Oscar Anderson House, the Kimball and Wendler buildings, and the Pioneer Schoolhouse and log cabins in Crawford Park. Among the recently built high-rise towers are tucked the old and new Federal Buildings and City Halls, the interesting Heritage Library, and several prestigious additions to the city's facilities. These include the Convention Center, across from the magnificent Performing Arts Complex, with its new concert hall and refurbished Sydney Laurence Auditorium, the home of the Alaska Repertory Theater. There is also a huge extension to the Historical and Fine Arts Museum, where excellent collections of Eskimo, Aleut, and Indian art are displayed. Another new structure is the versatile Sullivan Arena, used for various spectator sports, just five minutes from downtown.

People who prefer to take part rather than watch are often found at Delaney Park, a long green expanse on 9th Avenue that is known locally as "Park Strip" and was once used as an airfield. The park contains facilities for all kinds of sports and recreational activities and hosts popular outdoor concerts in the summer.

All over town there are shops and stores where you can buy locally made goods, including fur hats and coats, reindeer-leather items, and soapstone carvings. Anchorage also has excellent restaurants, some of which specialise in local king crab, salmon, and other seafood dishes. For evening entertainment, there are dinner shows and night clubs, symphony concerts and choral performances, opera, shows, and theater to suit a wide range of tastes. And among the city's many festivals are the Anchorage Fur Rendezvous in February and the Alaska Music Festival in September. With its numerous attractions, Anchorage clearly has a promising future as a major tourist center.

Evening sunshine lights up the high-rise buildings of downtown Anchorage against the backdrop of snow-capped peaks in the surrounding scenic wilderness. Anchorage has grown rapidly in recent years as the gateway port to Alaska.

Atlanta GEORGIA

The Phoenix Reborn

Above: In Atlanta's Hyatt Regency Hotel, part of the impressive Peachtree Center complex, a futuristic glass-bubble elevator speeds visitors from the spacious atrium up to the revolving Polaris restuarant more than 320 feet above street level.

Opposite: The striking architectural forms of the Peachtree Center are given added excitement when photographed through a fish-eye camera lens. Dominating the complex is the distinctive towering cylinder of the 70-story Peachtree Plaza Hotel (background left), with its thrilling exterior elevators.

Gone with the Wind, Martin Luther King, Jr., the Braves, Coca-Cola, the Peachtree Center – when people have Georgia on their minds, it is amazing how varied their first thoughts are at the mention of Atlanta. Yet this is understandable when you remember that this thrusting modern metropolis of 425,000 people has always imposed itself on the nation's consciousness, for as Scarlett O'Hara remarked, "Atlanta is full of pushy people." For years, this proud city has taken center stage as the gateway to the South: the hub of interstate rail, road, and air networks; a major manufacturing center; and, in recent times, a favorite choice for conventions.

Throughout their history, Atlantans have demonstrated their determination and boldness to the rest of the nation, a spirit most forcefully revealed in the rebuilding of their city from the burned-out ashes of the Civil War and later in the campaign for racial equality that was courageously waged by their honored son, Dr. Martin Luther King, Jr. Under their civic symbol, the phoenix – the mythological bird that dies by fire only to be reborn – Atlantans are today forging their city's second renaissance, an economic resurgence that is changing not only the face of the city, but also its image of itself. Atlanta is now staking its claim to be a cosmopolitan city of international stature.

The architectural profile of ultramodern towers of mirrored glass and steel that graces the downtown area is a long way in time from the smoking shell left behind by General William Tecumseh Sherman's fire-raisers in 1864, and even farther from the simple log cabin built some 30 years earlier by Hardy Ivy at a crossroad now known as Five Points at the heart of the city. Atlanta really took off after 1837 when the Western and Atlantic Railroad ended here, and a settlement known as Terminus was founded around the spot now marked by the famous Zero Mile Post. Soon the place was being called Marthasville after the governor's daughter; but in 1847, its present name was invented, derived with southern charm from the feminine form of the "Atlantic" part of the railroad's title.

Growing rapidly into an important communications center as other railroads came in to link up here, Atlanta, now a city of 20,000 people, became the industrial giant of the South and supplied the Confederate armies during the Civil War – hence its destruction by the Union army under Sherman. But the city's indomitable spirit survived both the shameful holocaust and the indignities imposed by the North during Reconstruction.

Atlanta, therefore, retains all the grace and charm of a southern city, encapsulated in the lovely old homes, tree-lined streets, and springtime explosions of azalea and dogwood in its attractive suburbs – pleasant neighborhoods such as Druid Hills, Buckhead, and Morningside. It also has its traditions and celebrations, none more colorful and enjoyable than the annual Dogwood Festival in April. At the same time, Atlanta has modern manufacturing industries based on the latest technology and is the headquarters of many of the nation's leading corporations. Here you will also find some of the finest hotels, shops, and restaurants, the most exciting night life, and the most imaginative architecture in all America. Expeditions around this lively city, either on foot or on the bus and rail system of the Metropolitan Area Rapid Transit (MARTA), soon reveal the wide range of Atlanta's attractions.

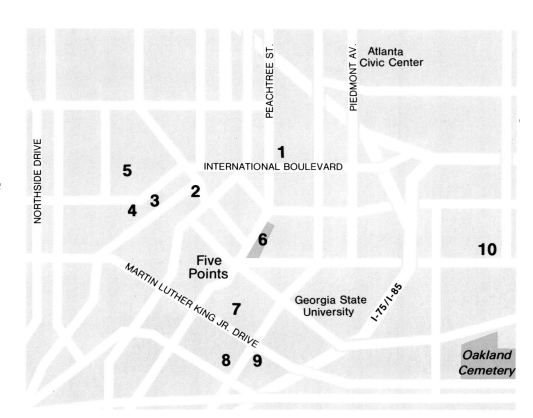

For first impressions, there is a spectacular view over the city from the revolving Sun Dial restaurant at the top of the Peachtree Plaza Hotel, a gleaming 70-story cylinder that reputedly is the world's tallest hotel. The breath-taking ride in one of the elevators on the outside of the building and the magnificent seven-story lobby enclosing a half-acre lake are matched only by the architectural wonders in the adjacent Hyatt Regency Hotel. Both hotels are part of the vast Peachtree Center complex designed by John Portman to accommodate stores, restaurants, and offices linked by enclosed elevated walkways and decorated with hanging plants and bubbling fountains.

Some blocks west are the huge World Congress Center and another multipurpose megastructure, the colossal, futuristic Omni International complex; its 5.5-acre, 14-story atrium encloses an ice-skating rink, and its 17,000-seat arena is used by the city's basketball and ice-hockey teams, the Hawks and the Flames.

A haven of greenery among the downtown high-rise blocks can be found in Central City Park, a favorite lunchtime spot for city workers that was donated to Atlanta by Robert Woodruff, a former president of Coca-Cola. Not far away to the south, by the Zero Mile Post, is the colorful four-square-block restored historic district known as Underground Atlanta, an atmospheric collection of shops, restaurants, and clubs submerged beneath a traffic viaduct in the late nineteenth century and later revived as a symbol of Atlanta's renaissance. In this area, too, is the gold-domed Georgia State Capitol.

On the edge of the southeastern suburbs, the Atlanta–Fulton County Stadium provides an opportunity to see the city's football team, the Falcons, and baseball stars, the Braves. To the east, popular Grant Park offers a fine view over the city from the site of old Fort Walker; the park also contains a pleasant zoo, with an excellent reptile collection, and the renowned Cyclorama, a huge three-dimensional painting that portrays the Civil War struggle for Atlanta. Some of the Confederate dead are buried on the heights of Oakland Cemetery in this part of the city, as is Margaret Mitchell, author of *Gone with the Wind*. And a few blocks north, the tomb of Martin Luther King, Jr., can be seen at the Ebenezer Baptist Church on Auburn Avenue, where he once preached.

A trip to the southwestern suburbs is worth the trouble in order to visit the Wren's Nest, the lovely cottage on Gordon Street where Joel Chandler Harris created Uncle Remus and such beloved, immortal "critters" as Br'er Rabbit and Br'er Fox. But it is into the northern suburbs that Atlanta has packed most of its treasures. In the revitalized Midtown area near Piedmont Park, there are, for instance, several theaters and museums worth a visit, among which the Atlanta Memorial Arts Center and the Fabulous Fox Theater are widely known. Here, too, is the pleasant Colony Square complex of shops, restaurants, and offices.

Farther out, in the expensive Buckhead neighborhood, the opulent Swan House of 1928 and the lovely Tullie Smith House, a restored plantation farmhouse of around 1840, can be seen on the grounds of the Atlanta Historical Society. This area also contains the delightful Atlanta Toy Museum and the beautiful home of Georgia's chief executive, the Governor's Mansion.

A drive north from Atlanta rewards history buffs with Fort Peachtree, built near the former Indian settlement of Standing Peachtree, which has given the city its 30 Peachtree Streets! And, 23 miles out of the city, there is Kennesaw Mountain Battlefield Park, which commemorates a major Civil War encounter with the Yankees. But perhaps the most enjoyable places for all the family are the fascinating Stone Mountain Park to the east of Atlanta and, to the west, the spectacular Six Flags over Georgia amusement park.

Unfortunately, it is not possible to visit the lovely mansion of Tara described in *Gone with the Wind*, since it was merely the product of Margaret Mitchell's vivid imagination. So was Scarlett O'Hara herself; yet somehow her determination and vitality seem to live on – reborn like the phoenix – in this vibrant, confident city of tomorrow.

The skyscrapers of downtown Atlanta provide a dazzling panorama from a viewpoint near the Atlanta-Fulton County Stadium. Completed in 1965, the stadium holds more than 50,000 spectators at Falcons football and Braves baseball games.

Austin TEXAS

Lone Star Capital

Above: Second in size only to the Capitol in Washington, D.C., the Texas State Capitol, in Austin, is a massive but elegant structure built from Texas pink granite and other local materials. Completed in 1888, it is the fifth statehouse to be built in the city since 1839.

When you drive north across the Texas plains from San Antonio during the evening, you know when you have reached Austin by what looks like 21 hovering moons casting a cool blue light over various parts of the city. As you get closer you see that the moonbeams are made by mercury-vapor lamps at the top of 165-foot (50 m) metal towers, the survivors of the original 31 towers erected in 1895 to light the whole city. Popular with residents and visitors alike, the moonlight towers are a unique feature of Austin and just one of the many attractions that make the Lone Star State's capital such a fascinating place.

Austin straddles the Colorado River (not the one that flows through the Grand Canyon) where it leaves the beautiful Hill Country to flow south-eastward across the coastal plain to the Gulf of Mexico. Northwest of the city, the river has been dammed to create a 150-mile chain of seven Highland Lakes, which provides a magnificent recreational playground within easy reach of town. With a climate that produces sunshine 300 days of the year and encourages a life style in which outdoor activities take up a good deal of time, Austin has earned high ratings in recent years as one of the most livable cities in the United States.

Well-manicured residential districts with attractive tree-shaded streets and big shopping centers reach into the central part of the city from the suburbs. Just north of the river – a stretch bordered by pleasant parkland and known as Town Lake – the downtown district occupies a square-mile grid of streets in which the lofty State Capitol is a prominent landmark. Farther north is the huge campus of the University of Texas, dominated by its famous 307-foot (94 m) tower. In this district, the historic heart of the city, are many old buildings that reflect Austin's growth since its birth 150 years ago.

In 1835, Jacob M. Harrell pitched his tent by the Colorado River and became the future city's first permanent resident. After other people moved in, the little community, now known as Waterloo, was chosen as the site for the capital of the Republic of Texas following its breakaway from Mexican rule in 1836. It was renamed Austin in honor of Stephen F. Austin, leader of the first Anglo settlers in the region during the 1820s. A square-mile area was laid out in what is now the downtown district, and lots were sold to prospective residents, including a site for the still surviving French Legation. After the United States annexed the young republic in 1845, Austin was confirmed as the permanent capital of the new state of Texas. Despite the Civil War, during which the city's inhabitants had divided sympathies, Austin continued to grow and to improve its amenities, becoming a thriving trading center that transported local cotton and cattle after the arrival of the railroad in 1871. In the 1890s, it was declared "the most beautiful and wealthiest city of its size in the United States," its prosperity continuing until today. Now a city of more than 350,000 people, Austin has an economy in which the major employers are the state government, higher-educational institutions led by the University of Texas, the Bergstrom Air Force Base, and "clean" high-technology industries involved in electronics, computers, and research.

There are fine views over Austin from the top of 775-foot (236 m) Mount Bonnell, on the west side of the city, and from the State Capitol, in the heart of downtown. This magnificent pink-granite building, completed in 1888, stands on a hill in 43 acres of lovely wooded grounds, offering marvelous views of the city from its fifth-floor verandah. With a delightful touch of Texas pride, the dome was completed just 7 feet (2 m) higher than that of the Capitol in Washington, D.C.

Among the surrounding streets are several public buildings of special historic interest, such as the stately Governor's Mansion of 1855, the Land Office Building of 1857, and the Texas Archives and Library Building. Other buildings reflect past life styles: the Millet Opera House, where many great nineteenth-century actors performed; the Old Bakery and Emporium; the distinguished Driskill Hotel; and old homes like those in the famous

Austin's two best-known landmarks, the Texas State Capitol and, beyond, the sleek University of Texas tower, stand out among the high-rise buildings in the downtown district north of Town Lake.

Bremond Block, the Neill–Cochran House, and the writer O. Henry's home, both of these now museums.

Other interesting museums are to be found on the University of Texas campus, among them the fine Texas Memorial Museum, with its collections on history and natural history; the impressive, modern LBJ (Lyndon Baines Johnson) Library and Museum; and the prestigious Harry Ransom Center, which houses art and literary exhibits.

Near the university are two special attractions for shoppers: the stretch of Guadalupe Street known as "The Drag;" and the colorful People's Renaissance Market, with its arts and crafts stalls, where various entertainers often amuse the crowds. An assortment of entertainments also attracts people to Symphony Square on the east side of downtown, where there are concerts under the stars. But for livelier nighttime activity, as well as for shopping, 6th Street, once known as Pecan Street, is the place to go. This former business district now swings with bars, restaurants, and night clubs where you can get a taste of the country music that has earned Austin fame as the "second Nashville."

If you prefer classical ballet to the cotton-eyed joe, then an evening with the Austin Ballet Theater at the downtown Paramount Theater or with Ballet Austin at the university's Performing Arts Center should fit the bill. At the Center, you can also hear the Austin Symphony Orchestra or enjoy other shows. But the place to go for any other kind of event, including sports, is the Frank Erwin Special Events Center on Red River Street. The city also offers a selection of fine theaters, including the Zachary Scott Theater, which stages plays by the Austin Community Theater, and the Paramount Theater, where, in addition to ballet, you can see varied productions, including some by Broadway touring companies.

More than 8,000 acres of parks around Austin await people looking for relaxation or with energy for recreational pursuits; they offer hiking and biking trails as well as facilities for golf, tennis, horseback riding, swimming, and countless other activities. Zilker Park, just south of Town Lake, contains one of the city's most popular highlights, the Barton Springs Pool, a favorite swimming hole that is fed by natural springs. In August, the landscaped parks along Town Lake are the setting for Austin's big Aqua Festival, a ten-day celebration that features colorful parades and over 75 other exciting events.

Then there are the seven Highland Lakes to the northwest of the city, where city dwellers enjoy picnicking, camping, boating, and fishing in the midst of the delightful Hill Country scenery. Among the many fascinating natural features of this beautiful region are countless caverns and springs, including the Longhorn Caverns in Burnet and the Aquarena Springs in San Marcos. But the most popular attractions in the area around Austin include the birthplace and the ranch of President Lyndon B. Johnson, some 50 miles west of the city.

Baltimore MARYLAND

The Monumental City

O! Say can you see, by the dawn's early light,
What so proudly we hailed at twilight's last gleaming,
Whose broad stripes and bright stars, through the perilous fight,
O'er the ramparts we watched, were so gallantly streaming.

Everyone knows how the immortal words of "The Star-Spangled Banner,"
America's beloved national anthem, were scribbled down by the young
lawyer Francis Scott Key as he watched the Stars and Stripes still bravely
flying through the mist and smoke over Baltimore's Fort McHenry after a
terrible bombardment by British ships during the War of 1812. A deep-
water harbor in a protected inlet near the head of Chesapeake Bay,
Baltimore was of strategic importance on the supply route to nearby
Washington, D.C., the nation's capital. Despite epidemics of disease and
frequent floods of Jones Falls, it had grown steadily since its foundation as
the port for the colony of Maryland, which had been established by Lord
Baltimore in 1632.

With the coming of the first railroad, the B & O, and the development
of industry in the nineteenth century, the rugged city acquired the elegant
trappings of fine mansions and gracious streets and squares, many of which
survive in such desirable neighborhoods as Bolton Hill and Guilford.
Immigrant workers who swelled Baltimore's population in the later years of
the nineteenth century endowed the city with the rich ethnic and cultural
mix so evident today, while rich entrepreneurs – men like Johns Hopkins,
George Peabody, Enoch Pratt, and William and Henry Walters – founded
institutions that still bear their names. But despite this prosperity and the
rebuilding done after a devastating downtown fire in 1904, Baltimore
emerged from the Great Depression of the 1930s as an aging backwater in
need of rejuvenation.

Always overshadowed by its more glamorous neighbors, Washington,
D.C., and Philadelphia, Baltimore seemed to be off the beaten track for the
traffic that sped by between the east coast's great cities. In spite of its many
attractions and advantages, it had failed not only to capture the people's
imagination sufficiently to entice visitors, but also, significantly, to persuade
to country's leading corporations to set up their headquarters here. The
provincial image was not helped by the local way of talking, which only
"Bawlmer sidsins were lahble t'unnersteand, not Mairkan torsts from
Warshnin, D.C., or ignert farners from Yerp." It is not surprising that
H. L. Mencken, that provocative Baltimore journalist, became so engrossed
with the American language. Mencken's fellow citizens, however, seemed
content to go their own way, self-sufficient with the varied life style that
their city provided, and enjoying their annual City Fair and Preakness
Festival in the time-honored manner.

After World War II, things began to change, and various modernization
projects have put new life into the city, while of course preserving the best
of the past. Rebuilding, for example, has totally removed the rotting
wharves of the Inner Harbor area, and Baltimore's "homesteading" scheme,
in which decaying old houses could be won in a lottery for a dollar, has
rehabilitated such downtown neighborhoods as Otterbein and Stirling
Street. With its historic buildings rubbing shoulders with gleaming new
structures, with its beautiful parks and squares, varied cultural activities,

*Star-shaped Fort McHenry, built between
1798 and 1803, guards the approach to
Baltimore Harbor from the sea. Its successful
resistance to an all-out bombardment by
British ships in the War of 1812 inspired the
American lawyer Francis Scott Key to
compose the words of "The Star-Spangled
Banner." Today the Stars and Stripes flies over
the fort 24 hours a day by presidential decree.*

*Overleaf: Baltimore's renovated Inner
Harbor is a bustling center of activity where
visitors can spend days exploring the many
attractions. From Federal Hill, on the south
side, the scene is dominated by the elegant
World Trade Center tower, designed by the
celebrated architect I.M. Pei (right). Other
notable landmarks overlooking the Inner
Harbor are the USF & G Building,
Baltimore's tallest structure (left), and the
distinctive Art Deco Maryland National
Bank Building, with its huge neon "MN"
sign that changes color as it forecasts the
weather (center, left).*

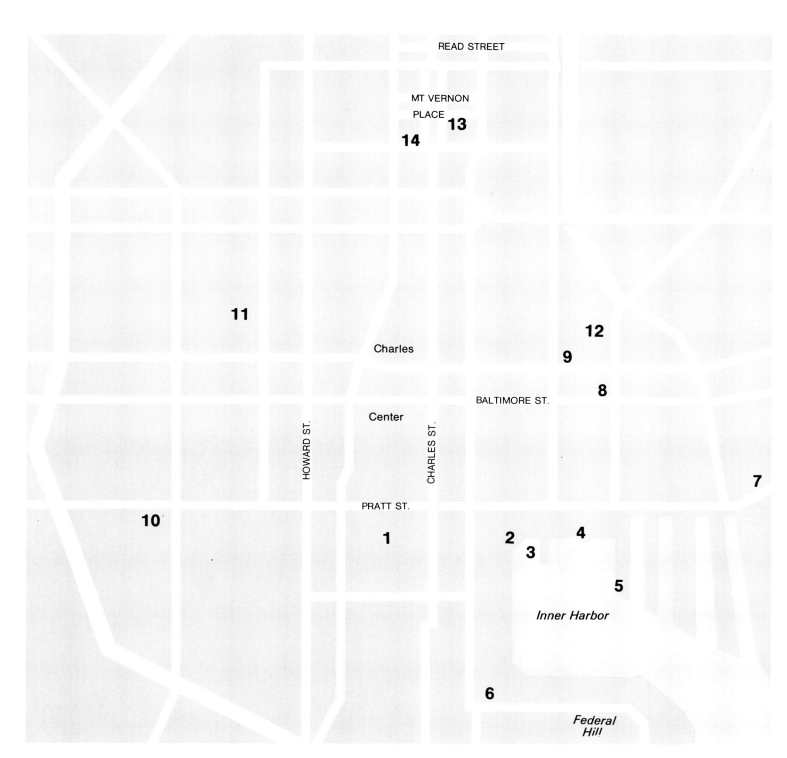

READ STREET

MT VERNON
PLACE **13**
14

11

Charles

12

9

8

BALTIMORE ST.

Center

HOWARD ST.

CHARLES ST.

7

PRATT ST.

10

1

2 **4**

3

5

Inner Harbor

6

Federal
Hill

Baltimore, City Center

lively festivals, and excellent restaurants that serve some of the finest seafood in the country, Baltimore is no longer a place to pass by. Still a major seaport with a population of around 768,000, the "Monumental City" is now also an exciting place with a thousand and one places of interest.

If you happen to be attending a gathering at the downtown Convention Center, it is but a short walk to the sparkling new waterfront area of the Inner Harbor, with its open promenades, brand-new buildings, and bustling activity. A magnificent view over this impressive spectacle and the surrounding city is available from the Top of the World observation deck in the magnificent 30-story World Trade Center, which was designed by I. M. Pei and built right on the waterfront. Below are the twin pavilions of Harborplace, with their dazzling array of shops, restaurants, and cafés; the proud old frigate *Constellation*, launched in 1797; and, on the wharves to the east, the futuristic shapes of the fascinating National Aquarium and the Pier 6 Concert Pavilion. Across the harbor is another bold structure, the

windowless, brick Science Center, which contains wonderful exhibits and displays and a fine planetarium. A superb view of the entire harbor area and the city beyond can be enjoyed from the top of nearby Federal Hill.

A wander through the downtown streets immediately behind the Inner Harbor reveals a wealth of interesting places, such as the Star-Spangled Banner Flag House, where Mary Pickersgill made the original flag that flew over Fort McHenry and inspired the national anthem; the once sleazy "Block" area, famous for its dancing girls; the beautiful Baltimore City Hall, now painstakingly restored; and the wonderful Peale Museum of 1814, with its fine collection of paintings and photographs. Here, too, are the birthplace of Babe Ruth, the grave of the writer Edgar Allan Poe in the churchyard of historic Westminster Church, and, farther west, the little row house on Amity Street where Poe lived for a time, not far from the present-day B & O Railroad Museum.

In the retail district of Howard Street is one of Baltimore's best-known city markets, the fabulous old Lexington Market, a gastronome's delight of two covered buildings filled with stalls brimming with tempting food. Not far away, the 33-acre Charles Center complex presents a contrasting note, its bold modern structures, one by the celebrated architect Ludwig Mies van der Rohe, marking the start of Baltimore's renewal in 1956. North of here along Charles Street, Baltimore's "cultural and culinary corridor," is a much older complex, gracious Mount Vernon Place, laid out in 1831 and now a National Historic Landmark. This comprises four lovely garden squares, embellished with trees, fountains, and sculptures, that converge on a central square dominated by the lofty column of the George Washington Monument. Lining the surrounding streets are elegant town houses and buildings occupied by the Peabody Institute, the celebrated music conservatory, and by the magnificent Walters Art Gallery.

After a pleasant morning in this lovely district, you can enjoy a good lunch in one of the superb restaurants crowded into the nearby Read Street area, and then continue north along Charles Street to admire the outstanding art collections in the Baltimore Museum of Art. If the day and time are right, you might then be able to complete a rewarding day at Memorial Stadium in this part of the city, watching the Baltimore Colts play football or a baseball game with the Orioles.

But if you prefer to spend a relaxing time just wandering through one of Baltimore's many fine old neighborhoods, then a trip to the quiet west-side district of Dickeyville or to the atmospheric port-side community of Fells Point is a special adventure. Baltimore has something for everyone, since here visitors can experience all the special delights of a rejuvenated old city where twentieth-century life goes hand in hand with the monuments of the past.

Above left: Launched in 1797, the restored frigate Constellation *has had a long and glorious history as the first commissioned warship of the United States Navy. Now a floating museum, the beautiful ship is moored in Baltimore's Inner Harbor, where it is a popular attraction for visitors.*

Above: A fascinating collection of locomotives, cars and other railroad relics is displayed in the huge roundhouse at the old Mount Clare Station, which is now used as the Baltimore and Ohio (B & O) Railroad Museum.

Birmingham ALABAMA

Vulcan's Southern Forge

Poised on its lofty pedestal atop Alabama's Red Mountain the impressive 55-foot (17 m) cast-iron statue of Vulcan, the Roman god of the forge, looks down over the sprawling industrial city at its feet. Vulcan is an appropriate symbol, for this is Birmingham, Alabama's great iron- and steel-making center. The industrial giant long known as the "Pittsburgh of the South," Birmingham nestles snugly in the lovely Appalachian foothills in the north of the state.

Iron-making began in the area in the early nineteenth century, when the Tannehill furnaces were set up to use local ore and limestone near Elyton, a little town surrounded by the cotton fields of the Jones Valley. Here the Confederate army got supplies of cannon balls and gun barrels for use in the Civil War, before the furnaces were destroyed by an enemy raid late in the hostilities. During Reconstruction, Elyton was renamed Birmingham, after the great industrial city in England; in the 1880s, a new iron-making industry, led by the Sloss Furnace Company, was established using coke made from local coal instead of charcoal. Now able to compete with foundries in the North, Birmingham entered a period of economic growth that was so phenomenal that the city was hailed as America's "Magic City," and people streamed in to share in its prosperity.

Although the Tannehill and Sloss furnaces have long since ceased to operate and are now honored historic sites, iron- and steel-making continue to be important factors in Birmingham's economy. In addition, the city now has a diversified range of manufacturing industries – including chemicals, components, furniture, textiles, and clothing – and has acquired a fine reputation for its superb Medical Center at the downtown University of Alabama campus. The city's economic progress has been aided by its excellent location at the hub of a rail and road network that gives easy access to all parts of the South and the industrial Northeast.

Today, around 284,000 people live in the city, the black community forming a considerable proportion. Residential areas such as Hoover and Vestavia have grown up around the central city, which itself has undergone much renewal and redevelopment in recent years. Like all old industrial centers, Birmingham has its share of urban problems, yet it also has many modern attractions and amenities and retains much of the flavor and charm of the Old South. Residential areas bright with spring azalea and dogwood, and outdoor summer barbecues with southern fried chicken and deep-dish cobbler, mint juleps and bluegrass music together form a kaleidoscope of sensations conjuring up the image of Old Dixie. But the sight that remains most deeply impressed on the mind as a symbol of an era long gone is that of Arlington Historic House, a graceful antebellum mansion constructed in Elyton in 1842 and now lovingly restored in its outstandingly beautiful gardens beside Cotton Avenue.

Three miles east of here, along Cotton Avenue and 1st Avenue North, is downtown Birmingham, its high-rise stores and offices lining the regular grid of numbered streets. A good place to start a tour of downtown is the spectacular Birmingham Jefferson Civic Center, a complex of buildings occupying a four-block site north of 9th Avenue North. Its four major buildings are the Exhibition Hall, Concert Hall, Theater, and Coliseum, which are used for a wide assortment of events and activities, including

The gigantic statue of Vulcan, one of the world's few monuments to industry, overlooks the industrial city of Birmingham from the landscaped gardens of Vulcan Park on the crest of Red Mountain. Including its pedestal, the monument rises to a height of 179 feet, offering magnificent views of the city from its observation deck.

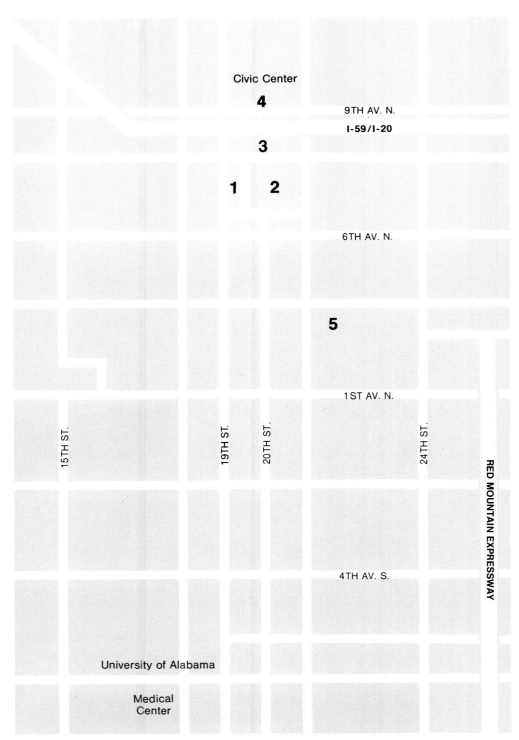

Civic Center

4

9TH AV. N.

I-59/I-20

3

1 **2**

6TH AV. N.

5

1ST AV. N.

15TH ST.

19TH ST.

20TH ST.

24TH ST.

RED MOUNTAIN EXPRESSWAY

4TH AV. S.

University of Alabama

Medical
Center

The gracious mansion of Arlington, built in 1842, captures the refined elegance of the Old South of pre-Civil War days. Originally named "The Grove" by its first owner, Judge William S. Mudd, the house has been beautifully restored and is now listed on the National Register of Historic Places.

Downtown Birmingham
1 City Hall
2 Woodrow Wilson Park
3 Museum of Art
4 Alabama Sports Hall of Fame
5 St. Paul's Cathedral

conventions, symphony concerts, ballet, and plays. With seats for 9,000 people, the Coliseum is a spacious entertainment and sports arena where there is often high excitement among basketball fans during home games of the University of Alabama's Blazers. Also in the complex is the Alabama Sports Hall of Fame, with memorabilia of the state's greatest sporting personalities, such as the famous checked hat worn by coach Paul "Bear" Bryant.

Long known as the "Football Capital of the South," Birmingham also boasts the excellent facilities of the Legion Field stadium, a 70,000-seat arena that vibrates to the roar of the crowd at the home games of the professional Stallions and of the University of Alabama's Crimson Tide, and hosts the annual postseason Hall of Fame Bowl game, which is fought between leading college teams. There is also Rickwood Field, where the professional, minor-league Barons enjoy a good following of baseball fans.

A short walk from the Civic Center, facing Woodrow Wilson Park and

The rugged outlines of steel-making plants mark the skyline of the old industrial city of Birmingham, long known as the "Pittsburgh of the South." In more recent years, however, the growth of a wide range of manufacturing industries and medical research facilities has helped to diversify the city's economy.

Opposite, top: Sailboats and pleasure craft offer pleasant relaxation as they ply the calm waters of the Charles River in the shadow of Boston's John Hancock Tower. This sleek, mirrored-glass structure of 60 stories is the city's tallest building.

Opposite, bottom: Built in 1660, the John Hancock House on Salt Lane, where the Revolutionary leader lived from 1764 to 1785, is the oldest brick building still standing in Boston.

City Hall, is the Museum of Art, which contains fine collections of modern paintings and old masters, Remington bronzes, silver, and porcelain. A short distance away, 20th Street provides a change of mood with its swinging night life; here an assortment of clubs and bars comes to life after dark to the sound of jazz and country music and the chink of glasses.

East of here, past St. Paul's Cathedral, are the old Sloss furnaces, now preserved as a National Historic Landmark at the 1st Avenue North viaduct. Contrasting with this silent symbol of the South's industrial heritage, the complex of research laboratories and hospital facilities at the University of Alabama's Medical Center bustles with activity on the south side of downtown. Overlooking these buildings from Red Mountain is the colossal statue of Vulcan, the world's largest cast-iron figure. Designed by the Italian sculptor Giuseppe Moretti and cast locally for showing at the Louisiana Purchase Exposition in St. Louis in 1904, the statue was later mounted on its pedestal amid the trees of Vulcan Park. The observation deck at its base affords the best panoramic view of the city.

Red Mountain also has a celebrated geology museum whose exhibits explain the rock formations that have given the area the iron ore, coal, and limestone for its iron- and steel-making industry. A mile or so away, in Park Lane Road, are the renowned Botanical Gardens, with over 67 acres of floral beauty and famous for their outstanding rose garden, conservatory, and Japanese garden, all of which are a delight at any time of the year. In the same area, Birmingham's fine zoo, the South's largest, offers the irresistible appeal of more than 1,000 kinds of animals and, for tired feet, a chance to ride on a miniature train.

Birmingham's well-known Festival of the Arts gets the year off to a good start each spring with a lively program of entertainment and cultural activities ranging from craft exhibits to ballet performances. And before the October Alabama State Fair sets people thinking about winter, there are countless other events to provide amusement. One of the most outrageous must be the annual Bed Race, in which beds of all shapes are propelled, amid raucous hilarity, along the city's main boulevard. Despite its dour image as a hard-working industrial city, Birmingham certainly has its moments of fun.

Boston MASSACHUSETTS

The Cradle of Liberty

Like a gigantic, upturned clenched fist grasping a sparkling emerald, the great city of Boston, Massachusetts, clusters along its blunt peninsula around the green space formed by its adjoining Common and Public Garden. The fist might indeed be a symbol of this historic city, for, as everyone knows, it was here that in colonial days the British were to feel the first blows in the fight for America's freedom. The Boston Massacre, the Boston Tea Party, Paul Revere's ride, the clashes at Lexington and Concord, and the slaughter on Bunker Hill – all those stirring events that sparked off the Revolutionary War were enacted in Boston's domain.

Many of the buildings and sites where the momentous drama was played out still remain, preserved among the concrete and glass towers that now bristle along Boston's skyline. Several of these soar above new development projects along the peninsula's spine, such as the Copley Place complex and the Prudential Center, with its prestigious Hynes Auditorium. The Skywalk on the fiftieth story of the Prudential Tower and the Observatory on the nearby 60-story John Hancock Tower afford breathtaking views of the vast city laid out below.

To the north you will see the broad sweep of the Charles River, dotted with sailboats and sleek rowing craft, separating the city of Cambridge on the far bank from Boston's Back Bay district. Laid out on reclaimed mud flats in the nineteenth century, Back Bay comprises an orderly grid of broad streets flanking impressive Commonwealth Avenue, with stately brownstone and brick houses that were once fashionable residences, although few are now used as homes. The district, however, now has a new role as Boston's center of cultural life.

To the east are the green oases of the Public Garden, with its lake upon which glide the famous swan boats, and of lovely Boston Common, the nation's oldest park. North of here, on rising ground, is the beautiful Beacon Hill district, where Nathaniel Hawthorne observed "the irregular and often quaint architecture of the houses," a maze of gaslit, tree-lined cobblestone streets that transport the mind back to an earlier age. Beyond the historic center and downtown business area, the oldest part of Boston, the North End district, occupies the tip of the peninsula facing the city's huge natural harbor. Now a lively Italian neighborhood, this charming old quarter of narrow brick streets stands at the northern end of the renovated waterfront area, where colorful shops and restaurants, pleasure craft and cruise boats bustle with life beneath the pointed shadow of the famous Customs House Tower.

If you are constantly reminded of history in this city, you cannot escape its cultural atmosphere. With its countless institutions of learning, museums, art galleries, and theaters, Boston has long lived up to its reputation as "the Athens of America;" for many people, it is the most liveable, civilized city in the United States. Among Boston's many outstanding museums, the Museum of Fine Arts and the Isabella Stewart Gardner Museum, both near the Fenway, and Harvard University's Fogg Museum, in Cambridge, are of international stature, as is the Boston Symphony Orchestra, whose home is the magnificent Symphony Hall in Huntington Avenue. The city also has opera and ballet companies and a flourishing theater district on Tremont and Boylston streets. And for those

who like music of a different sort until the early hours of the morning, there are disco clubs in Kenmore Square and jazz sessions at Inman Square.

In addition to its vigorous cultural life and night entertainment, Boston can boast many other things that make living in this city special. There are, for instance, its lovely parks: the Fenway Public Garden, Boston Common, and – the favorite haunt of joggers – the Esplanade along the Charles River, not to mention the smaller, but equally pleasant green spaces by the waterfront, such as North End Park, Paul Revere Mall, and, of course, Waterfront Park. Shopping in Boston is a special delight, not only in the big stores at places like Downtown Crossing and Newbury Street, but also in the tangy little neighborhood shops of North End and Chinatown or among the colorful stalls of Haymarket and Faneuil Marketplace. Boston is also packed with excellent restaurants, where you can relish the city's celebrated seafood or international specialties of every description. And there are places where you can watch an assortment of spectator sports, including baseball, basketball, football, and ice hockey.

Although his words are perhaps somewhat overpersuasive, you can understand the underlying pride of one of William Dean Howells's characters in *The Rise of Silas Lapham* when he growled, "The Bostonian who leaves Boston ought to be condemned to perpetual exile." Certainly, the first Pilgrim settlers, who in 1620 arrived in the *Mayflower* at Plymouth harbor, had no wish to return to Europe, despite the hardships they suffered during their early days in the New World. Nor did the Massachusetts Bay colonists, who prospered from the moment they established their own settlement of Salem in 1628. Two years later, they founded Boston on its fine natural harbor at the mouth of the Charles River, and the community flourished through fishing, farming, shipbuilding, and trading by fast ocean-going clippers. After the drama of the Revolution, the nineteenth century brought the rise of leather and textile industries and sufficient affluence for the reclamation and building of the Back Bay district. Since World War II, Boston has emerged as a leading high-technology center, involved in computers, office automation, and electronics, a field of activity reinforced by the research facilities available at such prestigious institutions of learning as Harvard University and the Massachusetts Institute of Technology (M.I.T.) in neighboring Cambridge. Despite a fall in the city's

Boston

1 *Prudential Center*
2 *John Hancock Tower*
3 *Copley Place*
4 *Museum of Fine Arts*
5 *Symphony Hall*
6 *State House*
7 *Old South Meeting House*
8 *Old State House*
9 *Faneuil Hall*
10 *Paul Revere's House*
11 *Old North Church*
12 *Bunker Hill Monument*
13 *U.S.S.* Constitution
14 *Boston Tea Party Ship*
15 *Custom House Tower*

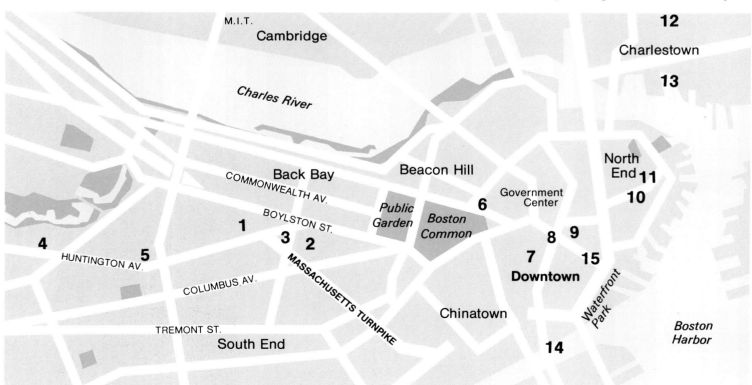

population to 562,994 in 1980, the business world's confidence in Boston's continuing prosperity remains unshaken, as evidenced by the number of new office buildings and hotels that have risen in recent years.

To see Boston's many attractions, you can ride on its buses, tourist trolleys, or "T," the underground rapid-transit system, or take one of its pleasant harbor cruises, but walking is by far the most rewarding way to explore its many intimate corners. To help visitors find the city's most treasured historic sites, the famous Freedom Trail walk has been devised through the downtown and North End districts, marked along its 1.5-mile route by red bricks set into the sidewalk. It begins near Park Street subway station by Boston Common in the heart of the city, and as you walk along it, you are transported back in time to colonial days and the Revolutionary War.

Among the highlights along the trail is the magnificent State House, designed by Charles Bulfinch and completed in 1798, which now preserves historic documents in its archives. The building stands majestically on the north side of Boston Common, its gold dome a well-known landmark on the city skyline. Farther on are Park Street Church; the Granary Burying Ground, containing the graves of Paul Revere, three signers of the Declaration of Independence, and other illustrious citizens; King's Chapel of 1754; and the old City Hall, with its statue of Benjamin Franklin. Beyond the Old Corner Book Store, the meeting place of Boston's literary circle, are the Old South Meeting House, the scene of mass meetings – one

Northeastward along Huntington Avenue, the skyline of Boston's Back Bay district is dominated by the soaring Prudential Tower (center left), which overlooks the adjacent modern complex of the Prudential Center and the prestigious hotels of nearby Copley Place.

Opposite: Copper-domed Quincy Market, one of the three 500-foot-long buildings of Faneuil Hall Marketplace, is packed with a colorful assortment of food stands, delicatessens, restaurants, and cafés. First opened in 1826 close to the Boston Harbor waterfront, the marketplace stands directly behind historic Faneuil Hall and is a popular attraction for some 15 million tourists each year.

In Boston's North End district is the house where the famous patriot and silversmith Paul Revere was living with his large family when he set off on his historic ride to Lexington in April, 1775, to warn the Colonists that British soldiers were on their way. The two-story wooden structure, built in 1676 and Boston's oldest building, is on the Freedom Trail.

of which roused adventurous citizens into organizing the Boston Tea Party – and the Old State House, built in 1712 as the seat of colonial government. From its balcony the Declaration of Independence was read out to the people, and across the street a ring of cobblestones now marks the site of the Boston Massacre of 1770.

At this point on the trail is Faneuil Hall, built in 1742 as a market, but because of the many political meetings held there, it became known as the "Cradle of Liberty." As a result of the revitalization of the adjacent Quincy Market, the ground floor of Faneuil Hall now buzzes with shoppers. Continuing north, you come to Paul Revere's house, built in 1676 and the oldest structure in Boston, and a little farther on, his statue and Old North Church, the city's oldest religious building. It was here that two lanterns were hung in the steeple on the night of April 18, 1775, to warn the revolutionaries that the British were crossing by water to Charlestown on their way to Lexington. Over the Charlestown Bridge, the trail leads up the winding streets to the Bunker Hill Monument, which marks the site of the bloody 1775 battle, and along the waterfront to the U.S.S. *Constitution*, the nation's oldest warship, launched in 1797.

To crown a journey back into history, you can relive the Boston Tea Party at the full-size replica ship and museum near Congress Street Bridge, south of downtown. You can also visit Lexington and Concord, the Harvard University campus in Cambridge, and other places of interest around the city. To the south are Harbor Islands State Park, Plymouth, and Cape Cod; to the north, the spectacular scenery of North Shore and, beyond, the mountains and lakes of New Hampshire.

Boston, the most European of American cities, is, in the words of one of its citizens, "a city to caress, one you can almost cup in your hands and admire at your leisure."

Buffalo NEW YORK

Queen City of the Lakes

When you try to guess the identity of a city from a list of its special features, chances are you will get a surprise. Take this example. A large, tough industrial metropolis and port at the mouth of a river in America's Northeast, with numerous monuments and statues; architectural masterpieces designed by architects of international renown; a huge central park landscaped by the celebrated Frederick Law Olmsted; an assortment of ethnic communities, predominantly Poles, Italians, Irish, and blacks; and cultural attractions that include a thriving theater district, a world-class orchestra, and an internationally famous museum of art. New York City seems the obvious answer. But when you are told that, in addition, the mystery city has an encircling necklace of beautiful parks, then it must surely be Boston. Yet, in fact, the surprising solution is Buffalo, New York State's second city, long thought to be just an industrial jungle with not much to recommend it.

The poor image is unjust, and undue emphasis has been given in the past to the city's problems at the expense of its very real attractions. It is true that after World War II, many people left the central area to take advantage of better conditions in the suburbs as the central core declined with a fall in industrial activity. By 1980, the population had declined to 357,870. But over the years, valiant efforts have been made to reverse this trend by the revitalization and renewal of the central business area, the construction of encircling highways, educational institutions, and hospital and research facilities, and the adoption of measures to reduce air pollution. On the business front, Buffalo is still the biggest grain-milling center in the country and a major steel producer, but its manufacturing industry has now diversified considerably to include high-technology products, aided by research facilities in the fields of electronics and aerospace.

Buffalo's growth as an industrial city and port stems partly from its

The old Erie Canal, which played a vital part in Buffalo's growth in the early nineteenth century, still bustles with tugs and barges that serve the industrial complexes along its banks.

One of the finest Art Deco public buildings in the United States, Buffalo City Hall is a richly ornamented reddish structure completed in 1931 in Niagara Square in the heart of downtown. An observation deck on the 28th floor offers spectacular views of the lakeside city and surrounding area.

Downtown Buffalo

1 City Hall
2 Prudential Building
3 Naval and Servicemen's Park
4 Erie Basin Marina
5 Memorial Auditorium
6 Theater District
7 Allentown National Historic District
8 Wilcox Mansion
9 Kleinhans Music Hall
10 Buffalo Museum of Science

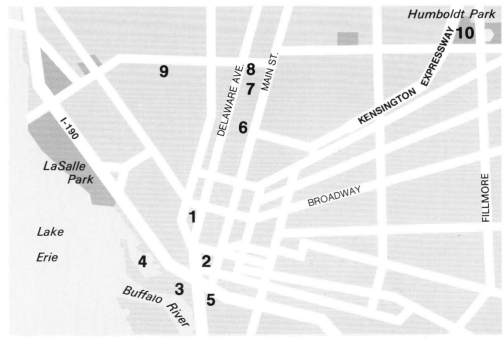

location at the extreme eastern end of Lake Erie at the hub of an area that encompasses almost 50 percent of the population of the United States and more than 60 percent of that of Canada. As "Queen City of the Lakes," Buffalo is a key center of communications, transporting raw materials and finished goods by land on its excellent rail network and by water via the Great Lakes and the St. Lawrence Seaway.

Although the whole of this St. Lawrence region was first explored and claimed by the French, the site of Buffalo was not settled until 1804, when Joseph Ellicott laid out the village of New Amsterdam at the mouth of Buffalo Creek. According to one of the many stories on the subject, the name Buffalo arose because local Indians mispronounced the French term *belle fleuve*, meaning "beautiful river" (referring to the Niagara River), and the Americans who settled here later preferred this Indian version to New Amsterdam. After the Erie Canal opened in 1825, the community experienced a dramatic boom through the growth in Great Lakes trade, and New Englanders and European immigrants streamed in to work in its burgeoning industries, bringing not only their wide-ranging skills, but also a rich cultural diversity. Today, Buffalo has the biggest St. Patrick's Day parade outside New York City, and the German and Polish restaurants in its Broadway and Fillmore district serve national cuisine to satisfy the most fastidious of gourmets.

Tourists who take time to explore the Niagara area surrounding the famous falls discover that, despite its obvious concern with industry, Buffalo has many attractions and a climate that is never excessively hot, due to the breezes that blow off the lake and, incidentally, help to clear away polluting factory smoke. An enjoyable cruise can be taken on Lake Erie aboard the *Miss Buffalo*, which docks in the Erie Basin Marina at the mouth of the Buffalo River. Along the waterfront is a series of pleasant green spaces, such as LaSalle Park on the lake and, along the north bank of the river, the Naval and Servicemen's Park, where several World War II ships are now preserved.

Behind the lakeshore, the downtown business district contains many architectural gems. Among them is the magnificent and richly ornamented City Hall on Niagara Square, a ruddy Art Deco masterpiece facing the monument to President William McKinley, who was assassinated in Buffalo in 1901. The nearby Church Street area boasts one of Louis Sullivan's finest creations, the Prudential (formerly Guaranty) Building of 1896, with its red terracotta decoration; St. Paul's Episcopal Church, Richard Upjohn's masterpiece of 1851; the famous Ellicott Square Building of 1896; and the elegant M & T Bank Building, Minoru Yamasaki's 1966 contribution, with its plaza where you can enjoy midday concerts during the summer. Students of architecture will also find Henry Hobson Richardson's impressive Buffalo State Hospital north of downtown and five lovely private houses designed by Frank Lloyd Wright at various sites in the city.

North of Church Street, the mile-long pedestrian mall along Main Street passes through the lively theater district, a potpourri of shops, restaurants, offices, and, of course, theaters. Outstanding among these are the Studio Arena Theater, acclaimed for its excellent dramatic productions, and the beautiful Shea's Buffalo Theater, a former 1920s movie house that boasts a magnificent Wurlitzer pipe organ and is lit by priceless chandeliers in its opulent interior.

Parallel to Main, on the west, the bustling Victorian stretches of Franklin and Delaware avenues lead north into the National Historic District of Allentown, Buffalo's bohemian enclave brimming with antique shops, art galleries, and fine restaurants. On Delaware Avenue, once Buffalo's "millionaire's row," is the old Wilcox Mansion, where Theodore Roosevelt was inaugurated after President McKinley's assassination; it is now a National Historic Site. To the west is the renowned Kleinhans Music Hall, a magnificent 2,839-seat building with near-perfect acoustics designed

In recent years imaginative building programs have helped to dispel Buffalo's unjustifiable image as a dowdy, run-down industrial city. Smart new office towers, spacious plazas, and enchanting fountains and waterfalls have swelled the city's proud heritage of architectural excellence.

by the world-famous architects Eliel and Eero Saarinen and the home of the Buffalo Philharmonic Orchestra.

Delaware Park, laid out by Frederick Law Olmsted, the creator of New York City's Central Park, is one of Buffalo's outstanding outdoor attractions. It contains not only a superb zoo and golf course, but also the internationally acclaimed Albright–Knox Art Gallery, with its excellent collection of contemporary art, and the Buffalo and Erie County Historical Society Museum, which houses exhibits on local nineteenth-century life. One of the city's other major institutions, the wide-ranging Buffalo Museum of Science, is located on the east side of town, whose streets often throng with baseball fans packing into the district's War Memorial Stadium to watch the Bisons. Buffalo's other main sports arenas are the 80,000-seat Rich Stadium, the Orchard Park home of the football Bills, and the downtown Memorial Auditorium, which seats 17,000 spectators for Braves basketball and Sabres ice-hockey games.

Several other places of interest are within easy reach of downtown Buffalo, including the Tifft Farm Nature Reserve; the South Park Botanical Gardens; the Darien Lake Fun Country theme park; the family entertainment and cultural center of Artpark in Lewiston; and the most thrilling experience of all: Niagara Falls, which, despite commercialization, remains one of the world's most spectacular wonders. It is also the source of the electric power that turns the wheels of this great industrial city.

One of the world's great natural wonders, Niagara Falls is a major tourist attraction only a short distance from downtown Buffalo. As it races north from Lake Erie toward Lake Ontario, the short Niagara River divides around little Goat Island and plunges spectacularly over a rocky ledge to create the 182-foot-high American Falls and the 176-foot-high Horseshoe Falls.

Charleston SOUTH CAROLINA

Historic Charles Towne

Soon after the settlement of Charles Towne was founded in South Carolina in 1670, a leading local figure named Dr. Henry Woodward received a small quantity of rice seeds from a certain Captain Thurber, recently arrived after a voyage from Madagascar. Some 70 years later, a teenage girl named Eliza Lucas got some seeds of the indigo plant from her father, then on the West Indian island of Antigua, and experimented in their cultivation at their family home near Wappoo Creek. Not, you might think, particularly dramatic events; yet it was from these simple beginnings that colossal exports of rice and indigo developed in the century prior to the Revolutionary War and created the wealth to build the beautiful and gracious city of Charleston we see today. It is a city of lovely mansions, scented gardens, and cobblestone streets lined with palmettos and shade trees, a place where time seems to have stood still for centuries.

On Broad Street, in Charleston's beautiful historic district, is the city's oldest church, St. Michael's Episcopal Church, completed in 1761. George Washington worshiped here when visiting Charleston during his tour of the South in 1791.

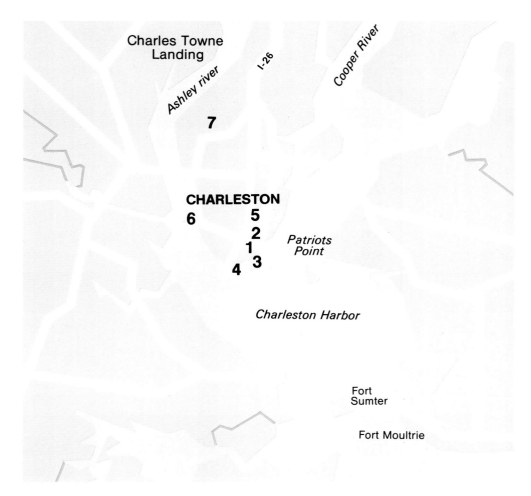

Charleston is located on a narrow finger of land between the Ashley and Cooper rivers in one of those long tidal inlets that cut deep into America's Atlantic coastline. Protecting its huge natural harbor on the seaward side are sandy islands built up over the centuries by the currents and tides. The restricted site occupied by the old city has meant that its suburbs and industrial areas are separated from it by the rivers and creeks that abound in this tidewater area, although linked to it by a system of modern highways, and that only 69,000 people, just over one-sixth of metropolitan Charleston's population of 411,000, live in the old city.

The first Europeans to arrive in this marshy "Low Country" landed in 1670 on the west bank of the Ashley River at a spot they first named Albemarle and then Charles Towne, in honor of the English king. Ten years later, they moved across the river to a better-protected site, where the present city stands, and there they built a walled settlement that was open to immigrants of every religious persuasion. Through trade in rice, indigo, and, later, cotton, the community grew into a major seaport, which saw action against the British during the Revolution. On April 12, 1861, the first shots of the Civil War were fired against federal troops holding Fort Sumter in the harbor; from then on, Charleston entered a period of decline in its fortunes, from which it has only begun to emerge in recent years. Today, Charleston is developing as a manufacturing and financial center, its economy aided by the siting here of military and naval installations and by the growing tourist industry.

Three hundred years of elegant, European-style living, supported in the early days by the labor of black slaves, produced a conservative, but religiously tolerant society that recently has had to think long and hard before accepting the challenge of industrial development and tourism. Since 1975, however, change has come about; it is evident, for example, in the revitalization of the old City Market and the conversion of old warehouses near Market Street to house an assortment of boutiques, restaurants, and expensive homes. The success of the first Spoleto Festival U.S.A., held in 1977, helped to bring in the tourists, and the secret of Charleston was out. Since then, thousands of people have come here every year to admire the beauty of this historic city, to enjoy its many attractions and its southern hospitality and charm, and to bask in its semitropical climate.

Perhaps the logical place to begin a tour of Charleston is at the original settlement. It is now enclosed in Charles Towne Landing State Park, 80 acres of beautiful, landscaped gardens with lagoons and moss-draped live oaks, where you can see the reconstructed palisade and earthen walls, a seventeenth-century vessel moored along the creek, and wild animals of the kind that roamed the area in those early days.

You can then spend several days walking or riding in a horse-drawn carriage through the tree-shaded cobblestone streets and alleys of the old city, a remarkable treasure trove of historic buildings and beautiful gardens whose flowers perfume the air. Many of the houses that belonged to prominent early citizens are open to visitors as museums and offer a taste of the gracious life style of past centuries. Among them are the Thomas Elfe House, a small Charleston "single house" of about 1760 that was occupied by the local cabinetmaker of same name, and such larger homes as the charming Heyward–Washington House, built around 1772 and exquisitely furnished, and the Nathaniel Russell House of 1809, famous for its floating staircase. There are also the Joseph Manigault House (1803), the Edmonston–Alston House (1828), the Aiken–Rhett Mansion (1830s), the Calhoun Mansion (1876), and the many old private properties that are specially open to the public during the annual springtime Festival of Houses.

Everywhere there are beautiful old churches of all denominations, testifying to the religious freedom established here by the early colonists.

The stunningly beautiful gardens of the famed Magnolia Plantation, about 10 miles northwest of Charleston, are ablaze with camellias and azaleas in the early months of the year. The ancestral home of the Drayton family since the 1670s, the plantation is now listed in the National Register of Historic Places and is one of the most popular visitor attractions in the Charleston area.

Among them are the city's oldest church building, St. Michael's of 1761, and the colony's mother church, St. Philip's. Of special interest are the eighteenth-century College of Charleston, the Exchange Building and its grim Provost Dungeon – used as a prison by the British during the Revolution – and the Dock Street Theater, still used for productions of plays and shows. A mine of information about past times is to be found in Charleston's many museums, the most notable including the comprehensive Charleston Museum, founded in 1773 and America's oldest museum, the Confederate Museum, and the Old Slave Mart Museum. And for paintings reflecting local history, the City Hall Gallery and the Gibbes Art Gallery should not be missed.

Spring is a particularly enchanting time of year in Charleston, for then its gardens burst into dazzling displays of colorful azaleas, camellias, magnolias, rhododendrons, and wisteria. It is a time when every visitor drives north out of town to see the world-famous Magnolia Plantation and Gardens; Middleton Place, America's oldest landscaped gardens; and the mysterious Cypress Gardens, a shady swamp garden ablaze with flowers. Also to the north of the city are two other outstanding attractions on everyone's list: the former cotton plantation of Boone Hall, with its avenues of moss-covered live oaks, used in the filming of *Gone with the Wind*; and Drayton Hall, a magnificent Georgian-style mansion.

Boat cruises around Charleston's harbor provide an opportunity to see historic Forts Sumter and Moultrie and the impressive collection of modern naval vessels, including the aircraft carrier *Yorktown*, at the Patriots Point Naval and Maritime Museum.

Charleston has many facilities for outdoor recreation, especially golf, tennis, and water sports; it also boasts excellent public and private resort beaches along its Atlantic coastline, such as Folly Beach, the Isle of Palms, and Kiawah Island. For shoppers, there are the delightful specialty shops along Church, King, and Market streets in the historic district, where excellent restaurants serve locally caught seafood. Now that Charleston has emerged from its shell, tourists are bound to stream in to sample its varied year-round attractions.

Located about 7 miles north of Charleston, the magnificent former cotton plantation of Boone Hall, dating from 1681, is open to visitors throughout the year. Renowned for its majestic avenue of live oaks planted in 1743, the mansion also has beautiful formal gardens and slave cabins of pre-Revolutionary War days.

Charlotte NORTH CAROLINA

Queen Charlotte's City

"Thar's gold in them thar hills!" Not California in 1849, or even the Klondike in 1897 – but Charlotte, North Carolina, a whole century earlier. One day in 1799, while wallowing in a stream that ran through his father's farm some 20 miles northeast of that city, 12-year-old Conrad Reed came across a 17-pound nugget that dramatically switched the family business from agricultural pursuits to hunting for gold. For his efforts, father John Reed was soon rewarded with the discovery of a 28-pound nugget at his mine – and the rush was on. Between 1800 and 1845, 100 mines in this part of North Carolina were America's main suppliers of the precious metal, and a branch of the United States Mint opened in Charlotte in 1837 to handle it. The old building, reconstructed and relocated, now holds a proud place among Charlotte's attractions as the Mint Museum of Art.

The Mint Museum is only one of the relics of history preserved in this thriving modern city, North Carolina's largest metropolis. Located in the Piedmont Plateau region of the state, Charlotte is the central buckle in the industrial belt known as the Carolinas Crescent. Concentrating mainly on the manufacture of textiles, the city is also a major financial and distribution center at the hub of a good network of communications. By no means a sleepy southern city, Charlotte has an atmosphere of vibrant excitement, symbolized by its revitalized central, or Uptown, district and neighborhoods, its lively and varied cultural life, and its wide range of sports and recreational events and facilities. With its beautiful parks, open spaces, and trees and its bold modern buildings, Charlotte is creating a pleasant, livable environment for its rapidly growing population. The 1980 census revealed that over 314,000 people were living in the city itself, a considerable increase over the previous ten years.

The first people to settle here were German and Scots-Irish migrants who arrived around 1750 from the colonies farther north. The town they founded was diplomatically labeled Charlotte in honor of Queen Charlotte, the German-born consort of England's king, George III. The surrounding county they named Mecklenburg after her duchy of Mecklenburg-Strelitz in Germany. In 1768, Charlotte was incorporated as a city and six years later it became the county seat. During the Revolution, after a brief occupation by British troops under Cornwallis, it became the headquarters of the American general Horatio Gates. The discovery of gold at the turn of the century helped to boost the growing city's fortunes, before the debacle of the Civil War brought humiliating defeat with North Carolina's surrender to General William Tecumseh Sherman's Union forces. Fortunately, Charlotte avoided destruction during the war, the most drastic alterations to its skyline coming only in recent years with the construction of gleaming office towers and elevated walkways in the attractive Uptown area. At the same time, old neighborhoods have been renovated; one example is the pleasant Fourth Ward, with its lovely Victorian homes.

Charlotte boasts many historic places both in and around the city, among them the Hezekiah Alexander Homesite, known as the "Rock House," a former dairy farmhouse built in 1774 and now Mecklenburg County's oldest dwelling. Also at the site is the Mint Museum of History, which houses exhibits emphasizing local events. North of the city is Latta Place, a restored river plantation house of about 1800 with a 326-acre

The exciting modern architecture of Charlotte's downtown district is visible evidence of the city's growing prosperity as a leading financial, transportation, and textile-manufacturing center.

wilderness area and nature park, while a few miles on the other side of town, the James K. Polk Memorial recalls the life and times of America's eleventh president at its log-cabin site.

Among the exciting twentieth-century architecture that lines Charlotte's Uptown streets is the Civic Center, which provides modern facilities for conventions and trade shows right in the heart of the city. Not far away are two other popular attractions. One of these, Discovery Place, is a science and technology museum where you can play laser pinball, experience a jungle thunderstorm, or take part in other fascinating adventures into knowledge. The other is a gracious old church now transformed into a center for the visual and performing arts known as Spirit Square.

Charlotte's cultural scene harnesses the talents of various theater groups and leading organizations such as the Opera Association, Dance Charlotte, and the Charlotte Symphony, whose performances are hosted by several theaters and halls to the south and east of the city center. Among these are the Children's Theater, the Charlotte Little Theater, the Golden Circle Theater at the Mint Museum of Art, and the well-known Ovens Auditorium on Independence Boulevard, the home of touring Broadway productions.

Near the Ovens Auditorium is the Charlotte Coliseum, a popular venue for country-music and rock concerts, circuses, basketball games, and wrestling contests. Sports lovers in Charlotte also make their way to the Memorial Stadium, which hosts equestrian events that include the prestigious U.S. Open Jumping Championship, and to the Jim Crockett Memorial Park, where the minor-league Charlotte Orioles play their home baseball games. Thousands of people regularly drive north out of town to enjoy the excitement of stock-car and motorcyle racing at the famous Charlotte Motor Speedway, while others prefer the more peaceful pleasures of one of the city's many fine golf courses. Charlotte has excellent facilities for all kinds of sports, not least of which is fishing at Lakes Wylie and Norman.

Several places with a broader family appeal are located on the south side of the city center, such as the Nature Museum, the bird sanctuary and garden of Wing Haven, and the lovely recreation and amusement park at Heritage Village and Fort Heritage. About 11 miles south of town is the 77-acre Carowinds theme park, a must for everyone who loves the thrill of the roller coaster. In the opposite direction, about 17 miles north of town, is the Buffalo Ranch, which offers a fascinating stagecoach ride to see herds of buffalo, Texas longhorn cattle, and wild animals roaming free on its land.

Charlotte
1 *Civic Center*
2 *Spirit Square*
3 *Discovery Place*
4 *Park Center and Memorial Stadium*
5 *Mint Museum of Art*
6 *Charlotte Coliseum and Ovens Auditorium*
7 *Mint Museum of History and Hezekiah Alexander Homesite*
8 *Jim Crockett Memorial Park*
9 *Nature Museum*

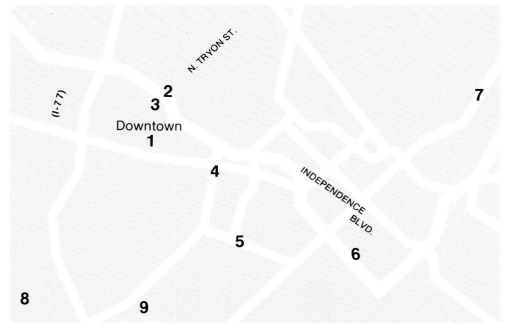

Action-packed entertainment awaits visitors to the Carowinds theme park south of Charlotte. Among the attractions is the thrilling roller coaster, which makes many a brave heart quake as it races round four vertical loops.

For the more adventurous, Charlotte is well located for drives farther afield to the lovely Appalachian Mountains, which enclose the magnificent Great Smoky Mountains National Park and where there are breath-taking vistas along the Blue Ridge Parkway.

To add to the pleasure of visiting or living in Charlotte, there are various festivals and events throughout the year, beginning in early spring with the Southern Living Show, St. Patrick's Day parade, and Springfest, and followed by the Festival in the Park in September, the Carolinas Carrousel Parade on Thanksgiving and the Southern Christmas Show.

Visitors to Charlotte can always find something to remind them of their stay in this pleasant city by wandering around the bustling Uptown shopping area, with its interconnecting walkways above street level, or by browsing through the large number of mill-outlet stores and outlying shopping centers, such as the immense South Park and Eastland malls. Young Conrad Reed would certainly find a lot of things to spend his gold nugget on if he returned to Charlotte today.

Chicago ILLINOIS

The Windy City

Run a finger down the listing in the Chicago telephone directory, and you will be surprised to see just how many Polish names you find there. Chicago has, in fact, more residents of Polish origin than does any other city in the world except Warsaw, plus a fair number of people from almost everywhere else – including Germans, Italians, Greeks, Irish and Chinese – not to mention the pioneer Americans who flocked in from the east during the early days of westward expansion. It is therefore a city with a strong cosmopolitan flavor, its life style enriched by the various ethnic communities through their colorful customs and festivals, restaurants and crafts, and even museums that preserve their cultural heritage.

But more than just adding spice to the city's way of life, the immigrant communities, through their skills and their labor, have helped to make Chicago the Midwest's most powerful industrial, commercial, and financial giant – a powerhouse of enterprise second only to New York City. If Chicago were a nation, the value of the goods and services it produces would make it the ninth richest state in the world. Although no longer America's food-processing and meat-packing center – "hog butcher to the world," as the poet Carl Sandburg called it – Chicago is the country's biggest grain market, and its O'Hare Airport is the busiest in the world, bringing in some 8 million convention delegates and tourists each year.

Clinging tightly to its 29-mile shoreline along Lake Michigan, Chicago is a long, narrow city of some 3 million people, with a six-county metropolitan area whose population is around 7.6 million. Although long known as the nation's "Second City," it is now the third largest city in the United States, having been overtaken by Los Angeles in recent years. Despite its bitterly cold, snowy winters and its hot, humid summers that take your breath away as you step out of air-conditioned buildings, Chicago has been fortunate in its geographical location. Placed near the heart of the nation at the southern end of Lake Michigan, the city was destined to become both a major Great Lakes port and the hub of east–west transportation routes by road, rail, and air. It was therefore almost inevitable that, in 1673, the first French explorers in the area, Jacques Marquette and Louis Joliet, should have passed by the lakeside spot that local Indians called Checagou, a name variously interpreted to mean "strong," "powerful," "wild garlic" or, unflatteringly, "skunk."

Although a French trading post was set up on the site in 1779, followed by the building of Fort Dearborn by Americans in 1803, it was not until 1830 that a permanent settlement was established. The village grew rapidly as a trading center for the Midwest, its population increased by large numbers of American and foreign immigrants. After the Great Fire of 1871 had left 18,000 buildings destroyed, the need for new, cheap, and efficient buildings in the reconstruction of the city gave birth to the invention and use of the steel-framed structure and the "skyscraper" (of up to 16 stories) by architects of the famous Chicago school. Buildings designed in the 1880s and 1890s by such masters as Louis Sullivan and Frank Lloyd Wright still grace the streets of the city, and the suburb of Oak Park, where Wright designed many homes and the famous Unity Temple, is a mecca for students of architecture.

During the present century, Chicago has experienced many ups and

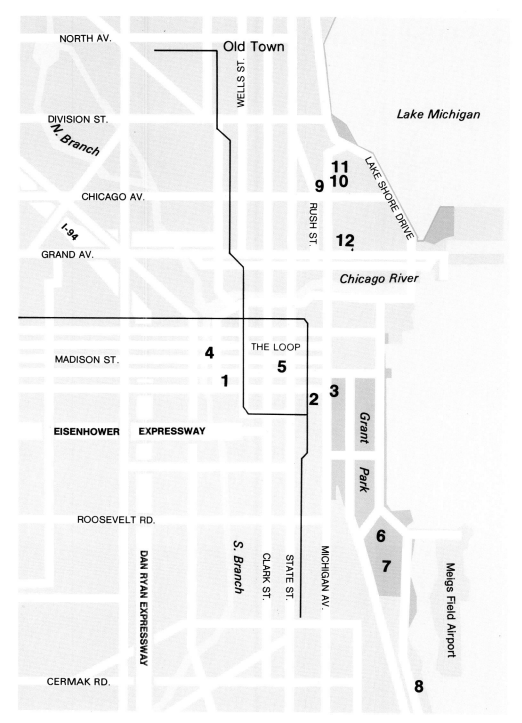

NORTH AV.

Old Town

WELLS ST.

DIVISION ST.

N. Branch

CHICAGO AV.

I-94

GRAND AV.

Lake Michigan

LAKE SHORE DRIVE

RUSH ST.

11
9 **10**

12

Chicago River

THE LOOP

MADISON ST.

4

5

1

2 **3**

EISENHOWER EXPRESSWAY

Grant Park

ROOSEVELT RD.

DAN RYAN EXPRESSWAY

S. Branch

CLARK ST.

STATE ST.

MICHIGAN AV.

6

7

Meigs Field Airport

CERMAK RD.

8

downs in its fortunes. The first two decades saw a cultural renaissance that gave the city its opera, its symphony orchestra, and such writers as Hamlin Garland, Theodore Dreiser, and Carl Sandburg. Then there were the race riots of 1919; Prohibition in the 1920s, when Al Capone's gangland activities culminated in the notorious St. Valentine's Day Massacre; the Great Depression of the 1930s; and the post-World War II flight of residents from the decaying center city to the suburbs.

It is hardly surprising that over the years Chicago acquired an unenviable reputation as a tough, cynical place: "stormy, husky, brawling; City of the Big Shoulders," was how Carl Sandburg described it in its early years. But now the old image is history, as the city presents a more sophisticated, cosmopolitan face to the world. A bold, imaginative program of urban renewal has revitalized much of the city in recent years, and fine new buildings pierce the magnificent skyline. Chicago has a new image as an outward-looking, international metropolis, with countless sightseeing and cultural attractions to interest the visitor.

Overleaf: The narrow Chicago River winds through the heart of the great lakeside city between the Loop and North Side districts, crossed by numerous bridges and flanked by tall buildings. Among these are the distinctive twin towers of the Marina City office and residential complex (in the background, right).

Thanks to Daniel Burnham's imaginative 1908 plan for the city's development, Chicago's urban sprawl is broken by hundreds of parks and "forest preserves," with a lakeshore free from industrial and commercial development. The view of the city skyline from a boat on Lake Michigan or from a plane flying in from the east is unquestionably breath-taking. Behind the beaches that front the lakeshore on each side of the mouth of the little Chicago River is a string of green parks – Lincoln to the north, Grant and Jackson to the south – and then a crop of glistening modern skyscrapers – some white, some dark – sprouts into the sky from the downtown district beyond. On the lake, yachts and cruise boats bob in the two harbors, Monroe Street and Burnham Park, and small executive jets line up in their varied liveries along the waterside runway of Meigs Field Airport. Dramatic views of the city and the surrounding area can be enjoyed from the Skydeck on the 103rd floor of the 110-story, 1,454-foot (443 m) Sears Tower, the world's tallest building, or from the 94th-floor Observatory in the 100-story John Hancock Center, farther north.

The downtown area straddles the Chicago River just below the point where its North and South branches converge. A narrow, meandering waterway, the river is crossed by a series of bridges that link the North Side with the main business and shopping district, which is known as the Loop. The name derives from the loop in the Chicago Transit Authority's elevated railroad, popularly referred to as the "El," which circles the district above street level. Laid out in the traditional American pattern, the downtown streets are numbered from the intersection of State and Madison streets in the Loop. Along State Street, now a bustling pedestrian mall, is a whole galaxy of shops, restaurants, theaters, and such

The 53-foot-high red "Flamingo" stabile by the celebrated artist Alexander Calder provides an eye-catching focal point in Federal Center Plaza in Chicago's downtown business and retail district. It is one of several monumental works of art by internationally renowned artists that now embellish the plazas among the high-rise office buildings in this part of the city.

elegant department stores as the famous Marshall Field and the majestic Carson Pirie Scott & Company, Louis Sullivan's architectural masterpiece of 1904. Scattered throughout the Loop are many other architectural gems of the same period, including the famous Rookery Building of 1886; the sturdy, masonry-built Monadnock Building of 1893; and the Manhattan Building, also dating from the 1890s, the city's first steel-framed structure and the pioneer of the modern skyscraper. Another interesting structure is the Art Deco-style Board of Trade Building, where you can watch the traders on the Grain Exchange at work. More recent architectural projects have given the Loop magnificent office towers and lively plazas embellished with sculptures by such world-famous artists as Pablo Picasso, Joan Miró, Henry Moore, Alexander Calder, and Claes Oldenburg, while the plaza at the foot of the futuristic, A-shaped First National Bank Building is adorned with Marc Chagall's famous *Four Seasons* mosaic.

Take a walk north along Michigan Avenue, and you pass other imposing city landmarks; the elegant, white 80-story Standard Oil Building; the twin-towered Wrigley Building; the Tribune Tower; and, upriver on the left, the celebrated double towers of Marina City, a residential and office complex. North of the river, Michigan Avenue as far as Oak Street has become known as Chicago's "Magnificent Mile," a broad, tree-shaded thoroughfare lined with plush hotels, elegant shops, restaurants, and airline offices, where one of the city's most famous landmarks, the Gothic-style Water Tower, stands as a survivor of the Great Fire of 1871. Across the street, overshadowed by the soaring John Hancock Center, is Water Tower Place, a magnificent shopping mall with smart stores, shops, restaurants, and movie theaters on several levels around its impressive atrium. Bustling

Still standing as a lone survivor of Chicago's Great Fire of 1871, the old Gothic-style Water Tower is a well-known landmark amid the modern offices and stores of North Michigan Avenue. It now serves as a visitor information center, providing a multimedia presentation of Chicago's many attractions.

Left: Since 1924 the white twin buildings and clock tower of the Wrigley Building have been a familiar sight by the Chicago River at the start of the "Magnificent Mile" of North Michigan Avenue.

nighttime activity to the sound of jazz or the blues can be found in the swinging clubs, bars, and restaurants on nearby Rush Street and some blocks north along Wells Street in the rejuvenated Victorian district of Old Town.

While in this part of the city, you should not fail to visit the fascinating Chicago Historical Society Museum on North Clark Street and to stroll through the open spaces of nearby Lincoln Park, a huge recreational playground with a beautiful flower conservatory and a 35-acre zoo that boasts a fine collection of apes. Drive north along the lakeshore from here, and you will see the luxurious apartment buildings of the aptly named Gold Coast.

Among Chicago's many sightseeing attractions are countless museums of all kinds, many of which are world famous. The Chicago Art Institute houses excellent collections of Impressionist and Post-Impressionist paintings and twentieth-century art. There is also the superb Museum of Contemporary Art, while the most popular of all is the captivating Museum of Science and Industry, where visitors can get involved in exhibits that demonstrate the latest advances in science and technology. The stories of mankind, the animal and plant worlds, and our earth are the subjects that draw people to the excellent Field Museum of Natural History on South Lake Shore Drive, close to the outstanding Shedd Aquarium and Adler Planetarium.

Theater figures high on Chicago's list of cultural attractions, with the Blackstone, Goodman, and Shubert among a group of fine downtown playhouses offering a wide range of entertainment that includes musical comedies, Broadway shows, classical drama, and contemporary plays. There are also many "Off-Loop" theaters that stage experimental drama and the works of new playwrights.

One of the highlights of the city's music scene is the prestigious Chicago Symphony, which offers wintertime concerts at the downtown Orchestra Hall and summertime performances at the renowned Ravinia Festival in Highland Park. The famed Lyric Opera stages its fine productions at the 3,500-seat Civic Opera House, and there is also the excellent Woodstock Opera House, a historic theater in the suburbs. Among the city's dance and ballet companies is the Chicago City Ballet, which performs at various theaters and throughout the Midwest. During the summer months, many musical events are held at various places in the city, among them the concerts performed at the Petrillo Bandshell in Grant Park. The city's many festivals include a two-week music bonanza in the annual ChicagoFest, held at the Navy Pier in July.

Baseball fans in Chicago have a choice of watching either the Cubs at Wrigley Field or the White Sox at Comiskey Park, while followers of football or soccer make their way to the lakeshore's Soldier Field Stadium to shout for the Bears or, if they prefer the game with the round ball, the Stings. Chicago Stadium, just west of downtown, is the choice for supporters of the Bulls basketball and the Blackhawks ice-hockey teams. Several tracks in the Chicago area offer the excitement of horse racing, while thrilling auto-racing events are held at Raceway Park and the Santa Fe Speedway.

Other kinds of thrills can be enjoyed at the celebrated Marriott's Great America entertainment center to the north of the city in Gurnee, where the highlights for the strong and adventurous include stomach-churning rides on the American Eagle roller coaster and The Edge.

A century or more ago, Chicago's over-talkative politicians earned it the often misunderstood nickname of "Windy City," which does not refer to the weather, and over the years, many words have been written about it. But Chicago is a city of action rather than of words, a city bursting with the energy and vitality that make it an exciting place both to live in and to visit.

Below: Buckingham Fountain, one of Grant Park's impressive sights, was donated to the city of Chicago by Kate Sturges Buckingham in 1927 as a memorial to her brother. Built of Georgia pink marble, the fountain has sculptured groups of seahorses and 133 jets spouting 15,000 gallons a minute. During the summer months the spectacular cascades are beautifully illuminated at night.

Cincinnati OHIO

Ohio's Queen City

Downtown Cincinnati forms a backdrop of high-rise buildings, dominated by the lofty Carew Tower and pointed Central Trust Tower, on the north bank of the Ohio River, where the colossal Riverfront Stadium is a prominent landmark.

In her zealous campaign against demon drink at the turn of the century, Carry Nation, the formidable archpriestess of American temperance, smashed her way with an ax through the saloons of Kansas before going on to the bigger cities. No item of glass – whether window, bottle, or barroom nude – was safe from her fierce depredations, which she called her "hatchetations of joints." But when she arrived in Cincinnati, Ohio, in 1901, the sheer number of liquor parlors there defeated her. "I would have dropped from exhaustion before I had gone a block," she confessed to the eagerly awaiting press. Even today, it is true that Cincinnati folk enjoy the good things in life, although they do so with considerably more reserve and gentility than did their nineteenth-century forbears, whose riotous life style inspired future president William Henry Harrison to look on the city as "the most debauched place I ever saw."

Cincinnati's unenviable reputation in those days went hand in hand with its role as the busiest port on the Ohio River, through which came migrant families, aristocratic travelers, tradesmen, and all kinds of riffraff eager to stake their claims in the newly opened-up West. In Longfellow's phrase, Cincinnati was "Queen City of the West," and the writer Charles Dickens, no mean observer of urban life, found it "a beautiful city; cheerful, thriving and animated. I have not seen a place that commends itself so favorably and pleasantly to a stranger at the first glance as this does."

Cincinnati really does occupy a beautiful setting on the north bank of the Ohio River across from Kentucky, surrounded by an amphitheater of gentle hills, each now surmounted by its own distinct neighborhood. The site, in southwestern Ohio, was chosen in 1788 for a settlement called Losantiville, an unmusical name that was quickly changed by the first governor of the territory to Cincinnati, in honor of the Society of the Cincinnati, to which he belonged. This was an organization of Revolutionary War officers who admired the ideas of Lucius Quinctius Cincinnatus, a Roman general of the fifth century B.C. who believed that soldiers should remain at home as private citizens when not needed to fight.

Grown sufficiently to receive its charter as a city in 1819, Cincinnati boomed with the opening of the Miami Canal to Ohio's interior and the coming of the railroads. By mid-century, it was the most important port on the Ohio River, handling huge volumes of trade with the South via the Mississippi, while its jetties thronged with crowded passenger steamboats. Large numbers of German and other immigrants arrived at this time, contributing their skills and their culture to the life of the city. Now a metropolis of some 385,000 people, Cincinnati remains the nation's largest inland river port and a major hub of communications, although its industries now produce high-technology goods and a wider assortment of manufactures including machine tools, jet engines, soap products, and playing cards.

With its strong German atmosphere, the Queen City is a businesslike, conservative place with a cosmopolitan flavor. Not given to flamboyance, its citizens nonetheless enjoy the lively cultural life, colorful festivals, excellent restaurants, and facilities for sports and recreation that have earned Cincinnati recent praise as one of America's top five livable cities. Meantime, they get on with the task of urban renewal that has already seen

Eden Park borders the charming hilltop neighborhood of Mt. Adams, now enjoying a renaissance as a renovated bohemian enclave of smart boutiques, nightspots, and restaurants, among which The Pavilion claims one of the best views of the city.

Cincinnati's other major attractions are scattered among the surrounding suburbs and outlying communities. They include the excellent zoo, renowned for its Big Cat Canyon – with its rare white tigers – and its Gorillas Outside and Insect World exhibits. There are also the Harriet Beecher Stowe House, where the famous novelist did her research for *Uncle Tom's Cabin*; and the College Football Hall of Fame, on the grounds of the vast Kings Island theme park, a popular family-entertainment center that boasts a replica of the Eiffel Tower and the most terrifying roller coaster of all, named The Beast. For those who prefer the peace of natural surroundings, there is Mt. Airy Forest, the nation's largest municipal park, comprising 1,447 acres of greenery in the northwestern part of the city. History buffs will enjoy the collection of restored nineteenth-century buildings that re-creates Ohio pioneer life at the Sharon Woods Village to the north of town.

For shoppers, Cincinnati has many special places outside the downtown area in which to hunt for souvenirs or just simply browse, among them the lively outdoor Findlay Market; the gracious Art Deco-style Union Terminal mall, which was once a railroad station; the Markets International in suburban Springfield; and the huge Florence Mall across the river in Kentucky, where the community of Covington offers much to the explorer. But perhaps the most pleasurable souvenirs of Cincinnati are its ebullient Oktoberfest, its unique local chili, and the gourmet cuisine at the Maisonette on East 6th Street, one of the Queen City's truly royal experiences.

Framed by a thrilling roller coaster loop, a miniature-scaled Eiffel Tower overlooks 1,600 acres of family entertainment at Kings Island theme park north of downtown Cincinnati.

Cleveland OHIO

North Coast City

For years, the industrial metropolis of Cleveland, on Ohio's Lake Erie shore, bore the brunt of much scoffing and snickering as a symbol of all that was wrong with the older American cities. The image was fueled by inescapable facts. Its steel mills, oil refineries, and factories had polluted not only the air, but also the Cuyahoga River, on which the city stands, and Lake Erie itself. A decline in manufacturing had brought job losses and an exodus of people, who left behind a decaying central city inhabited mostly by the poor and elderly and with deteriorating services. The biggest sick joke of all came in 1978, when, unable to meet its debts, Cleveland became the first American city to default since the Great Depression of the 1930s.

Dramatic things have happened in Cleveland since then. Thanks to a vigorous recovery program launched by a new mayor, the city is now seeing a turnaround in its fortunes, having already made good its loans without state or federal aid. Industrial pollution is on the decline. Greater emphasis is being placed on more diversified manufacturing, technological and medical services, and research at the expense of heavy industry. With the recovery of business confidence, work has begun on several prestigious new office buildings in the downtown district, and revitalization and renovation throughout the city are saving many old neighborhoods and buildings from decay. The last census revealed that the city population had declined from around 1 million in 1950 to 573,822 in 1980, but now people are beginning to return. Cleveland's recovery in the 1980s is probably the

Downtown Cleveland
 1 *City Hall*
 2 *Convention Center and Public Hall*
 3 *Old Stone Church*
 4 *Terminal Tower*
 5 *Rockefeller Building*
 6 *The Arcade*
 7 *New Central Market*
 8 *Playhouse Square*

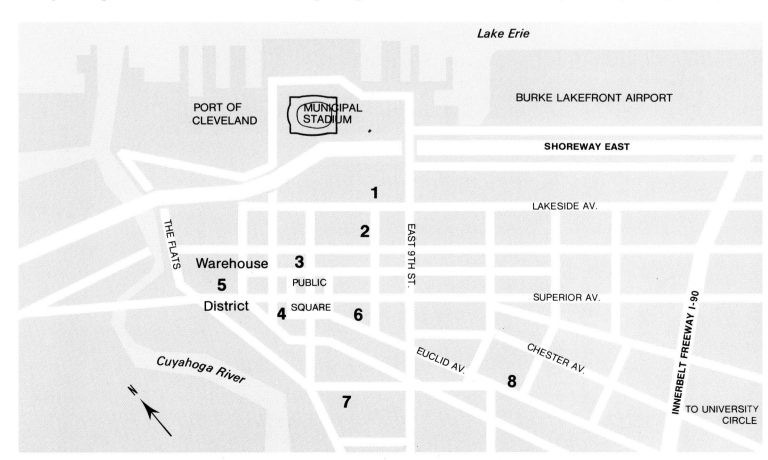

Sprawling along 30 miles of Lake Erie shoreline, Cleveland offers excellent facilities for fishing and boating enthusiasts, and even boasts more yacht clubs than San Diego. High-rise office towers punctuate the downtown skyline behind the port and the nearby Municipal Stadium.

most exciting event in the city's history since its birth nearly 200 years ago.

In 1796, General Moses Cleaveland surveyed a strip of forested territory along Lake Erie for the Connecticut Land Company and founded a settlement on the east bank of the Cuyahoga River. Named for its founder – although without the middle *a* because of a newspaper misprint – the new community developed as a trading and shipping center under its nickname of "Forest City." With the completion of the Ohio and Erie Canal in the 1830s, followed by the arrival of the railroads, Cleveland became a link between Ohio's interior and the markets in the east-coast states. Iron ore imported from Minnesota and coal from Pennsylvania established a vigorous iron and steel industry, and Cleveland became a thriving manufacturing and business center vying with Detroit by the end of the century as the nation's leading automobile-making city. Meantime, John D. Rockefeller had shrewdly harnessed the oil bonanza ushered in at Titusville, Pennsylvania, in 1859 and made himself a billionaire by creating the vast refining empire of Standard Oil, which he based in Cleveland. The city was to benefit considerably in later years from his philanthropic donations, as it did from those of such magnates as Mark Hanna and Sam Mather. The fortunes of these tycoons were based largely on the sweat of the immigrant labor force that had streamed into Cleveland from the eastern states and from Europe and had created a rich patchwork of ethnic neighborhoods across the city.

General Cleaveland's original plan, with its neat pattern of streets laid out around a central public square, is now swamped in the midst of the urban sprawl that extends on both sides of the Cuyahoga River and up into the surrounding suburban heights as far as the ring of parks so elegantly named the "Emerald Necklace." Shaker Heights and Chagrin Falls, with their affluent executive mansions, and Lakeside, with its "Gold Coast" of expensive apartments and condominiums, are just three of the desirable residential areas around the city within easy reach of the downtown business district. Down by the river, where it winds under quaint old bridges into the lake, the industrial eyesores known as the Warehouse District and the Flats are sprouting new life, as old buildings are converted into restaurants and shops. Across the river, the neighborhood of Ohio City, once the stronghold of the steel-mill workers, is witnessing the rejuvenation of its many fine Victorian homes, as younger and more affluent people move in. In this convenient area is the splendid West Side Market, packed with stalls selling ethnic foods of every description.

Behind the lakefront, with its docks and parks, the 80,000-seat Cleveland Municipal Stadium is the setting for some of the city's most exciting and noisy sports action when the crowds turn out to see home games of the baseball Indians and the football Browns. A few blocks south, the city's most prominent landmark, the 52-story Terminal Tower, soars above the business district in the central Public Square, the site of the Old Stone Church of 1855 and the new Standard Oil Company of Ohio's headquarters, one of several exciting glass and steel structures in this part of town.

East of here, on Euclid Avenue, is the 1892 Arcade, a beautiful, multi-tiered enclosed shopping center on the way to Playhouse Square, now being restored to its former glitter and glamor as a center of cultural activity that offers top-rate shows, plays, opera, ballet, and music concerts in its Palace, State, and Ohio theaters. Farther along Euclid is the Cleveland Play House, the country's oldest professional theater company, which now boasts the new Bolton Theater designed by the celebrated Cleveland architect Philip Johnson.

Continuing along Euclid in the same direction, you come to a remarkable and unique cluster of cultural, educational, medical, and religious institutions in a beautiful 500-acre parkland setting known as University Circle. Here you will find the world-famous Cleveland Museum of Art; the captivating Frederick C. Crawford Auto–Aviation Museum; the lovely Severance Hall, the winter home of the acclaimed Cleveland Orchestra; the Actors Company's Eldred Theater, which helped to start actors like Joel Grey and Paul Newman on their way to stardom; and a host of other prestigious places too numerous to describe.

There is, however, one other cultural attraction that enjoys special popularity among Clevelanders: Blossom Music Center, an hour's drive south of downtown in Cuyahoga Falls, where you can hear the summer concerts of the Cleveland Orchestra in a lovely open-air setting. You can also take a delightful steam-train ride in the same direction to the Hale Farm and Village, a living museum of early-settler life in the beautiful countryside of Cuyahoga National Recreation Area.

Other special pleasures of life in Cleveland are its assortment of first-rate ethnic restaurants all over town and its excellent selection of big stores, specialty shops, and malls ranging from the exciting treasure troves of Antique Row in Ohio City to plush, contemporary Beachwood Place, a suburban mall out in Beachwood. And, of course, there is Lake Erie, a place for relaxing cruises, yachting, or even fishing, now that the fish are coming back.

Voted one of the top ten All-American Cities for 1981/82 by the National Municipal League, Cleveland is making a rapid comeback from its recent difficulties as a good place both to visit and to live in.

An elegant, old-world atmosphere captivates shoppers in the ornate, glass-enclosed interior of the Arcade on Cleveland's Euclid Avenue. Built in 1892, this historic shopping center has five tiers of specialty stores, boutiques, and restaurants.

Columbus OHIO

The Buckeye Capital

The 41-story red granite Ohio State Office Tower stands out on the downtown Columbus skyline on the east bank of the Scioto River. In recent years Columbus has been the only major city east of the Mississippi River and north of the Mason-Dixon Line to continue to grow in population.

For the celebration of Columbus Day in 1955, the industrial city of Columbus, Ohio, received the gift of a 20-foot (6 m) bronze statue of Christopher Columbus from its sister city of Genoa, Italy, the birthplace of the famous fifteenth-century explorer. Despite the donation, the American city does not have a large Italian community. Unlike many of the great industrial centers of the northeastern states, Columbus did not receive large numbers of immigrants from foreign countries in its early years, except for German settlers who in the 1850s established the city's one major ethnic neighborhood, south of downtown. To their adopted city they bequeathed the German Oktoberfest, the principal ethnic event in its cultural calendar.

Columbus is a planned city, established in 1812 when the Buckeye State authorities were looking for a suitable site for Ohio's political center. They found it in the rolling country near the middle of the state, at a place on the east bank of the Scioto River opposite the earlier settlement of Franklinton. Named Columbus, the new city became the state capital officially in 1816, after which it served not only as the seat of state and county government, but also as a manufacturing and distribution center for the surrounding area. With its economic development boosted by the arrival of the Ohio and Erie Canal in 1831 and the first railroad nearly 20 years later, the

city became a leading manufacturer of buggies. Further growth came after 1940, when the federal government set up an aircraft factory here, and other industries followed. Today, Columbus gives its citizens employment in the manufacturing of machinery, aircraft, and auto assemblies; in printing; in wholesale and retail business; and in finance, banking, and government services. As a leading technical and scientific research center, the city is also proud to be home to the vast campus of Ohio State University, one of America's largest.

After World War II, efforts were made to improve environmental conditions in the city after decades of industrial development and wear and tear. The Inner and Outer Belt highways were built to relieve traffic congestion; measures were taken to control air and river pollution; and urban rehabilitation and renewal projects were begun. Now Columbus is the only large industrial center in the Northeast to show continued economic progress and an increase in its central-city population, which has risen since 1970 to more than 565,000.

New office and hotel towers now mark the heart of the city, which you can see from a height by riding in the external elevator on the Nationwide Insurance Company building. Among the grid of streets is the long major thoroughfare of Broad Street, where the statue of Christopher Columbus stands by the City Hall, not far from the 41-story State Office Tower, an elegant modern structure built in red granite. Contrasting in style is the beautiful white-limestone State Capitol, which has stood in dignified majesty in nearby Capitol Square since 1861, the finest example of Greek Doric architecture in the country.

A walk farther east along Broad Street reveals two other treasures: the exciting Center of Science and Industry, with varied exhibits and displays that include a see-through talking woman; and the prestigious Columbus Museum of Art, with splendid art collections that embrace painting by the

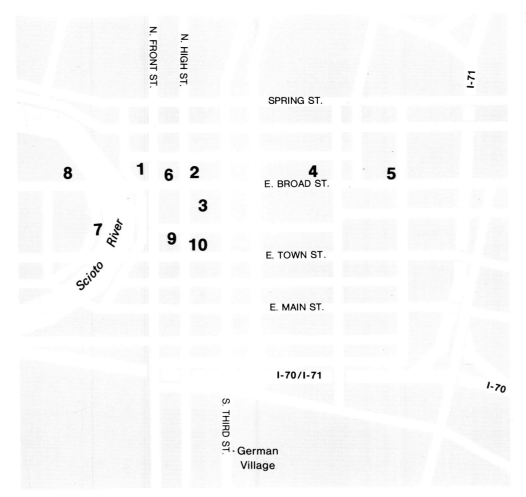

Downtown Columbus
1 City Hall
2 State Office Tower
3 State Capitol
4 Center of Science and Industry
5 Columbus Museum of Art
6 Palace Theater
7 Riverfront Amphitheater
8 Veterans Memorial Auditorium
9 Ohio Theater
10 Centrum

Columbus-born artist George Bellows. In the other direction, you will find the magnificent Palace Theater, opened in 1926 and recently renovated to create an opulent setting for touring Broadway shows, and on the west bank of the river, the Riverfront Amphitheater, a popular outdoor venue for summer concerts. Father west along Broad Street are the Franklin County Veterans Memorial Auditorium, another place for concerts and shows as well as trade expositions, and the historic home of William Henry Harrison, the ninth president of the United States.

More cultural life is in evidence on State Street, the location of the grand Ohio Theater, another renovated building where you can enjoy a wide range of entertainment – including symphony concerts, opera, ballet, Broadway musicals, and plays – in its plush auditorium, plus a summer season of movies preceded by recitals on the Mighty Morton organ. Along High Street, a popular meeting place is the sunken plaza known as the Centrum, where you can roller-skate in summer and ice-skate in winter. Also on High Street are the huge F & R Lazarus store and the Ohio Center convention complex and shopping mall, the place to make for during the annual Oktoberfest celebrations. South of here, along South Third Street, is one of Columbus's most popular attractions, the 233-acre German Village, a restored neighborhood of brick-paved streets lined with quaint houses, antique and specialty shops, and tempting German restaurants with its own special atmosphere. For another experience in European-style shopping, you can travel to the northern part of the city to the Continent shopping center, with its specialty shops, food stalls, and restaurants.

On the east side of town, garden lovers will find two places to interest them: the Franklin Park Conservatory and Garden Center, which has magnificent displays of exotic plants; and the Dawes Arboretum, a lovely

A statue of President William McKinley stands before the majestic Ohio State Capitol, a magnificent example of the Greek Doric style of architecture and a National Historic Landmark. Built in white limestone between 1839 and 1861, the building contains an impressive rotunda embellished with murals depicting events in American History and, in the 158-foot-high dome, a stained-glass representation of the Great Seal of Ohio.

900-acre park of trees and shrubs, containing a pleasant Japanese Garden with a lake and teahouse. And in the northern part of town, along North High Street, there is the acclaimed Park of Roses, where over 400 varieties provide a dazzling kaleidoscope of color.

This part of the city is dominated by the extensive campus of Ohio State University, with its huge football stadium, but there are many other places of interest, particularly for the history buff. There are the Victorian Village, an elegant old neighborhood of graceful homes that are now being restored; the Ohio Historical Museum, with its marvelous exhibits on the state's early period and its collection of nineteenth-century buildings in the adjacent Ohio Village; and, in Worthington, the Benjamin Hanby and Orange Johnson houses, dating from the same years, and the fascinating Ohio Railway Museum. North Columbus also has the Columbus Zoo and nearby Amusement Park, and the State Fairgrounds, which hosts the largest state fair in the United States.

Facilities for sports and outdoor recreation are scattered throughout the city, and there are also two outstanding horse-racing tracks in the southern districts: Scioto Downs, a showplace of harness racing; and Beulah Racetrack, for thoroughbred and quarter-horse events.

Located at the hub of an excellent network of highways, Columbus is a good starting point for excursions into the pleasant rural areas around the city. One of the choicest spots is Hocking Hills State Park, with its impressive gorges and waterfalls. There are many things to see and do in and around Columbus, and it comes as no surprise that with its high quality of life and wide range of business opportunities, the city is succeeding in persuading people not only to stay here, but also to explore, like Christopher Columbus, a new world of fulfillment.

Dallas/Fort Worth TEXAS

"Big D" and the Cow Town

Will Rogers, the humorist from Oklahoma, once remarked that "Fort Worth is where the West begins and Dallas is where the East peters out." It was a shrewd observation that seized on the essential differences between the two cities, companions in the rapidly growing "metroplex" that sprawls across the flat plains of northeastern Texas by the Trinity River. Between 1970 and 1980, the population of the combined eleven-county metropolitan area increased by 25 percent to almost 3 million, of which 904,078 people lived in Dallas, the second largest city in Texas and seventh in the nation, with 385,114 people living in Fort Worth, its neighbor to the west.

Served by the biggest airport in America – it is bigger than Manhattan Island – the two-city metroplex epitomizes all you imagine about Texas, with superlatives like *biggest*, *best*, and *richest* at the front of your mind, although the stereotyped images hide some surprises. Dallas – "Big D" – is glossy and sophisticated, vibrant and affluent, a flourishing business center involved in banking, insurance, and the operations of scores of top-ranking corporations. As the "Buckle of the Bible Belt," Dallas nurtures strong religious beliefs and conservative attitudes, a suitable climate for the location here of the Southern Methodist University (S.M.U.) campus. At the same time, it is a fun-loving city whose resident are not ashamed to spend their wealth on a wide range of entertainment activities and the performing arts. Fort Worth takes a more easy-going view of life; here, the earthly pleasures of the rodeo or the cattle auction are in keeping with the city's image of a cow town. And yet this is a city that can boast some of the finest art collections in the nation. Fort Worth is the lean Texas cowboy, clad in jeans; Dallas, the well-dressed, cigar-toting city businessman; and both shade their heads from the hot Texas sun with their big, wide-brimmed Stetsons.

Proud of their achievements, Dallas folk will tell you that theirs is a city that really should not exist at all. There were no natural advantages to the site on the Trinity River where John Neely Bryan built the area's first simple trading-post cabin back in 1841. Yet he managed to persuade others to settle here, and over the years, the community slowly grew. Historians argue whether its name was chosen to honor someone known to Bryan ("my friend Dallas") or George Mifflin Dallas, a United States vice president. But they all agree that the arrival of the railroads in the early 1870s put the place firmly on the map, so that by 1890, it was the biggest city in Texas, with more than 42,000 residents. Today, well-manicured suburbs with their big shopping malls surround the central city, served by a network of interstate highways and encircling loop freeways.

The wealth and success of Dallas are manifested most obviously in its affluent residential areas, its numerous Cadillacs and Rolls-Royces, its thriving business districts, and its continually changing downtown skyline. Here the city's best-known landmark, the 50-story Reunion Tower, rises above the surrounding glass and concrete structures, the light-studded globe at its top enclosing a revolving restaurant and an observation deck that affords magnificent views for miles around. From here, you can see the Trinity River snaking away through the green parkland that lines its banks and, below, the old Union Station and the Reunion Arena, where basketball fans gather to cheer on the Mavericks.

The downtown streets contain many places to capture the visitor's interest, although only a few stately buildings remain from the nineteenth century. One notable survivor from the earliest days is the John Neely Bryan cabin, preserved and relocated in the Dallas County Historical Plaza. Nearby are the moving John F. Kennedy Memorial and the Texas School Book Depository, from where Lee Harvey Oswald is believed to have fired the shots that killed the thirty-fifth president. Elsewhere among the streets is Thanksgiving Square, which offers passers-by a moment of quiet relaxation and reflection in its unique spiral chapel and beautiful garden before they go on to admire the architect I. M. Pei's imaginative New City Hall and Central Library buildings, separated by a lovely plaza containing Henry Moore's sculpture *The Dallas Piece*, and the new Museum of Art in the arts district that is being developed north of Ross Avenue. Two downtown parks are of particular interest: Pioneer Park, an old cemetery that contains the famous Confederate Memorial Statue and is adjacent to the impressive Convention Center complex; and Old City Park, with its interesting collection of nineteenth-century buildings.

The downtown streets are also, of course, a paradise for shoppers, although there are special delights, such as the renowned Neiman-Marcus department store, the assortment of shops in the Plaza of the Americas complex and the Underground system, and the colorful bustle of Farmers Market.

After dark, fun seekers enjoy the night life provided by downtown hotels or congregate in the restaurants and clubs on Greenville Avenue and elsewhere. Theatergoers can choose among such top-ranking attractions as Theater Three in the Quadrangle, the Dallas Repertory Theater in North Park, or the Dallas Theater Center – designed by Frank Lloyd Wright – in the affluent Turtle Creek area. Those who like opera, ballet, or symphony concerts are sure to find something to their taste at the downtown Majestic Theater, on the S.M.U. campus, or at the famous Music Hall at Fair Park, 2 miles east of downtown, where the popular summer musicals are well attended each year.

Fair Park, a 277-acre entertainment, recreational, and cultural center,

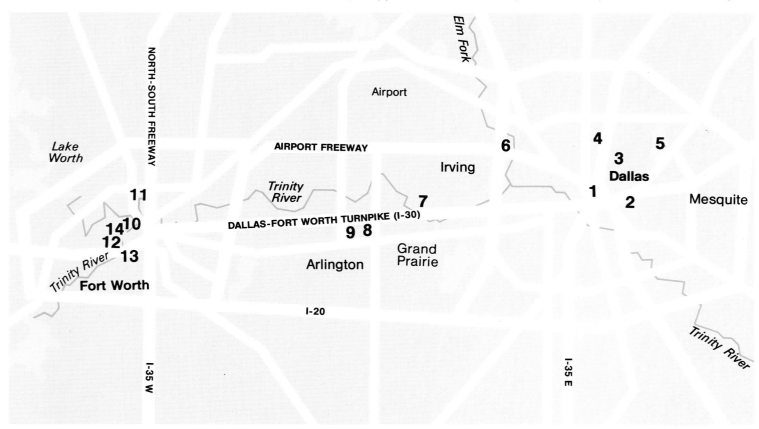

offers a wide range of attractions, including a group of museums, an aquarium, fairground rides, Shakespeare plays, an assortment of shows and exhibits, and college football in the Cotton Bowl stadium. The park also hosts the spectacular 17-day Texas State Fair in October.

Scattered widely around Dallas are countless other notable attractions, among which must be mentioned White Rock Lake Park to the east, with its water activities and the lovely De Golyer estate, and the weekly rodeos farther out in Mesquite. There are also the Marsalis Park Zoo in the attractive suburb of Oak Cliff, south of downtown, and the celebrated South Fork Ranch to the north of the city, where members of the Ewing family work out their complex lives in the glossy television series.

Along the Dallas–Fort Worth turnpike to the west of downtown Dallas, a cluster of theme parks, amusement centers, and other attractions is concentrated in the communities of Arlington, Grand Prairie, and Irving. You can lose your inhibitions in the rip-roaring fun at Six Flags Over Texas, the area's number-one amusement park, or join the water frolics at the Wet 'n' Wild and White Water centers. You can also sample the varied attractions of the International Wildlife Park, the Wax Museum of the Southwest, the Texas Sports Hall of Fame, and, some way south, the famous flea market at Traders Village. If in a mood for spectator sports, you can take in a Texas Rangers baseball game at Arlington Stadium or drive north to Irving to see the Dallas Cowboys play football at Texas Stadium. Irving is also the location of the delightful Sesame Place amusement park, which fun-loving youngsters find hard to resist.

If you continue driving west along the turnpike from Arlington, you eventually see modern glass skyscrapers rising on the horizon at a spot on the Trinity River where the city of Fort Worth began in 1849. In that year, Major Ripley Arnold set up a military camp during the campaign against Comanche Indian raids and named it Fort Worth in honor of his commander, General William Jenkins Worth.

After the Civil War, the little community became a stopping point for cowboys driving great herds of Texas longhorn cattle along the famed Chisholm Trail from Texas to the railheads in Kansas. As the last outpost

Opposite: The simple log cabin built by John Neely Bryan, the founder of Dallas, stands in the heart of downtown, reminding citizens of today's prosperous ultra-modern city of their pioneer heritage.

The Fort Worth Stockyards are a scene of noisy festivity every June as the Chisholm Trail Round-up gets under way, with a big parade, a trail ride, rodeos, gunfights, dances, and races to commemorate the days of the great cattle drives from Fort Worth to the railheads of Kansas in the 1880s.

75

of civilization on the way north and the first place to offer opportunities for carousing on the way back, Fort Worth developed into a classic cow town, its central streets, known as "Hell's Half Acre," throbbing with lively gambling halls and saloons like the Dixie and the White Elephant. Here, fun-starved cowboys let off some steam after weeks in the saddle, and such characters as Wyatt Earp, Doc Holliday, Butch Cassidy, and the Sundance Kid stalked around the streets.

Over the years, things calmed down as the city grew, its development spurred by the hard-won arrival of the first of its railroads in 1876, the discovery of oil in the surrounding country some 40 years later, and the establishment of its aircraft industry during World War II. It was a long and hard struggle in which prominent citizens like Amon G. Carter played a significant role. Today, Fort Worth is still actively engaged in the livestock business, although its economy has now diversified into the oil industry, manufacturing, and finance.

There is still great affection here for the colorful past, which lives on at the revitalized Stockyards on the north side of town. Here, you can stroll along the boardwalks among renovated stores and saloons, join in the whooping at the Cowtown Rodeo held in the Coliseum on Saturday night, or enjoy such annual festivals as the Chisholm Trail Round-up in June or the Pioneer Days celebrations in September. To round off a visit, you can sample the delights of Billy Bob's Texas, a vast entertainment complex that claims to be the world's biggest honky-tonk. Elsewhere in Fort Worth are other reminders of the old ranching days, which can be found by taking a ride on one of the attractive green and yellow trolleys that serve the central area. Among them are the Cattle Raisers Museum, west of downtown, and the restored Thistle Hill mansion, once a rich cattle baron's home, on Pennsylvania Avenue.

Parts of downtown have undergone revitalization in recent years, and interesting sights now await the visitor. Among the highlights are the renovated turn-of-the-century Sundance Square, the immense Tarrant County Convention Center complex and, nearby, the imaginative Water Gardens created by the architect Philip Johnson, which never fail to captivate the visitor.

On the west side of town, the Trinity River flows by the pleasant green expanses of Forest and Trinity parks. On a walk through Forest Park, you can wander through the magnificent zoo, ride on the world's longest

miniature railroad, and relive the past at the Log Cabin Village, a living museum that features a collection of restored and refurnished buildings of the mid-nineteenth century. Trinity Park encloses the beautiful Botanic and Japanese Gardens, which are on every visitor's list.

As a city with important higher-educational establishments, Fort Worth counterbalances its brash cow town image with many top-rate cultural institutions and flourishing performing-arts organizations that provide opera, ballet, choral music, symphony concerts, and various other forms of entertainment. Many of these are to be found concentrated to the west of Trinity Park between West Lancaster Avenue and Crestline Road, an area of museums, theaters, and music centers embellished with sculptures by top-ranking artists. Three distinguished art museums here are of outstanding interest: the magnificent Kimbell Art Museum, acclaimed as much for its architecture as for its superb international collections; the Amon Carter Museum of Western Art, featuring the works of Frederic Remington, Charles M. Russell, and other American artists; and the Fort Worth Art Museum, noted for its twentieth-century art. Not to be missed either is the marvelous Museum of Science, with its Noble Planetarium.

Theater lovers in the area have the choice of several outstanding playhouses, the most notable of which are the Casa Manana, renowned for its summer musicals and children's playhouse, and the prestigious William Edrington Scott Theater, the home of the Fort Worth Theater Company. Both are on West Lancaster Avenue near the Will Rogers Memorial Center, which hosts, among various other events, the renowned Southwestern Exposition and Fat Stock Show in January.

Having solved the problem of its water supply many years ago, Fort Worth has several man-made lakes in pleasant surroundings outside the city that are used for a wide assortment of recreational activities. Offering a wonderful escape from the pressures of modern urban living is the refreshing Fort Worth Nature Center and Refuge near Lake Worth, a 3,400-acre wildlife park to the northwest of the city. There are also many ranches in the surrounding country that provide facilities for horseback riding and other entertainments.

When Robert E. Lee remarked on a visit to Fort Worth long ago, "I hear the incoming march of thousands of feet," he might well have been referring not only to future settlers, but also to the increasing number of visitors and vacationers who are now discovering the varied and exciting attractions of this interesting part of America's Southwest.

Denver COLORADO

The Mile High City

Lined with fine department stores, specialty shops, and restaurants, downtown Denver's 16th Street Mall is a pleasant, tree-shaded thoroughfare always bustling with activity. At one end of the Mall, at the intersection with Arapahoe Street, the famous old Daniels & Fisher Tower still stands amid the surrounding ultra-modern skyscrapers.

In the annals of the Old West, the story of Horace ("Haw") Tabor, the Colorado tycoon, and his young wife, Baby Doe, is the stuff of Greek tragedy. Raised from a storekeeper to fabulous wealth by lucky speculations in mining activities, Tabor lived like a king, until a collapse in silver prices in 1893 left him ruined. A few years later, he died, leaving Baby Doe to guard the Matchless Mine in Leadville, where she lived in dire poverty waiting for better times until, in 1935, she was found frozen to death. The magnificent Tabor Hotel and Grand Opera House, which the speculator built in Denver, the state capital, have also long since gone, but today his memory is honored again in the impressive new Tabor Center complex, a prestigious office, hotel, and shopping development rising over 50 stories above the downtown streets.

The Tabor Center is only one of the many construction projects that have reshaped the face of downtown Denver in recent years. Like another Dallas, the cluster of gleaming skyscrapers that now marks the central business district rises abruptly out of the Great Plains; but unlike Dallas, Denver is set against the breath-taking backdrop of the Rocky Mountains, which rise sharply like a wall to the west, with 14,264-foot (4,351 m) Mount Evans towering behind. At an altitude of 5,280 feet (1,610 m) above sea level (as a brass plaque on the steps of the State Capitol records), the "Mile High City" is the business and cultural capital of the whole Rocky Mountain region, its financial district along 17th Street known as the "Wall Street of the West."

Although, like many cities, Denver has its air-pollution problems, it impresses the visitor with its comfortable dry climate, its clean downtown streets, and its numerous well-watered parks and tree-lined residential districts, which contrast with the drier plains outside the city. With its suburbs now spreading as far as the Front Range of the Rockies, the metropolitan area has a population of more than 1.5 million, with about 491,000 people in the city itself.

Denver has come a long way since a few huts were erected in 1858 at the site of a modest gold strike near the junction of the South Platte River and Cherry Creek. The following year, strange rumors of richer pickings in the nearby mountains brought a stampede of prospectors – rallying to the cry "Pike's Peak or bust!" – to the area, where General William H. Larimer had shrewdly invested in real estate. Larimer did well, and his settlement grew. Named for General James W. Denver, the territorial governor of Kansas, which then stretched as far west as the Rockies, the community prospered as the gateway to newly opened-up gold and silver mines in the mountains, its roisterous saloons raking in the coins as quickly as the miners dug out the metal.

Designated Colorado's capital in 1867, Denver emerged from its isolation three years later when a railroad was built to link up with the Union Pacific line at Cheyenne, Wyoming. Gradually, the city became the financial center of the region, involved in its mining, agricultural, and ranching activities, and much of its wealth was channeled into the creation of prestigious buildings, elegant mansions, tree-lined streets, and beautiful parks, kept permanently green by the construction of extensive irrigation networks. In this century, the location in Denver of federal-government agencies and military establishments, the growth of diversified manufacturing industries, and, more recently, the development of space and energy research have added further dimensions to the city's economy, confirming its status as "Queen City of the Plains."

Glittering among the new skyscrapers in the ever-changing downtown business district, the 24-carat-gold dome atop the gray State Capitol is an appropriate symbol of Denver's mining origins. The Capitol stands on a slope in the lovely Civic Center gardens facing the elegant City and County Building, which at Christmas is illuminated with thousands of colored lights. Behind it, the largest horde of gold bullion in the country outside of Fort Knox is stored in the modest-looking United States Mint, which is open to visitors. Treasures of other kinds are housed in a variety of museums nearby. The most important of these are the celebrated Denver Art Museum, a gray-tiled sculptured structure like some futuristic castle that contains priceless collections of Western American and international art, and the fascinating State Historical Museum in the Colorado Heritage Center.

One of Denver's most impressive developments is the huge Center for the Performing Arts, between 12th and 14th streets: it encompasses three theaters; a movie house; the Boettcher Concert Hall, where the Denver Symphony plays; and the glass-covered Galleria shopping mall, next to the enormous Currigan Exhibition Hall. A block away, old Denver lives again in Larimer Square, a delightful restoration of Victorian brick buildings now buzzing with activity as restaurants and specialty boutiques set amid pleasant courtyards lit by gaslights. Another block from here is the city's principal shopping street, the broad tree-lined 16th Street Mall, a pleasant oasis in the midst of the skyscrapers. A notable landmark in this area is the 325-foot (99 m) D & F (Daniels and Fisher) Tower of 1910, designed to recall the famous Campanile in Venice.

Of the many other fascinating places in downtown Denver, mention

Downtown Denver
1 *City and County Building*
2 *U.S. Mint*
3 *Denver Art Museum*
4 *Colorado Heritage Center*
5 *Convention Center and Center for the Performing Arts*
6 *Currigan Exhibition Hall*
7 *Daniels and Fisher Tower*
8 *Brown Palace Hotel*
9 *Molly Brown House*

Top: Facing the State Capitol across the attractive gardens of the Civic Center, the Denver City and County Building is an elegant, classical-style structure, whose beauty is further enhanced when illuminated for the Christmas season each year.

Above: Nestling among dramatic rock formations in the Rocky Mountains foothills near Morrison west of Denver, Red Rocks Amphitheater is an impressive open-air setting for summer concerts and other events, with spectacular vistas of the rolling Great Plains to the east.

must be made of the historic Brown Palace Hotel, an elegant hostelry where royalty and the famous have lodged over the years, and the Victorian house on Pennsylvania Street where the "unsinkable" Molly Brown, a survivor of the 1912 *Titanic* disaster, held court among local society.

On the east side of town, in attractive Cheesman Park, are the Denver Botanic Gardens and conservatory; not far away is the much larger City Park, whose attractions include the excellent Museum of Natural History and the pleasant Habitat Zoo. For family fun, there is a choice of three amusement parks in different places around the city; Elitch Gardens, Lakeside, and Heritage Square Artisan's Market. There are also opportunities to see spectator sports at the Mile High Stadium, the McNichols Arena, and other sites, as well as facilities for those who like to fish, play golf or tennis, or ride. If you happen to be in Denver at the right time, you can also enjoy the thrilling rodeo at the National Western Stock Show at the Coliseum in January, the big St. Patrick's Day parade in March, or the lively Oktoberfest in the fall.

As the gateway to the Rockies, Denver is well placed for lovely drives through the spectacular mountain scenery and historic mining towns to the west. Beyond Golden, with its famous Coors Brewery and railroad museum, are the Red Rocks Amphitheater, an impressive natural setting for outdoor concerts; Buffalo Bill Cody's grave atop Lookout Mountain; and magnificent views of the Great Plains below. The scenic highlight of this mountain wonderland, however, is some way to the north – breath-taking Rocky Mountains National Park, one of the world's most beautiful and unforgettable places. In these mountains, too, are the colorful towns that once thronged with prospectors, now bustling with sightseers and winter skiers. Among them are Central City, Idaho Springs, and, of course, Leadville, where "Haw" Tabor's other opera house still stands – not only a reminder of Colorado's flamboyant past, but also a symbol of the fickleness of fortune.

Des Moines IOWA

The Corn State Capital

As you drive through the rich rolling farmlands of the Corn State of Iowa, a scene of tranquil, timeless beauty on the way to the state capital, Des Moines, it is hard to believe the old-timer who reportedly contended: "Anyone who was fool enough to move into such a hell of a country as Iowa deserved to starve." The harrowing struggles and bitter disappointments that the pioneer settlers experienced on the prairies in the nineteenth century now seem very far removed from this idyllic landscape. Yet if you drive to the west side of Des Moines, you can get a lasting impression of what life was really like here in those days by walking around the marvelously realistic reconstructions at the Living History Farms, a 600-acre museum that features five historic farms and communities from different periods since the 1700s. If you then take Interstate 235 downtown, you can fill in more details about Iowa's story at the State Historical Building and Museum near the State Capitol.

In 1843, a fort was built at the junction of the Des Moines and Raccoon rivers in central Iowa to protect local Indians during the tense period of settlement after the Black Hawk War of 1832. The name chosen for the fort came from the French term for the river, *la rivière des moines*, which historians argue can mean either "river of the friars," referring to the first French missionaries in the area, or "middle river," describing its location halfway between the Mississippi and Missouri rivers. Either way, the French term is itself a corruption of the Indian name, Moingonia, meaning "river of the mounds." Whatever the derivation, the little community that grew up as a market town around the fort became known simply as Des Moines, and within 12 years of its foundation became a city and the state capital.

Agriculture, of course, has always been the basis of Des Moines's economy, and several companies concerned with farming activities have facilities in the city. But diversification has also created the city's strong insurance business – Des Moines is now second only to Hartford, Connecticut, as the nation's major center – and its printing and publishing interests. Over the years, the growth in population and movements of people out of the central city, particularly the west side, have created West Des Moines and residential areas such as Windsor Heights, Clive, and Urbandale. The city itself now has a population of around 191,000, a decline since 1970.

Rejuvenation of the downtown area began in 1955, and the last few years have witnessed the construction of several fine buildings. Among them are the 34-story Ruan Center, built in 1975; Capital Square, a more recent office and retail complex noted for its impressive eight-story atrium; and the Convention Center at 5th Avenue and Grand. Many of the buildings here are linked to the growing elevated-walkway system, which is transforming the downtown street scene and giving pedestrians climate-controlled protection from Des Moines's freezing winter and hot summer days. Another new project is the mall on Walnut Street.

One of the finest structures in the central city is the Civic Center, a magnificent modern building beside Nollen Plaza, a beautifully landscaped space containing a 2,000-seat amphitheater, fountains, and a pool dominated by a huge iron umbrella sculpture by Claes Oldenburg. The Civic Center

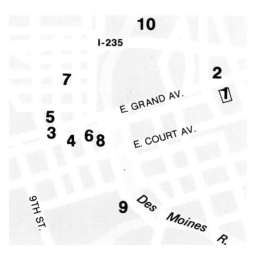

Downtown Des Moines
1 State Capitol
2 State Historical Building and Museum
3 Ruan Center
4 Capital Square
5 Convention Center
6 Civic Center
7 Veterans Memorial Auditorium
8 Polk County Heritage Gallery
9 Sec Taylor Stadium
10 Des Moines Botanical Center

itself can seat 2,700 people for its regular performances of concerts, Broadway plays, and ballet, while some blocks to the north, the Veterans Memorial Auditorium packs in crowds for pop concerts, basketball games, athletics competitions, and an assortment of conventions and other shows. Another highlight of the downtown scene is the Polk County Heritage Gallery, which has changing art exhibits in the lobby of the old Post Office building.

For sports lovers, the Greater Des Moines area also has Sec Taylor Stadium, which offers professional, minor-league baseball at the Des Moines and Raccoon rivers junction; the Drake University's stadium and other facilities for football, basketball, and track and field events; and the Des Moines Ice Arena for skating and professional hockey. There are also amenities for golf, tennis, and other sports, and recreational activities within easy reach of downtown and in the large number of parks throughout the metropolitan area. Many of these parks are particularly attractive in the spring, notably the Lilac Arboretum in Ewing Park and Water Works Park along the Raccoon River, which becomes a sea of color with its flowering crabs.

A drive west out of downtown Des Moines takes in many places of special interest, starting with the city's oldest art gallery, Hoyt Sherman Place. On Grand Avenue is Terrace Hill, a magnificent Victorian mansion of 1869 now used as the governor's residence, and farther west is Salisbury House, a fascinating replica of an English royal Tudor residence filled with sixteenth-century furnishings and standing majestically among the trees on its 11-acre estate. In this area, too, you will find the excellent Community Playhouse and, in Greenwood Park, the stimulating Center of Science and

Above: A block away from the fine Public Library, between Locust and Walnut streets in downtown Des Moines, is the city's prestigious new Civic Center auditorium for the performing arts. Adjacent to it, on the far side, is the landscaped open space of Nollen Plaza.

Opposite, top: The Iowa State Capitol, with its lofty central gold dome and four smaller domes at each corner, is an imposing sight in a parkland setting just east of downtown Des Moines.

Opposite, bottom: The home of Iowa's governor since 1972, the 20-room mansion of Terrace Hill, on Grand Avenue west of downtown Des Moines, is one of the finest examples of Victorian architecture in the Midwest.

Industry and Des Moines Art Center, the latter with exceptionally fine buildings designed by Eliel Saarinen and I. M. Pei. To round off a visit to this side of the city, West Des Moines offers an opportunity to browse through the specialty shops and antique stores of Valley Junction, one of the city's three major shopping malls and the scene of special music events and festivals during the summer.

A drive to the east side of town, across the Des Moines River along East Grand Avenue, takes in the city's most imposing building, the State Capitol, which dominates the downtown area from its hilltop site. This magnificent building, elaborately decorated inside, has a beautiful gold-leaf dome that is one of the largest in the country. Low down by the riverside to the northwest, you will see another dome, this one of glass, marking the location of the renowned Des Moines Botanical Center, a wonderland of exotic plants to delight every garden lover. And beyond the Capitol, to the east, there is a mecca for fun lovers, the huge Iowa State Fairgrounds and Heritage Village, the venue for an assortment of lively shows and events culminating in the spectacular State Fair in August. For more fun, it is an easy drive from here to Adventureland Park, a family-entertainment center that offers all kinds of amusements on the northeast side of the city.

In the summer months, people from Des Moines often take advantage of the facilities north of the city for boating, swimming, and other water activities at the man-made Saylorville and Big Creek lakes, or the quiet trails through the woods at Jester Park. Many enjoy more distant spots, such as the Amana Colonies, the Herbert Hoover birthplace near Iowa City, or simply the beautiful country that surrounds Des Moines on all sides. For Iowa in the Indian language means "The Beautiful Land."

83

Detroit MICHIGAN

The Motor City

Henry Ford, the automobile magnate, was one of those classic self-made men who, by their inventive genius and entrepreneurial sense, have made a tremendous impact on American life. Having hit on the idea of making a cheap, mass-produced car for ordinary working people, he manufactured some 16 million Ford Model-Ts, affectionately known as "Tin Lizzies," over an 18-year period starting in 1909 and helped to turn the great industrial city of Detroit, Michigan, into the automobile capital of the world. With a population of around 1.2 million, the "Motor City" is today America's sixth largest city. It extends along the north shore of the Detroit River, which forms southeastern Michigan's border with Canada between Lakes Erie and St. Clair.

One of Detroit's most prestigious automobiles took its name from the city's French founder, Antoine de la Mothe Cadillac, who in 1701 established Fort Pontchartrain on the site to guard the French fur trade in the Great Lakes area. Not surprisingly, Pontchartrain was too much of a mouthful for local settlers, who preferred to refer to their village by its location on the strait – in French, *détroit* – which was how they regarded the river.

The ensuing years saw Detroit emerge to maturity through British occupation for 36 years until 1796, Indian chief Pontiac's siege of 1763, a devastating fire in 1805, and the seesaw War of 1812, when it changed hands twice. The completion of the Erie Canal in 1825 opened up the Great Lakes region and brought a flood of American settlers and European immigrants into Michigan. A rapidly growing community during those years, Detroit served as territorial capital from 1805 to 1837, and for the next ten years as capital of the new state. Throughout the nineteenth century, a wide range of industries developed in the city, paving the way, with further influxes of immigrants, for the creation of the great automobile industry at the turn of the century by men like Henry Ford, Ransom E. Olds, and the Dodge brothers.

Over the years, the physical appearance of Detroit has undergone many changes, but the basic downtown-street pattern laid out after the fire of 1805 remains. Adapted from a plan for Washington, D.C., by the architect Pierre Charles L'Enfant, it comprises a grid of streets around the hub of Grand Circus Park, with broad avenues – Michigan, Grand River, and Gratiot – radiating from the central axis of Woodward Avenue. In recent years, many old buildings and slum areas have disappeared as wide freeways have been sliced through the city, and building projects have been completed as part of the program to entice people back to the central city following the general move to the suburbs after World War II.

One of these recent developments graces the waterfront area at the end of Woodward Avenue: the cluster of modern sports arenas, concert halls, and convention facilities that makes up the Civic Center complex. Here, the 10-acre Philip A. Hart Plaza provides an impressive setting for varied year-round activities, including summertime concerts, wintertime ice-skating, and a succession of colorful festivals culminating in the week-long International Freedom Festival shared with Canada in July. Nearby, the charming Old Mariners Church is now dwarfed by the towering futuristic forms of the Renaissance Center, a spectacular office, hotel, and shopping complex in which the 73-story tubular Detroit Plaza Hotel soars above its surrounding cluster of four 39-story office towers. From the revolving restaurant atop the 700-foot (214 m) hotel, there is a breath-taking view, and you can actually look *south* into Canada.

From the waterfront area, you can cross the Detroit River via the tunnel or the Ambassador Bridge to visit the interesting Canadian city of Windsor, Ontario; drive over another bridge to lovely Belle Isle, a pleasant park with entertainment and recreational amenities; or take a 26-mile boat cruise down to Boblo Island amusement park in the river off the Canadian town

Above: A breath-taking maze of walkways and dazzling atriums filled with greenery ana even a half-acre lake never fails to impress visitors to the magnificent Renaissance Center in Detroit. Several fine restaurants serve varied menus in the spectacular surroundings.

Left: One of the world's most spectacular architectural achievements in recent years, the glistening hotel and office complex of the Renaissance Center, designed by John Portman, soars 700 feet above Detroit's riverfront, dwarfing the charming red trolleys that pass by along Jefferson Avenue.

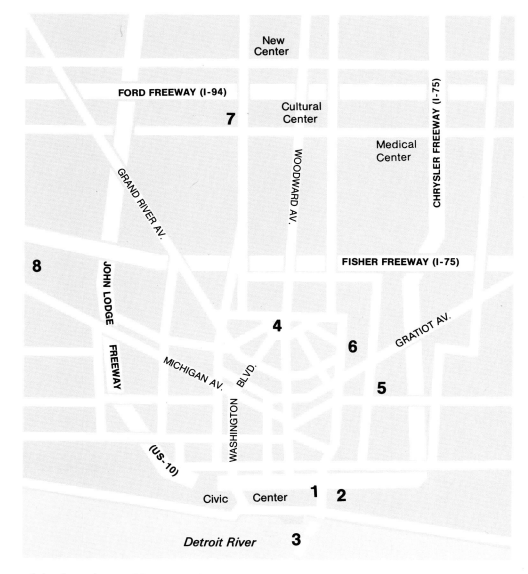

Opposite: Built on the site of old riverfront warehouses, Detroit's impressive Civic Center is a focal point of sport and cultural activities in the city. The complex includes (from top to bottom) the Joe Louis Arena, the home of the Red Wings ice-hockey team; Cobo Hall and Arena, a popular venue for conventions, expositions, and rock concerts; the Veterans Memorial Building; Philip A. Hart Plaza, with its famous fountain and spiraling pylon; and Ford Auditorium, the winter home of the Detroit Symphony Orchestra.

of Amherstburg. You can also catch an old red double-decker trolley for a delightful ride through downtown Detroit past the shops and outdoor cafés along Washington Boulevard to Grand Circus Park. Exploring the surrounding streets, you will discover such varied attractions as the excellent shopping mall along Woodward Avenue; a huge abstract sculpture by Alexander Calder; the fascinating Greektown district, with its marvelous restaurants and shops; and the Music Hall Center, which hosts a variety of theatrical, musical, and dance events.

North of Fisher Freeway is the extensive Medical Center, which encompasses several hospitals, research institutes, and other medical facilities not far from the Wayne State University campus. Between them, the area bordering Woodward Avenue contains a group of outstanding cultural and educational institutions collectively known as the Cultural Center and including the Detroit Institute of Arts, Public Library, Historical Museum, Science Center, and International Institute. Some blocks to the north is a lively office, retail, and restaurant area along West Grand Boulevard known as the New Center, the site of the General Motors Corporation headquarters and the superb Fisher Building, where you can shop, dine, or enjoy a Broadway show in its excellent theater.

As well as the Fisher, Detroit can boast several fine theaters, including the Repertory, Hilberry, Masonic Temple, and, north of town, Birmingham. Farther out, on the campus of Oakland University in Rochester, the beautiful gardens around Meadow Brook Hall, the luxurious home of motor magnate John Dodge's widow, contain a popular theater and a pavilion providing outdoor summer concerts of all kinds of music.

The basic original street plan of downtown Detroit, with broad avenues radiating from the central hub of Grand Circus Park, can be seen clearly from the air. Bordering the Detroit River, the Civic Center complex and the Renaissance Center represent prestigious developments of more recent years.

Among the top-ranking performers here is the Detroit Symphony Orchestra, which in winter can be heard at the Ford Auditorium in the downtown Civic Center.

The northern parts of the city also contain the Detroit Zoological Park, where more than 2,000 animals enjoy natural habitats in Royal Oak, and Cranbrook House, with its lovely gardens, Institute of Science, and Academy of Art Museum. Nearby Pontiac is a mecca for major-league sports fans, who pack into the 80,638-seat Silverdome to watch the Detroit Lions and Michigan Panthers play football or the Express team kick the round soccer ball. The Silverdome also hosts Pistons basketball and various other events. Downtown, the Red Wings ice-hockey team plays at the Joe Louis Arena in the Civic Center complex, while the Tigers use Tiger Stadium on Michigan Avenue for their home baseball games.

On the west side of town, history buffs can wander around old Fort Wayne by the river before driving to the special historic attractions awaiting in Dearborn. Here, you can tour the Ford motor plant and Henry Ford's 56-room Fair Lane Mansion. You can relive the past amid the collection of historic buildings associated with such famous Americans as Abraham Lincoln and Thomas Edison that has been gathered together at the Greenfield Village outdoor museum, and wander among the marvelous exhibits of American craftsmanship and industry – including, of course, automobiles – at the magnificent Henry Ford Museum and Hall of Technology.

Beyond Detroit's city limits, southeastern Michigan beckons the visitor with tempting and varied attractions, among which the state capital of Lansing, the lovely Dow Gardens in Midland, and the colorful Bavarian community of Frankenmuth are just a taste.

Hartford CONNECTICUT

America's Insurance Broker

Approaching the New England city of Hartford through the flat fields of tobacco bordering the Connecticut River, you get a marvelous distant view of the cluster of gleaming glass skyscrapers that marks the downtown district. No different from the aggressively modern skyline of countless other cities across the United States, the panorama suggests a city of rugged commercialism, alive with busy offices, plush hotels, and great stores packed with the goods of modern life.

And so it is. But when you enter this glittering metropolis and drive or walk along its downtown streets, you soon realize that hidden among its modern towers are many beautiful old treasures, more modest in scale but with many tales to tell of the city's past. Tucked away amid the new architectural wonders of Main Street, for example, is the Ancient Burying Ground, which, even in the eighteenth century, one angry citizen felt was being threatened by new building: "a really vandal-like invasion of the homes of the dead," as he put it. But, like so many other historic sites in Hartford, it has remained, to record in one of its glorious epitaphs how a certain Dr. Thomas Langrell "Drowned in the glory of his years, and left his mate to drown herself in tears."

Hartford, therefore, is a captivating mixture of old and new. As the capital of Connecticut, its history goes back 350 years, during which time its character has developed many facets. Apart from its involvement in state-government affairs, Hartford is a tough business center specializing in insurance. It is also a city with lively cultural traditions and fine museums, an apparent contradiction epitomized by the poet Wallace Stevens, who, unknown and unrecognized, worked here for years in the obscurity of an insurance-company office.

The shrewdness and pragmatism that make the wheels of Hartford's business life turn today were also much in evidence when the city was born. In 1636, the preacher Thomas Hooker marched into the area with a band of English followers to escape the strictures of Puritan life in Massachusetts. Boldly setting up a riverside community under the noses of Dutch settlers who had been here for 13 years, Hooker began the English colonization of Connecticut that finally drove the Dutch out. To the outraged Dutch, the newcomers were no better than thieves and pirates, or, as they put it in their own slang, *Jankes*. So the first "Yankees" in America were English, although it was not long before they showed the characteristic American love of liberty by getting themselves their famous royal Charter in 1662. This reflected the revolutionary ideas often expressed by Hooker and granted the people the right to control their own government. Apart from recognizing Hooker's role, therefore, as one of the founders of American democracy, Hartford citizens have to be grateful to him for having named their city after the town of Hertford in England, instead of adopting the original Indian name for the site: Suckiag, or "Black Earth."

Hooker's little seventeenth-century river port has become a large city of some 138,000 people that straddles the Connecticut River, its buildings representing American architectural history over three-and-a-half centuries. The downtown area lies to the west of the river, with West Hartford beyond and East Hartford across the river. A breath-taking view over the whole area can be enjoyed from the top of the 527-foot (161 m) Travelers

The shape of Hartford's historic Center Church, flanked by its Ancient Burying Ground, is echoed by the office building of the Travelers Insurance Company, one of the first insurance companies in the city. Crowning this building is the Travelers Tower, a famous city landmark. Hartford's founder, Thomas Hooker, is believed to lie buried near a corner of Center Church.

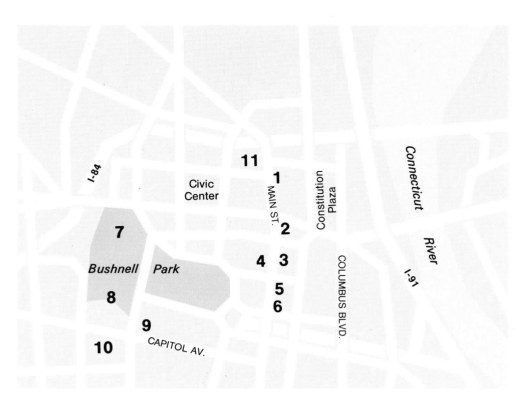

Downtown Hartford

The fall adds warm tints to the cool grays of office towers around Hartford's Bushnell Park. Reflecting the riot of color is the gold glass-walled office building that stands next to Center Church on Main Street.

Tower on Main Street, a good place to begin an easy walk around the major places of interest.

North on Main Street, the State House, used from 1796 to 1878, seems to crouch among the brash modern towers around it, a beautiful white-porticoed structure of red brick and brownstone designed by Charles Bulfinch, the architect of the Capitol in Washington, D.C. Three blocks away is the old brownstone building now known as The Richardson, created by another of America's great architects, Henry Hobson Richardson, to house elegant apartments and street-level shops and now restored to its original purpose. Behind is Constitution Plaza, a modern complex created when urban renewal first came to Hartford in 1962. It comprises shops, offices, and car-parking space, with open walks and a large fountain. An unusual feature is the tall glass office building contructed with only two sides, which curve like those of a ship. The day after Thanks-giving, the plaza is transformed into a delightful fairyland, as thousands of small white lights are turned on for the Festival of Lights.

Beside the Ancient Burying Ground opposite the Travelers Tower on Main Street stands Center Church, with its Tiffany-glass windows. Built in 1807 on the site of the church where Thomas Hooker once preached, this lovely building is now dwarfed by I. M. Pei's magnificent Bushnell Tower, built in 1969. Across the street, Alexander Calder's eye-catching Stegosaurus sculpture dominates the pleasant open space of Burr Mall

With its mixture of architectural styles, the Connecticut State Capitol, designed by Richard Upjohn and completed in 1879, is Hartford's most impressive building. Inside the majestic structure, the seat of state government, are many objects that commemorate Connecticut's history.

between the impressive Municipal Building and the renowned Wadsworth Atheneum, America's oldest public museum, whose outstanding collections include paintings, sculptures, and other masterpieces of art.

West of Main Street, Bushnell Park offers a pleasant relaxation area of grass and trees covering 41 acres. From a distance, you may hear the unmistakable sound of the Wurlitzer band organ on the old carrousel that delights children here through the summer months. But the most impressive sight in the park is the majestic Capitol Building, which stands on a hill on the south side. Opened in 1879, the building incorporates a range of architectural styles and is crowned by an imposing gold dome. The buildings around it include the splendid Bushnell Memorial Hall, a 2,728-seat auditorium in Art Deco style used for symphony concerts, opera, musical comedies, and ballet.

North of the park is the vast Hartford Civic Center complex, which brought life back to the downtown area with its three-level mall of shops and restaurants, its hotel, and its sports arena where you can watch Hartford's ice-hockey team, the Whalers, and the annual Aetna World Cup Tennis Championship.

Two of Hartford's most celebrated residents, Mark Twain and Harriet Beecher Stowe, once occupied grand houses that still stand at the old Nook Farm, west of downtown. The design of Twain's house is particularly interesting, with its echoes of a Mississippi steamboat. Here he wrote *Tom Sawyer* and *Huckleberry Finn*. West Hartford boasts several places of interest, including the University of Hartford, the delightful Children's Museum, and the home of the writer and dictionary compiler Noah Webster. The Wethersfield district, to the south, has two major attractions: the Buttolph Williams House of 1692 and the Webb–Deane–Stevens Museum, comprising three fascinating eighteenth-century homes.

Outside the city, the beautiful little towns and wooded hills of Connecticut are a special delight, especially when the trees are clothed in brilliant fall colors. It is easy to see why Hartford, with its considerable attractions, is rapidly becoming a favorite center for tourists.

Honolulu   HAWAII

Aloha Paradise

To every snowbound New Englander dreaming of a winter escape, the islands of Hawaii conjure up timeless images of sunny, palm-fringed beaches and glistening white surf, of garlanded hula dancers swaying to sensuous music, of a paradise on earth created to dispel worldly cares. As you fly over these lovely islands, set like jewels midway across the deep blue Pacific Ocean, the vision is confirmed. And then you look down on Honolulu, the capital city, sprawling over the luxuriant island of Oahu between the bustling harbors and beaches along its southern shore and the green mountain slopes to the northeast, and you realize that the dream is not the whole story: civilization has come to paradise.

Honolulu airport, one of the busiest in the United States, greets some 3 million tourists a year to the Aloha State of Hawaii and installs a large majority of them in the plush hotels lining Waikiki Beach, east of town. Already crowded into Honolulu are more than 681,000 local residents, representing nearly four out of every five people on the islands as a whole. Indeed, Honolulu is America's thirteenth largest city, and the old meaning of the Hawaiian name Oahu, "the gathering place," applies just as much today as it did when the island kings met here long ago.

Not surprisingly, Honolulu has the usual problems found in every modern metropolis, yet it is in many ways the most captivating of all American cities, with a considerable assortment of attractions to tempt the visitor. It is at the same time the least American, for here the original island cultures have managed to remain alive, although much watered down, beneath the glossy veneer of twentieth-century American civilization. Here, too, white Americans are outnumbered by islanders of Polynesian and oriental stock, who have intermarried and produced the lovely people so typical of these islands. Everywhere you can hear different languages spoken, often mingled with English in the local version of pidgin, the exotic atmosphere enhanced by the sound of Hawaiian music and the colorful ethnic festivals. All this is hardly surprising considering Hawaii's history and the fact that union with the United States came less than ninety years ago.

The first people came to Hawaii, experts tell us, probably from Tahiti in the sixth century A.D. The separate kingdoms they established were united only in 1795 after conquest by King Kamehameha I of the island of Hawaii. Shortly before this, Captain James Cook, the first European to visit the islands, had lost his life in a tragic skirmish here. After the unification of the islands, Pearl Harbor, on Oahu, became a major port for whalers and traders in sandalwood and furs, and in 1845, King Hamahameha III moved his court from the island of Maui to Honolulu, which he made the kingdom's capital city five years later. With the development of sugar cane- and, later, pineapple-growing, thousands of immigrants from China, Japan, and other countries began to stream in to work on the plantations and in the factories. Since the annexation of the islands by the United States in 1898 and the establishment of huge military bases here, Honolulu has benefited from the development of a wider range of manufacturing industries, and the economic explosion of recent years has been led by the huge growth in tourism.

Prosperity has brought many changes to Honolulu's skyline, as new

A black and gold statue of King Kamehameha I, who united all the islands of Hawaii under his rule in the early nineteenth century, stands outside the Judiciary Building in Honolulu's Civic Center. Cast in Italy in 1883, the statue is a replica of another that was lost at sea while on its way from Europe and later recovered and erected on the island of Hawaii.

7

PALI HWY.

8

2

3

4

5

6

9

KAPIOLANI BLVD.

ALA MOANA

KING ST.

University
of Hawaii

Ala Wai Canal

KALAKAUA AV.

10

11

H-1

Waikiki Beach

12

Diamond Head

Above: Flanked by the luxurious hotels and booming night clubs that make Honolulu the major vacation center of the Pacific, the sun-bathed sands of Waikiki Beach sweep round the bay as far as the landmark headland formed by the 760-foot extinct volcano of Diamond Head.

Opposite, top: Although Honolulu is a vibrant modern metropolis with gleaming new hotels and high-rise offices, the city has succeeded in retaining many nineteenth-century treasures and oases of greenery amid the bustle of twentieth-century life. And all round this paradise island are the deep blue water of the glorious Pacific Ocean.

Honolulu and Waikiki

hotels have mushroomed along Waikiki Beach and high-rise business towers have risen above the downtown streets. Pearl Harbor, too, has recovered from destruction in World War II to become a major United States naval base once more. Honolulu's own harbor is on a smaller scale, its busy waterfront overlooked by the famous Aloha Tower, which was once the city's tallest building. Nearby is the fascinating Chinatown district, with its colorful shops, markets, and restaurants representing the city's varied ethnic mix, not just the Chinese community.

From Chinatown, a walk through the downtown area's streets, pedestrian malls, and parks takes you past many buildings of special historic interest. You will see, at the Mission Houses Museum, the first buildings constructed on the island by nineteenth-century American missionaries; across the street, the Kawaiahao Church, where royalty were married and buried; the celebrated statue of King Kamehameha I, which is draped with garlands, called leis in Hawaii, during the annual June 11 celebrations in his honor; and the magnificent Iolani Palace, built in 1882 and America's only royal home, which stands next door to the impressive State Capitol, completed in 1969.

In the middle of downtown, the peaceful Foster Botanic Gardens provide a welcome relief from sightseeing and a chance to see remarkable displays of orchids as well as tropical trees and plants. At Thomas Square, you can admire particularly impressive collections of oriental and Western art at the Honolulu Academy of Arts or enjoy one of the many attractions at the Blaisdell Center, which hosts sporting events, plays, musicals, and concerts by the Honolulu Symphony Orchestra. A ride on one of Honolulu's red double-decker buses will take you to the city's other major museum, the prestigious Bishop Museum, which is in the neighborhood of Kalihi and houses a superb collection of Pacific islands art.

Two of the most visited places in Honolulu commemorate the dead of

World War II: the huge National Memorial Cemetery of the Pacific, more familiarly known as the Punchbowl, which overlooks the city; and in Pearl Harbor, the starkly moving *Arizona* Memorial, which marks the site of the battleship sunk in the Japanese attack on December 7, 1941.

On the other side of town is the golden resort of Waikiki, its magnificent 2.5-mile beach thronged with swimmers and surfers by day, its glittering night clubs, discos, and restaurants alive with swingers by night. A swamp not many years ago, this section of Oahu's coastline is now backed by a forest of magnificent hotels flanking Kalakaua Avenue. Rising at the eastern end of the beach is the famous dark, volcanic peak of Diamond Head, which you can walk around on a little trail. On the way, you can explore the wonderful Kapiolani Park, with its assortment of attractions, including a zoo, an aquarium, a lovely rose garden, and the renowned Waikiki Shell amphitheater, where you can see a delightful hula show. Two particularly interesting shopping centers are also within easy reach of Waikiki hotels: one of them, the lively outdoor International Market Place, is in Waikiki itself on Kalakaua Avenue; the other, the Ala Moana Center, is a huge complex to the west of the Ala Wai Canal.

Outside Honolulu, the mountains, beaches, and lush green countryside of Oahu provide an ever-changing kaleidoscope of scenic attractions that no one should miss. The breath-taking view over Honolulu from the famous Pali Lookout high in the Koolau Mountains is a special experience. And then there are the other islands in this paradise – Hawaii, Maui, Molokai, Kauai, and the smaller islands – which provide an endless source of delights for the traveler.

Houston TEXAS

Space City, U.S.A.

"Fly me to the moon," urge the words of an old popular song, and if there is one place in the United States that could do just that, it is Houston, Texas, where the awesomely spectacular Lyndon B. Johnson Space Center presides over the nation's manned space program. But if space technology is one major ingredient of Houston's booming economy, then another is oil, the fuel for a vast petrochemical industry that has brought growth on an undreamed-of scale. Manufacturing diversity, engineering, construction, finance, and scientific and medical research have also contributed, so that Houston today is the nation's fastest-growing city. It is also the fifth largest, with a population now numbering over 1,594,000 and still rising.

The immediately visible result of this burgeoning prosperity is Houston's dazzling downtown skyline, a constantly changing scene of sleek, glistening skyscrapers towering above the broad, clean streets below. To the east, lining the channel that connects Houston's busy port with the Gulf of Mexico, are the vast industrial plants that create so much of this wealth. And crisscrossing the urban sprawl is a snaking network of expressways that attempts to cope with the mass movements of people in this ant hill of a city, at the same time contributing to its serious air-pollution problems.

As an international business center, Houston also has the cosmopolitan appeal of a city that enjoys a thriving cultural life, nurtured by top-rate opera, ballet, and theater companies and a superb symphony orchestra. Yet beneath the city sophistication, the reassuring habits and attitudes of small-town Texas remain. As John Steinbeck observed, "Businessmen wear heeled boots that never feel a stirrup, and men of great wealth who own houses in Paris . . . refer to themselves as little old country boys." Houston is a city in which you can see people walking along downtown streets in western gear or in the latest Paris fashions, and where you can yell at a rip-roaring rodeo one night and sit entranced at the ballet the next.

Sometimes called "the most air-conditioned city in the world," Houston has to be, for its climate is hot. Its foundation by New York developers Augustus and John Allen in the flat, mosquito-ridden swamp country near Buffalo Bayou in 1836 did not seem to augur well for the future. Named for General Sam Houston, who had won Texas its independence from Mexico earlier that year, the little community at first scraped a living from timber-, cotton-, and cattle-shipping and spent much of its hard-earned cash in the saloons and gambling dens of Old Market Square or in the plush opulence of the opera house. Then in 1901, 90 miles away at Spindletop, came the first whoosh of black gold from the ground that transformed Houston's prospects and created the Texas oil industry. And when a 32-mile channel big enough for ocean-going ships was built in 1914 to link the city's inland port with the Gulf, industrial prosperity was ensured – and continues unabated today.

Not much remains of the original village by Buffalo Bayou, the site now being occupied by Allen's Landing park. But a group of old buildings gathered together and restored by the Harris County Heritage Society in downtown Sam Houston Park serves as a reminder of those early days, surrounded by the glass and steel towers of today. And the city's oldest building, an Indian trading post, survives on its original site in Old

Ready for blast-off, a Space Shuttle stands on the launch pad at the start of a thrilling journey into space. Its flight will be controlled from the Lyndon B. Johnson Space Center, a 1,620-acre complex about 25 miles southeast of downtown Houston which serves as the heart of the United States manned space flight program. Among the facilities open to visitors here are the famous Mission Control Center that monitored the early Apollo flights to the moon, and the full-scale trainers used to prepare astronauts for the more recent Space Shuttle missions.

Market Square, still a lively district for dining and entertainment.

A more recent downtown landmark is the 16-block Civic and Cultural Center complex, which includes a huge convention and exhibition hall, the acclaimed Alley Theater, and the magnificent Jesse H. Jones Hall for the Performing Arts, the home of the city's symphony orchestra and opera and ballet companies. A special downtown feature popular with shoppers is the system of underground tunnels linking concourses of boutiques and cafés beneath the bustling streets. Farther west, along Westheimer, are two other special attractions for shoppers: an 18-block district of antique stores, art galleries, bazaars, sidewalk cafés, bars, and nightspots known as the International Strip; and, farther out of town, the breath-taking Galleria shopping mall, with its three levels of stores and huge ice-skating rink.

A ride to this side of Houston also provides an opportunity to see how the city's rich live in the plush neighborhood of River Oaks. One of the fine mansions here, now called the Bayou Bend Museum, has a superb collection of early furnishings and can be visited.

South of downtown, along South Main, many of Houston's most important cultural institutions are located in the pleasant surroundings of Hermann Park, among them the excellent Museum of Fine Arts, the stark Contemporary Arts Museum, and the outstanding Museum of Natural Science and its superb planetarium. Here, too, are the delightful Houston Zoo and the Miller Outdoor Theater, where you can enjoy anything from pop concerts to Shakespeare. The neighborhood also contains the Rice University campus and the hospitals, colleges, and research facilities of the distinguished Texas Medical Center.

Farther along South Main, Houston's world-famous Astrodome, the "Eighth Wonder of the World," dominates the group of buildings that

Downtown Houston

1 Allen's Landing
2 Old Market Square
3 Old Sixth Ward: Sabine Historical District
4 Sam Houston Park
5 Albert Thomas Convention and Exhibit Center
6 Alley Theater
7 Jesse H. Jones Hall for the Performing Arts
8 Tranquillity Park
9 Music Hall
10 Sam Houston Coliseum
11 City Hall
12 Christ Church Cathedral

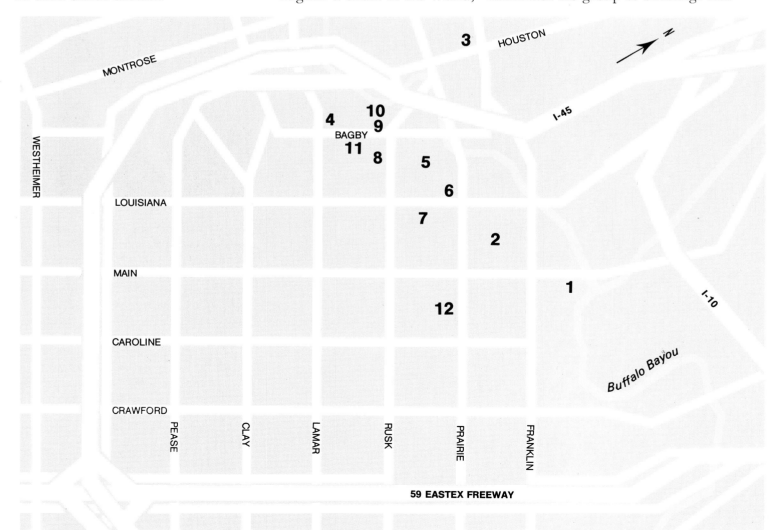

East of downtown Houston, on the Houston Ship Channel, the 570-foot San Jacinto Monument, completed in 1939, commemorates the decisive battle in 1836 that won independence for Texas from Mexico. Nearby is moored the battleship Texas, *which served in the United States Navy from 1914 to 1948 and saw action in two world wars. The ship is now preserved as a memorial and museum.*

Previous page, top: A stunning array of glistening futuristic skyscrapers punctures the continually changing skyline of downtown Houston, visible reminders that this prosperous city is America's fastest-growing metropolis.

Previous page, bottom: The immense enclosed interior of Houston's Astrodome is large enough to seat up to 66,000 spectators at the wide range of sports and other events held there. A notable feature of this architectural wonder is the huge electric scoreboard, which never fails to astonish with its dazzling display when the home team scores. However, lively action down in the arena keeps all eyes firmly fixed on the rodeo competitors during the two-week Houston Livestock Show and Rodeo held in late February and early March.

forms the Astrodomain complex. Seating 66,000 spectators, the world's largest indoor arena is the venue for Astros baseball, Oilers football, and many other games and events, not least of which is the exciting two-week Houston Rodeo and Livestock Show. Just across the nearby South Loop, the fabulous Astroworld entertainment park offers 70 acres of family fun, excitement, and, on the Sky Screamer, sheer terror.

On the east side of town, you can watch ocean-going ships as they glide by the observation deck on Wharf 9 at the port, or take a fascinating cruise among them along the channel. From here, it is only a short ride to see the magnificent battleship *Texas*, a veteran of two world wars now docked next to the colossal monument and museum commemorating the epic Battle of San Jacinto. South of here, in Clear Lake City, is the famous Space Center, on the way to the beautiful sandy beaches of Galveston Island, a sun-drenched resort for city dwellers some 50 miles out of Houston.

With its incredible prosperity, its lavish cultural and recreational amenities, its throbbing night life and fun places, and all those exciting attractions that make life in this city so varied and rewarding, Houston is the Los Angeles of the Southwest, the glittering "Golden Buckle of the Sun Belt." When you experience the fun of the bubbling ten-day Houston Festival, which takes over the city in March, you realize that there is really no reason to cry "Fly me to the moon" when you can enjoy Houston.

Indianapolis INDIANA

Home of the Speedway

On the last Sunday in May every year, thousands of auto-racing fans from all over the United States crowd into the world-famous Motor Speedway in Indianapolis to see one of the greatest events in the sporting calendar: the Indianapolis "500" car race, a tremendous spectacle in which the world's most powerful cars thunder around the magnificent 2.5-mile track. This is the thrilling climax to a whole month of celebrations that fill every hotel and motel room for miles around and turn this sports-loving city into one huge jamboree, highlighted by the "500" Festival Parade, the Queen's Ball, a mini-marathon, and various other events. The experience is unforgettable – and this is perhaps all that most people really know about Indianapolis, the nation's twelfth largest city housing a population of over 700,000. With its excellent network of interstate highways, which earned it the nickname "Crossroads of America," Indianapolis has been not only easy to get to, but also easy to leave.

Indeed, the accessibility of Indianapolis is the key to its foundation in the rolling country of central Indiana. The city did not simply grow here naturally around an eighteenth-century trading post or military fort; it was put here. The site was deliberately chosen for a state capital in 1820 by the first governor, Jonathon Jennings, and nine commissioners, who found the convenient, centrally located site they wanted close to the junction of the

Downtown Indianapolis
1 *Monument Circle*
2 *University Square*
3 *Indiana World War Memorial*
4 *Obelisk Square*
5 *Scottish Rite Cathedral*
6 *Old City Market*
7 *Market Square Arena*
8 *James Whitcomb Riley Home*
9 *Lockerbie Square*
10 *State Capitol*
11 *Indianapolis Sports Center*
12 *Natatorium*
13 *Indiana University Track and Field Stadium*

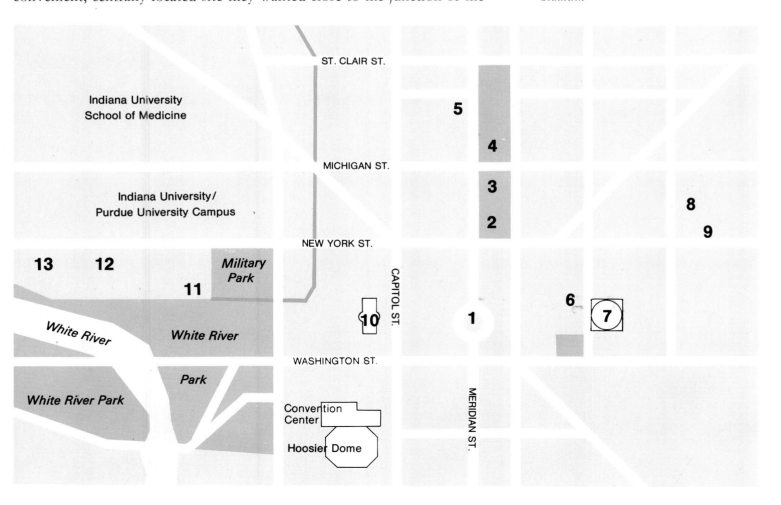

White River and Fall Creek. A name for it was coined by simply adding the
Greek work for "city," *polis*, to the name of the state. Building began,
following the mile-square plan laid out by the Washington architect
Alexander Ralston, and by 1835, the new capital's first state house was
finished. Soon, thriving agricultural and manufacturing businesses had
developed alongside the city's state-government activities, and prosperity
arrived.

Over the years, Indianapolis settled into a sedate, comfortable
Midwestern way of life. But as the affluent tree-lined suburbs were gradually
acquiring the supermarkets, shopping malls, movie houses, and other
conveniences of modern living that characterize the outskirts of so many
American cities, downtown Indianapolis, Ralston's Mile Square, was losing
its sparkle. The process was only halted when a progressive city
management began a program of revitalization in recent years that is not
only affecting the city center, but also reaching out to the surrounding
Marion County area. Among the graceful old buildings and parking lots of
downtown, gleaming modern structures have sprung up to create an
exciting new skyline and the vibrant atmosphere of a city on the move.

As a planned city, Indianapolis is an easy place to get around. Laid out
in the familar grid pattern with concentric rings of interstate highways, the
streets allow rapid access both in the compact downtown area and
throughout surrounding Marion County neighborhoods. The hub of the
plan is the tree-lined circular plaza of Monument Circle, although for street-
numbering purposes, the exact center of the city is the nearby intersection
of Washington and Meridian streets. On the ornate Soldiers and Sailors
Monument, which dominates Monument Circle, there is a balcony 230 feet
(70 m) above the ground that provides an impressive view over the city.
Another superb panorama can be enjoyed from the excellent La Tour
restaurant on the thirty-fifth floor of the nearby Indiana National Bank
tower.

North of Monument Circle, Meridian Street opens into an impressive
five-block mall linking University Square, Memorial Plaza, and Obelisk
Square. Here you cannot miss the huge Indiana World War Memorial and
the awesome Tudor Gothic cathedral used by the Scottish Rite Freemasons,
with its ornate interior and its tower containing a superb 54-bell carillon.
To the west of Monument Circle on West Market Street, you will find the
imposing 1888 State House and behind it, the State Library. To the east are
the delightful old City Market, now refurbished to house a colorful array of
restaurants and stalls selling all kinds of food, and, beyond, the colossal
Market Square Arena, a modern construction that seats up to 19,000
spectators at sporting events and other entertainments. There is, however,
another, even bigger stadium, the Hoosier Dome, not far away on South
Capitol, a brand-new addition to the Convention Center complex, which
can house as many as 63,000 people.

Into this cluster of impressive public buildings in the downtown Mile
Square, Indianapolis has packed many fine hotels, stores, shops, and
restaurants. Here, too, are museums and theaters offering a wealth of
cultural activities, including symphony concerts, ballet and opera
performances, and plays staged by the Indiana Repertory Theater. There are
also places of historic interest, such as the lovely Victorian house where the
Indiana poet James Whitcomb Riley once lived, the splendid home of
President Benjamin Harrison, and the beautiful Historic District of
Lockerbie Square.

Despite the many attractions to be found downtown, a ride past the fine
old mansions of Meridian Street into the suburban communities to the north
reveals even more places of interest to satisfy all tastes. Here you will find,
for example, the world-famous Children's Museum and the zoo, both of
which will delight the younger members of the family; the highly acclaimed
Clowes Memorial Hall, which hosts all kinds of musical events from pop to

The Indianapolis Motor Speedway, constructed in 1909, is the home of the celebrated "500" Mile Race, one of the world's greatest sports spectacles that attracts thousands of auto racing fans to the city each May. Inside the 2½-mile track is a fascinating Hall of Fame Museum.

opera; the magnificent Indianapolis Museum of Art; and the Indiana State Fairgrounds, a vast entertainment complex providing fun for all the family. Farther out of the city, at Noblesville, is the Conner Prairie Pioneer Settlement, a fascinating museum where nineteenth-century pioneer life in Indiana is re-created by highly trained actors.

For shoppers, this side of the city has superb shopping centers at Keystone at the Crossing and in the quaint old neighborhoods of Zionsville and Broad Ripple.

Sports lovers, however, would do better to make their way to the west side of downtown. Here there may be an opportunity to see top tennis stars competing in the annual U.S. Open Clay Court Championships, which are held at the excellent Sports Center on West New York Street. Farther west, on the combined campus of Indiana and Purdue universities, the superb Track and Field Stadium hosts many athletics meetings, and the excellent pools of the magnificent Natatorium are the venue for swimming events. It is in this part of the city, along the White River, that one of the most exciting development projects ever undertaken in Indianapolis has been located: White River Park, a vast, imaginative family-entertainment complex planned to give a tremendous boost to the city's growing tourist industry.

The people of Indianapolis certainly intend to persuade visitors to come to their city not only for the "500" race, but also to stay and sample the city's countless other delights.

Kansas City MISSOURI

The City of Fountains

Kansas City, Missouri, comes as something of a surprise to visitors expecting to find little more than grain elevators and stockyards, a cultural desert in the midst of flat, desolate prairies. While it is true that Kansas City is the nation's second largest wheat-flour producer and that steaks figure high on its restaurants' menus, there is much more to the city than that. As the French writer André Maurois once wrote, "Who in Europe, or in America for that matter, knows that Kansas City is one of the loveliest cities on earth?" For this bustling modern metropolis, a thriving distribution, underground storage, and manufacturing center producing such varied items as automobiles, trucks, instrument landing systems, and greeting cards, is indeed a beautiful and livable city that some 448,000 people are pleased to call home.

Scattered throughout the city, with its pleasant residential districts and tree-lined boulevards, are 125 lovely green parks and enough bubbling fountains, many embellished with beautiful statuary, for it to be known as the "City of Fountains." There are also numerous entertainment and cultural facilities, including museums and art galleries, flourishing theaters and music halls staging opera, ballet, symphony concerts, and Broadway shows, and night clubs where you can hear the jazz for which Kansas City is famous.

Geographically placed in the heart of America, Kansas City stands on Missouri's western border, adjoining Kansas City in neighboring Kansas. It spreads over hills on the south bank of the Missouri River where "Big Muddy" makes a broad eastward sweep below its junction with the Kansas River. The site was settled in 1821 when François Chouteau established a fur-trade post by the river. Twelve years later, wily John C. McCoy set up an outfitting store in Westport, 4 miles south, for traders passing along the Santa Fe Trail, and then helped to buy a 257-acre riverside patch, which is now the city's downtown district. Named Kansas after a local Indian tribe, a name that meant "smoky wind" – referring to prairie fires – the new plot outgrew both Chouteau's settlement and McCoy's Westport and became a wild frontier staging post for floods of westward-bound migrants. After 1869, when some shrewd political maneuvering brought the railroad from Chicago to Kansas City, the place really took off as a livestock-distribution center, its streets thronging with businessmen and such dubious characters as Wild Bill Hickok, Wyatt Earp, and Jesse James. Then along came the farsighted men who brought civilization to this muddy cow town, among them William Rockhill Nelson, who in the 1880s gave the city its boulevards and parks, and Jesse Clyde Nichols, who early in the twentieth century built the beautiful Spanish-style Country Club district and embellished it with statues and fountains.

There are many excellent vantage points for views of the city, including the hill where the famous Indian scout statue stands in Penn Valley Park and the thirtieth-story observation deck in the downtown City Hall. Bordering the Missouri River is the North End district, with the city's Italian community and the colorful City Market. South of here, the compact downtown area occupies a neat checkerboard inside an encircling ring of freeways, with glittering modern skyscrapers sharing the blocks with preserved older structures and parking lots. Apart from the Art Deco City

Kansas City
1 City Hall
2 City Market
3 Convention Center
4 Kemper Arena
5 Stockyards
6 Union Station
7 Liberty Memorial and Museum
8 Crown Center
9 Penn Valley Park
10 Westport Square
11 Nelson Art Gallery

Hall, interesting sights here include City Center Square; the restored Folly Theater, a former burlesque house now used for plays and concerts; the Lyric Theater, home of the Kansas City Opera and, in winter, the Philharmonic Orchestra; and the Convention Center, comprising the Art Deco Municipal Auditorium, with its arena, music hall, theater, and exhibition hall, and the H. Roe Bartle Hall, a huge, low modern structure used for all kind of expositions.

On the east side of town are the fine Kansas City Museum of History and Science and, farther south, the Harry S Truman Sports Complex, where Arrowhead Stadium seats 78,000 fans for Chiefs football games and nearby Royals Stadium holds 40,000 for baseball games featuring the Royals. Across town, near the railroad yards and stockyards, the well-designed Kemper Arena accommodates up to 17,650 people attending shows, celebrity concerts, sporting events that include home games of the Comets soccer and the Kings basketball teams, or the big American Royal Livestock and Horse Show and Rodeo in the fall.

Just south of downtown are three special points of interest: the magnificent old Union Station, third largest in the country; the 217-foot (66 m) Liberty Memorial and museum commemorating World War I; and the prestigious 85-acre Crown Center development area, a city within a city comprising hotels, offices, shopping complexes, and housing.

Farther south, you can recall the days of pioneer John McCoy among the restored brick buildings and courtyards of Westport Square, now a lively gathering place with shops, art galleries, restaurants, and nightspots. Not far away, you can bask in the exotic atmosphere of Country Club Plaza, created by Jesse Clyde Nichols years ago as a picturesque residential and shopping center whose architecture and fountains are reminiscent of those

Opposite, below: From April through October, major-league baseball fans following the progress of the Kansas City Royals flock to home games at the magnificent Royals Stadium, one of the twin arenas in the impressive Harry S Truman Sports complex east of downtown. The stadium features a 12-story computerized scoreboard and spectacular dancing fountains.

Below: An impressive panorama of Kansas City's compact downtown distict extends across the northeastern horizon from the famous Indian Scout statue in Penn Valley Park, one of several fine overlooks in this part of town.

of Spain. Every year, the buildings here are spectacularly outlined with thousands of lights throughout the Christmas season. Nearby are two of the city's major cultural attractions: the Helen F. Spencer Theater, home of the renowned Missouri Repertory Theater on the University of Missouri campus; and the world-famous Nelson Art Gallery, one of the finest in the nation, which boasts a particularly outstanding collection of oriental art.

Southeast is enormous Swope Park, one of the largest city parks in the country, 1,789 acres of woodland and greenery enclosing two golf courses, the city zoo, and the famous Starlight Theater, which seats 7,858 people for outdoor musicals and concerts on summer evenings.

A short drive away, on the Santa Fe Trail, you can walk through a town of the Old West re-created at the Benjamin Stables Trail Town, one of the many historic sites around Kansas City. Elsewhere are old Fort Osage; the historic river town of Weston; the stately Wornall House, around which the Civil War battle of Westport raged; and several places associated with Jesse James, including the family home in Kearney. East of Kansas City, the historic western frontier city of Independence includes in its treasures the Harry S Truman Library and Museum and the beautiful house in which the president once lived. Across the Missouri River from Independence and completely different in tone are the area's two major amusement parks, Worlds of Fun and Oceans of Fun, providing entertainment for all the family.

"A cracker town, but a happy town" was how the legendary jazz pianist Count Basie once described Kansas City. Although well adjusted to the modern world, this beautiful city has not forgotten its roots or traditional American values; it is a place where big-city sophistication blends happily with small-town homeliness and charm.

Below: Confirming André Maurois' opinion that "few cities have been built with so much regard for beauty," Kansas City's picturesque 55-acre Country Club Plaza, some 5 miles south of downtown, is a captivating residential and shopping center of Spanish-style architecture, gushing fountains, and beautiful statues.

Las Vegas NEVADA

Fun City, U.S.A.

Although a slogan on the control tower of the McCarran International Airport in Las Vegas, Nevada, reads reassuringly, "We don't gamble," it is a sure bet that most of the 9 million tourists who fly into this desert resort every year – plus those who arrive overland – will succumb to the blandishments of Lady Luck before leaving. For gaming – a more genteel word for gambling that is preferred here – is the life blood of this incredible city, where dreams of winning the riches of Eldorado seduce gamblers to contribute around $1.7 billion to casino revenues each year. Dumped miles away from anywhere in the dry, flat shimmering desert, where summer temperatures can soar above 100°F (38°C), Las Vegas has been dubbed the "Unreal City." It seems a reasonable tag when you walk into the lobby of one of its glittering hotel–casinos and are confronted with a barrage of flashing multicolored lights and clanking slot machines, set in rows like an army of space invaders. Elsewhere, pit bosses and dealers preside around the clock over players engrossed in the thrills of blackjack, roulette, craps, baccarat, poker, and keno.

Entertainment by such stars as Frank Sinatra, Sammy Davis, Jr., Liberace, Ann-Margret, and Wayne Newton; spectacular stage productions featuring variety acts and lavishly costumed showgirls; and well-known Broadway musicals like *Hello Dolly* and *South Pacific* lure audiences into the plush hotel theaters. Intimate lounges with live entertainment, singles bars, discos, and other nightspots, an assortment of restaurants, and cheap buffets subsidized by the proceeds of gaming – all combine to confirm that Las Vegas is the "Entertainment Capital of the World."

The action in Las Vegas is focused on the downtown area around Fremont Street – known as the Casino Center or, more colorfully, "Glitter Gulch" – and along 3.5-mile Las Vegas Boulevard – more familiarly labeled the "Strip." Behind their sparkling huge billboards, the hotel–casinos on the Strip display an astonishing variety of imaginative architecture: Circus-Circus is a pink-and-white-striped tent; the Holiday Casino, a Mississippi steamboat; the Aladdin, a sensuous palace out of *The Arabian Nights*. But the queen of them all, Caesar's Palace, stands back in cool elegance, suffused with soft green light behind its rows of spectacular illuminated fountains and copies of famous Roman statues.

Off the Strip, beyond the unmistakable Landmark hotel–casino tower, is the huge Convention Center, its 1 million square feet of space for trade shows, exhibitions, and meetings placing it among the top five such facilities in the country. The downtown Cashman Field Center extension also incorporates a 10,000-seat baseball stadium. Sporting events are major year-round attractions of this desert resort, and many prestigious competitions of golf, tennis, boxing, auto racing, and other sports are sponsored by the hotels. There are also facilities for a wide range of recreational activities, with golf courses forming lush green patches among the dry city blocks and numerous swimming pools and tennis courts offering relaxation at hotels on the Strip.

Despite the emphasis on gaming, spectacular shows, and outdoor recreation, Las Vegas can provide the culturally minded with more serious fare. On the 350-acre campus of the University of Nevada, the Artemus Ham Concert Hall hosts performances by world-famous orchestras and solo

Las Vegas
1 Casino Center
2 Convention Center
3 Caesar's Palace
4 Dunes Country Club
5 Tropicana Country Club
6 University of Nevada
7 Las Vegas Natural History Museum
8 Boulevard Mall

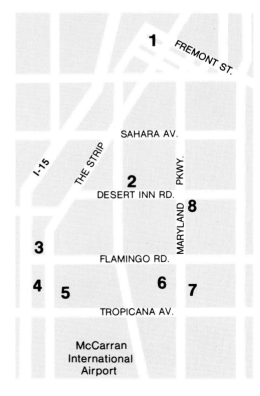

musicians during its celebrated Masters Series, while the Judy Bayley
Theater stages plays and productions by the Nevada Dance Theater. The
city also has the Meadows Playhouse and the Reed Whipple Cultural
Center, where the Civic Symphony and Ballet Company and the acclaimed
Rainbow Company Children's Theater provide a varied program of
performances.

For those interested in Nevada's colorful past and its natural
surroundings and wildlife, there are fascinating exhibits in such museums as
the Las Vegas Natural History Museum on the university campus; the
Nevada State Museum in Lorenzi Park; the Southern Nevada Museum, 13
miles south in Henderson; and the Lost City Museum, 60 miles northeast in
Overton. All around Las Vegas are the ruined remains of nineteenth-century
mining towns that once were thronged with prospectors hunting for the
state's rich silver, gold, and other mineral deposits.

The life of the early pioneers in the state has been entertainingly re-
created among the attractions and activities at the Old Nevada and Old
Vegas theme parks outside the city; the atmosphere is reinforced during the
spectacular Helldorado festival in May, when the Old West heritage of Las
Vegas is commemorated with a big parade, a beauty contest, rodeos, and
carnival events. But the Old Mormon Fort preserved on Las Vegas
Boulevard North is a monument of real-life significance, recalling the first

*Las Vegas Boulevard, better known as the
"Strip," is flanked by glittering hotel-casinos,
each with its gaudy billboard, along a
3½-mile stretch between the downtown
Casino Center and McCarran International
Airport.*

*Overleaf: A dazzling spectacle of illuminated
gaming house signs greets nighttime visitors
to Fremont Street in the Casino Center, the
heart of downtown Las Vegas. Among the
famous casinos here is the Horseshoe,
founded by the legendary Benny Binion,
where in 1980 an unknown gambler made
the highest single casino bet in history —
$777,000 — on the craps table, and won!*

Right: The serene and majestic exterior of Caesar's Palace, elegantly illuminated at night, gives no hint of the hectic gaming activity and lavish entertainment under way inside. Frank Sinatra, Sammy Davis Jr., and Andy Williams are just three of the many top show-business stars who have frequently appeared here.

Below: The thrill of gambling annually attracts millions of visitors to Las Vegas, where the plush hotel-casinos provide challenges to suit every taste. Roulette is a simple form of gambling, in which players bet which number will come up on the spin of the wheel by placing "chips" representing an amount of money on the appropriate numbered box on the adjacent layout.

settlers in the area back in 1855. The Mormons arrived some 25 years after Spanish trading explorers had passed by the spot, a grassy oasis watered by springs that the Spaniards referred to as "the meadows," or *las vegas*.

Abandoned by the Mormons within three years, the meadows were then farmed by settler families until the land was purchased for a town site and watering depot by the railroad (later the Union Pacific), which was then being built from Los Angeles to Salt Lake City. When the railroad eventually opened in 1905, the new town boomed, but it was the construction of the Boulder Dam (now the Hoover Dam) 30 miles away on the Colorado River in the 1930s and the legalization of gambling in 1931 at the railroad-supply depot of Las Vegas that really set the place on the road to prosperity, with nearby Henderson and Boulder City emerging as major industrial and residential centers for the area. After World War II hotels and casinos blossomed in Las Vegas, which was supplied with water and electricity by the dam. By 1982, the city had grown to 183,184 people, its economy boosted by additional revenues from the big Nellis Air Force Base and from new "clean" industries and ready to face the challenge from its gaming-resort rival, Atlantic City in New Jersey.

Like Reno, Las Vegas has liberal laws regarding marriage and divorce, and many couples take advantage of the possibility of marrying here without the usual waiting period or blood test. Many of the ceremonies are performed for a fee in the charming miniature wedding chapels dotted around the city under such colorful names as "The Hitching Post" or "The Wee Kirk o' the Heather." Afterward, there is no shortage of honeymoon entertainment, outdoor recreation, or sightseeing in the city, with trips farther afield to a variety of attractions. Among these are Hoover Dam and its accompanying recreational facilities at Lake Mead; the ruddy sandstone formations and petroglyphs in Valley of Fire State Park, 32 miles northeast; the spectacular Red Rock Canyon, 15 miles west near the attractive Spring Mountain Ranch, whose rich owners once included Howard Hughes; and the Mount Charleston recreation area, high in the cool forested Spring Mountains to the northwest of town. And if that is not enough, Grand Canyon, Bryce Canyon, and Zion national parks and awesome Death Valley are all within reach of Nevada's fabulous resort city.

Left: One of the most popular tourist attractions within easy reach of Las Vegas is Hoover Dam, some 30 miles southeast of the city. The 727-foot-high dam backs up the waters of the Colorado River to form Lake Mead, 115 miles long and the largest man-made lake in the United States. The lake is now the focus of a major outdoor recreation area in southern Nevada's desert country.

Below: Since 1926, when only 100 marriage licences were issued, Las Vegas has become an increasingly popular place for weddings because of Nevada's liberal marriage laws. Dotted around the city are charming little wedding chapels — Cupid's, the Candlelight, the Silver Bell, and many others with equally delightful names — where the splendor of the ceremony depends on the fee paid.

Los Angeles CALIFORNIA

The City of Angels

Images of sun-bronzed people basking under eternally blue skies, of luxurious swimming pools shaded by tall swaying palm trees, of Rolls-Royces and Cadillacs drawn up before palatial mansions that overlook the deep blue Pacific Ocean – all those dreams of success and the ultimate good life this side of paradise have for decades attracted people to southern California's magnetic city of Los Angeles. More than any other city in the United States, except perhaps New York, Los Angeles arouses strong emotional responses, and its character depends more on the eye and the mood of the beholder than on any absolute truths. A city that some believe

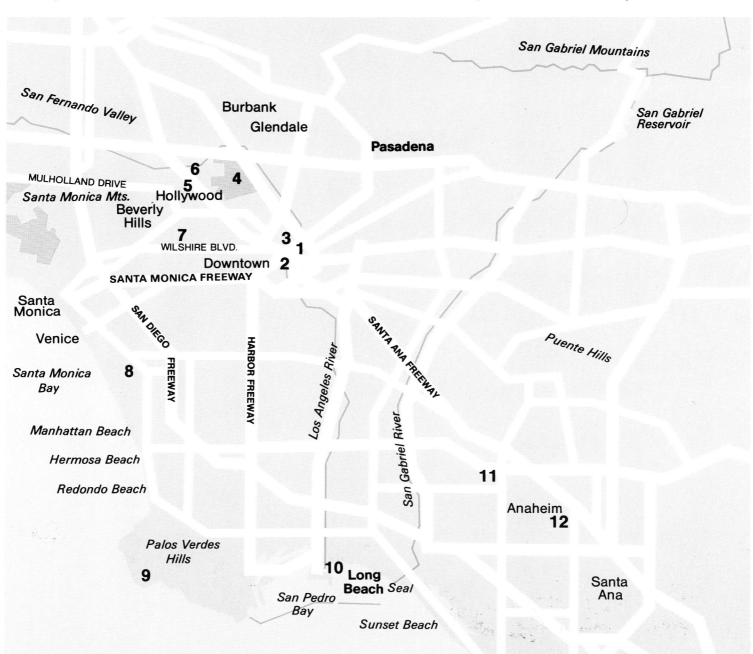

to be paradise, others regard as the last word in horror; a city that some claim to be exciting, dynamic, and romantic, others see as superficial, brash, and selfish. Long the center of the world's greatest movie-making industry, the city's Hollywood district has itself been the creator of such dreams, in which the great movie stars represented the epitome of success and glamor to ordinary folk engrossed in the more mundane and harsher realities of everyday life. Contrasts between myth and reality, success and failure, beauty and ugliness color the many-sided nature of this fascinating city and help to explain local attitudes and behavior, for here the worst disaster of all is to be old, poor, or ugly.

Think of Los Angeles as a modern work of art, an abstract mosaic of a subject not immediately recognizable and made up of small pieces – some brightly colored, others of somber hues; some parts appealing, other parts less so – and you get an impression of both the city's enigmatic character and its physical composition. For years rivaling Chicago as the nation's second city, L.A. spreads over an area of 464 square miles and has a growing population that in 1980 was just under 3 million. But Los Angeles is only one part of the vast megalopolis that takes in over 140 other communities and some 13 million people in Los Angeles County. The

Overleaf: The great efforts made by city officials, business organizations, and community groups in recent years to revitalize downtown Los Angeles as a thriving commercial, cultural, and residential area has resulted in the emergence of an exciting new skyline. Rapidly becoming an attractive place in which to work and live, the central business district is now increasing in population.

Below: Sprawling across the vast plain between the San Gabriel Mountains and the Pacific Ocean, the immense metropolis of Los Angeles, America's second city, is a glittering magnet that entices millions of visitors every year to experience the superb beaches of the Pacific coastline, the fascinating sights of Hollywood and Beverly Hills, and countless other places of interest.

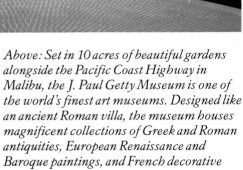

Above: Set in 10 acres of beautiful gardens alongside the Pacific Coast Highway in Malibu, the J. Paul Getty Museum is one of the world's finest art museums. Designed like an ancient Roman villa, the museum houses magnificent collections of Greek and Roman antiquities, European Renaissance and Baroque paintings, and French decorative arts.

Above right: The mirrored-glass round towers of the futuristic Bonaventure Hotel are a well-known landmark in downtown Los Angeles. Designed by John Portman, they rise above a fine shopping gallery of specialty shops, boutiques, art galleries, and restaurants at 5th and Figueroa Streets.

sprawl extends across the plain between the Pacific Ocean and the San Gabriel Mountains, forming a colorful patchwork that encompasses not only urban development, but also desert country, pine-clad mountains, and superb beaches, with graceful palm trees adding a subtropical flavor to the glittering sunlit cityscape.

Superimposed on the scene is a giant spider web of freeways, which gives some cohesion to the sprawl of buildings and makes traveling practicable – although incidentally contributing much to the blanket of hazy smog that often hangs over the city. If Los Angelenos spend much of their lives in their automobiles, at least they can reach the more distant parts of the city relatively easily, unless caught up in a traffic jam. A knowledge of the city's geography is therefore useful before setting out.

Greater Los Angeles meets the Pacific Ocean along Santa Monica and San Pedro bays and, between them, the rocky headland of Palos Verdes. Lining the Santa Monica Bay shoreline from Malibu in the north is a string of popular seaside communities, including Santa Monica; Venice, with the magnificent Marina del Rey boat harbor near the city's international airport; and the three beaches of Manhattan, Hermosa, and Redondo. Beyond Palos Verdes is the huge port city of Long Beach on San Pedro Bay, where the elegant former British luxury liner *Queen Mary* is berthed as a floating museum. Farther east, the inland cities of Anaheim and Santa Ana are fringed by the fabulous beaches of Orange County – including Seal, Sunset, Huntington, and Laguna – frequented by surfers.

Downtown Los Angeles lies some 12 miles inland behind Santa Monica, with the famed districts of Hollywood and Beverly Hills bordering the Santa Monica Mountains on the northwest, and with Burbank, Glendale, and Pasadena on the north and northeast, where the San Gabriel Mountains form a natural barrier. There are magnificent views of the whole of Los Angeles, particularly enchanting at night, from Mulholland Drive, which winds along the crests of the Santa Monica Mountains above Beverly Hills.

Two centuries of growth have created this breath-taking metropolis. In 1781, 11 Spanish-speaking families, totaling 44 people, established a small community by the Los Angeles River on the orders of General Felipe de Neve, the governor of California, and called it El Pueblo de Nuestra Señora la Reina de los Angeles de Porciúncula – Town of Our Lady the Queen of the Angels of Porciúncula – now shortened to simply Los Angeles. The surrounding area was used as ranching country until the 1880s, when settlers began to flood in after the arrival of the railroads, lured by cheap fares and the guarantee of a healthy climate. The dry, sunny weather also attracted the movie industry, which recognized the additional benefits of a cheap labor supply and of the varied natural scenery, which could be used for locations. And from beneath the ground came oil, which has contributed much to the city's prosperity as well as a forest of nodding well-heads to the urban landscape.

Taking advantage of the almost perfect climate, in which daytime temperatures rarely fall below 70°F (21°C) even in winter, Los Angelenos

The Los Angeles Memorial Coliseum was the impressive setting for the athletics events of the 1984 Olympic Games. During the two-week competition, spectators shared the conflicting emotions of the international athletes from the joy of victory to the despair and disappointment of defeat, from the triumph of Carl Lewis to the anguish of Mary Decker. Appropriately, America's show-business and movie capital brought the games to a breath-taking close with a stunning spectacle that ended with the arrival of a mock spaceship and a comforting speech from a space visitor.

spend a good deal of time outdoors, whether relaxing by pools or on the beaches or indulging in the wide range of recreational pursuits possible here, including not only the usual tennis and golf, but also such pastimes as roller-skating and ocean fishing. Many also enjoy spectator sports at the racetracks and stadiums, with large numbers of fans crowding into Dodger Stadium for Dodgers baseball games and into Anaheim Stadium for Rams football games. In the summer of 1984, the city's many sports facilities hosted the exciting events of the Olympic Games.

When the sun goes down, Los Angeles springs to life, with a wide assortment of excellent restaurants, swinging nightspots, and theaters to choose from. The theaters range from small workshop groups and try-out Equity-waiver theaters to such large playhouses as the famous Shubert in Century City, the renovated Pasadena Playhouse, and the prestigious downtown three-theater Music Center, which also stages musicals and ballet and is the winter home of the Los Angeles Philharmonic. For many years, one of the most popular attractions on the music scene has been the Hollywood Bowl, the renowned hillside amphitheater where music lovers can listen to concerts under the stars on warm summer evenings.

Lest you imagine that Los Angeles people are concerned with only the pleasures of the moment, the city boasts many fine museums and art galleries where the treasures of the past are carefully preserved. Among them are the beautiful J. Paul Getty Museum in Malibu, with its exquisite statues, furniture, and paintings; the George C. Page Museum, which houses the reassembled bones of prehistoric animals that were caught in the adjacent La Brea Tar Pits, and the excellent, wide-ranging Los Angeles County Art Museum, both on Wilshire Boulevard; the fascinating Southwest Museum in Highland Park, with exhibits on American Indian cultures; and the impressive Huntington Library, Art Gallery, and Botanical Gardens in San Marino.

Apart from museums, Los Angeles has countless other sightseeing attractions, many of which can be enjoyed simply by walking through the most interesting areas. Browsing in elegant stores, specialty shops, and enchanting boutiques is a particularly pleasant pastime on such fascinating streets as Melrose Avenue, Wilshire Boulevard, and Rodeo Drive in Beverly Hills, while downtown Los Angeles has such special shopping attractions as Arco Plaza and Olvera Street.

The downtown district is where the city began in 1781, and you can get an idea of its compact layout, encircled by freeways and traditionally centered on Pershing Square, from observation points high in the City Hall Tower or in new hotels like the Bonaventure or Hyatt Regency. Many such high-rise office and hotel buildings and residential developments have sprouted in the downtown district in recent years and have imposed on it an exciting ultramodern profile; among them is the prestigious California Plaza complex, begun in the mid-1980s.

Contrasting with these gleaming new structures, the birthplace of the city nestles just across the Santa Ana Freeway from the City Hall, the area around its majestic plaza and church now preserved as a State Historic Park. With its restored Mexican-style shops and restaurants, the adjacent pedestrian alley of Olvera Street bustles with twentieth-century activity and is a favorite sightseeing spot for visitors. Other special browsing attractions in the downtown district are the colorful Grand Central Market, the picturesque Chinatown area, and the Japanese quarter, known as Little Tokyo, on First Street.

Drive west from downtown along the freeway, and a big white-lettered sign on a hillside boldly announces HOLLYWOOD. Here are some of the places that everyone has dreamed of: Sunset Boulevard, Sunset Strip, Hollywood Boulevard, and some of the great movie studios, although much of the old glamor has long since faded away. Many of the studios, such as RKO and Warner Brothers, have now gone, while others are used

Exotic homes that reflect the individual tastes and interests of their owners line the elegant residential streets of Beverly Hills and other western suburbs of Los Angeles. Here are houses that seem to have been taken straight out of the movies.

by television companies or rented to other film-production houses. But fascinating tours are conducted around the huge Universal Studios (and, for those interested, around the NBC Television Studios in Burbank). Along Hollywood Boulevard, you can recall the great movie stars of the past in the names enshrined in bronze stars along the "Walk of Fame," in the hand- and footprints imprinted in cement outside Mann's Chinese Theater (formerly Grauman's Chinese Theater), or in the figures immortalized in wax at the Hollywood Wax Museum. And to get an idea of the stars' luxurious life style, you can drive past their graceful mansions, pastiches of many architectural styles, along well-manicured streets in the beautiful residential area of Beverly Hills.

While on this side of the city, a visit to Griffith Park, the largest municipal park in the United States, is a must. In its hilly 4,253 acres are areas of wilderness, golf courses and other recreational facilities, and numerous entertainment attractions, including a famous zoo, an observatory, and the popular outdoor Greek Theater, set in a canyon.

Many other top-ranking attractions are scattered around Los Angeles, although within easy reach via the freeways. Among them are such world-famous family-entertainment centers as the superb Disneyland in Anaheim, not far from Movieland and Knott's Berry Farm, a park with an Old West theme, in Buena Park. And overlooking the ocean on the Palos Verdes headland, performing dolphins, whales, and other sea creatures entertain the crowds at the wonderful Marineland oceanarium.

Places to visit farther afield include the beautiful resort of Santa Barbara, on the Pacific coast to the northwest of the city, and picturesque Santa Catalina Island, off Palos Verdes. History buffs will also enjoy trips to the three missions founded by Father Junípero Serra in the Los Angeles area: San Juan Capistrano, in Orange County; San Gabriel, northeast of downtown; and San Fernando, in the San Fernando Valley beyond the Santa Monica Mountains. And for those who wish to escape the city bustle, there are many captivating drives inland, with the Mojave Desert a unique and challenging experience.

For people who like to live life to the full, Los Angeles truly is a paradise city, appropriately nicknamed the "City of Angels."

Louisville KENTUCKY

Home of the Derby

If there is one American horse-racing event that everyone has surely heard of, it must be the world-renowned Kentucky Derby, the highlight of the spring race meet run on the first Saturday in May at Louisville's Churchill Downs track. The expectant excitement of the occasion is interrupted only briefly when the 100,000 spectators indulge in a spot of nostalgic sentimentality by singing "My Old Kentucky Home." The race itself is the climax of the annual Kentucky Derby Festival, which begins ten days earlier when the Bluegrass Region city springs to life with music, dancing, and a colorful assortment of events that includes a balloon race, a mini-marathon, a river-steamboat race, and the traditional Pegasus parade. Horses – breeding them, selling them, or racing them – are in the blood of Louisville. Apart from racing at Churchill Downs, there are harness races at the Louisville Downs track, horse farms around the city specializing in different breeds, and, in August, the famous Kentucky State Fair and World Championship Horse Show, which offers entertainment for all the family.

Louisville has also derived much of its prosperity from the rich agricultural produce of the broad valley of the Ohio River, on which the city stands, and from a wide range of manufactured goods such as bourbon whiskey, cigarettes, paint, chemicals, electrical appliances, and even books in braille. The success story began when Louisville, because of its location at the only falls on the river, became an important transshipment and distribution point in the early nineteenth century and then a major supply point for the Union forces during the Civil War after the construction of the first north–south railroad route across the river. Settlement at the site, however, dates from Revolutionary War days, when General George Rogers Clark camped here in 1778 during his campaign against the British and the Indians in the region. Locust Grove, the fine mansion where he later lived for nine years before his death in 1818, is today one of Louisville's cherished historic homes.

Named in 1789 to honour King Louis XVI of France for his country's aid during the Revolution, Louisville has matured into a pleasant modern city of just under 300,000 people. But, not surprisingly for the largest city of a border state that maintained a middle-of-the-road stance between the Union and the Confederacy in the Civil War (or War Between the States), the city has tried to strike an even position between preserving the old and adopting the new. So Louisville's industrial face is balanced by its atmospheric historic districts and lovely parks, its brand-new shopping complexes, by its lovingly restored old buildings. Yet changes are being made, and expensive redevelopment programs have been undertaken in recent years.

A panoramic view of the downtown area of this city of contrasts can be enjoyed from the restaurant and cocktail lounge at the top of the 38-story First National Tower Building at Fifth Avenue and Main Street. To the north, the broad sweep of the Ohio River is segmented by a series of old iron bridges that link the city with neighboring Indiana. On this stretch of the river, the old steamboats *Belle of Louisville* and *Bonnie Belle* ply up and down with their complement of sightseers during the hot, steamy days of summer. A good observation point for activity on the river is the Riverfront Plaza, where ice-skating is popular in winter and where many events

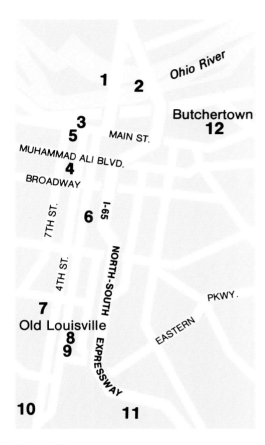

Louisville
1 Clark Memorial Bridge
2 John F. Kennedy Bridge
3 Riverfront Plaza
4 4th Avenue Mall
5 City Hall
6 Filson Club
7 St. James Court
8 Rauch Memorial Planetarium
9 J.B. Speed Art Museum
10 Churchill Downs
11 Kentucky Fair and Exposition Center
12 Thomas Edison House

Opposite, top: The graceful, tree-shaded neighborhood of Old Louisville is a National Preservation District south of downtown, where many beautiful Victorian mansions, some of them superbly restored, reflect the city's early prosperity. Many prominent citizens, including several writers, lived in St. James Court, now the site of a major art fair every fall.

Opposite, bottom: Among the assortment of traditional events that excite the crowds during the 12-day Kentucky Derby Festival held in Louisville in early May, is the Great Balloon Race, when up to 40 hot-air balloons create a colorful spectacle as they float silently over the green countryside of Jefferson County.

Below: Louisville sits beside the only falls on the Ohio River, linked to the neighboring state of Indiana by the Clark Memorial and John F. Kennedy bridges, two of the romantic old iron bridges spanning the river at this point. Although modern high-rise buildings are now sprouting above the downtown streets, the city still preserves much of its nineteenth-century heritage amid the new developments.

of the annual summer festivals are held. The most popular and enjoyable of these are the four summer weekends of music, dancing, and entertainment provided during the Heritage Weekend Celebrations by the city's many ethnic communities, and the lively foot-tapping Kentucky Fried Chicken Bluegrass Music Festival in September.

Behind the riverfront, the neat grid of streets making up the downtown area contains many interesting and surprising sights within walking distance from the riverfront. Running parallel to the river, West Main Street, a National Preservation District, sets the balanced tone between old and new that is so characteristic of Louisville. Here, restored nineteenth-century stone and cast-iron-fronted buildings are juxtaposed with the imaginative design of the new 27-story Humana Tower, and the modern complex of the Kentucky Center for the Arts – with its two halls for performing music, opera, theater, and dance – contrasts with the elegant, beautifully restored old bank building now used by the prestigious Actors Theater of Louisville. The repertory here includes not only old classics, of course, but also brand-new plays. West Main Street is also the location of the fascinating Museum of History and Science and the unique American Saddle Museum. One of the high points in Louisville's year takes place here in December, when citizens dress in nineteenth-century costume and celebrate a Victorian-style Christmas with traditional food and entertainment as part of the Christmas in the City festivities.

Fourth Avenue, which crosses the downtown district at a right angle to West Main Street, also offers interesting places for the visitor. Between Market Street and Broadway is a five-block pedestrian shopping mall, where newcomers to the city are sure to stand spellbound in front of the incredible Louisville Clock, an ingenious creation that marks the hour of noon by staging a race among five historic Louisville characters on an

elevated track. Not far away is the huge modern Galleria complex, which features a large greenhouse-like atrium containing shops and restaurants flanked by two 26-story office towers. Another redevelopment project, at the junction of Fourth Avenue and Broadway and including the restoration of the Brown Hotel, is the most recent scheme in the modernization of Louisville's downtown area. Yet amid all the changes on Fourth Avenue, the city authorities have had the foresight to preserve and restore a fine old movie theater and create from it the opulent Louisville Palace for popular Las Vegas-style shows.

If renovation is gradually changing the face of downtown Louisville, time seems to have stood still among the fine mansions and tree-lined streets in the lovely historic residential neighbourhood of Old Louisville just to the south. And in the equally old district of Butchertown, by the Ohio River east of downtown, the European atmosphere created by the early German residents has remained, the quiet, charming neighborhood erupting every fall with the noisy celebrations of the Oktoberfest. Here you can visit the old stockyards, which are still in use, and the house inhabited by Thomas Edison while he was working in Louisville for Western Union.

Louisville's attractions are many, and no visit to the city would be complete without wandering through the city's ring of fine parks and the zoo, browsing through the downtown Filson Club's pioneer-history exhibits and the superb art collections at the J. B. Speed Art Museum, or breathing the historic atmosphere of the Zachary Taylor National Cemetery and such graceful nineteenth-century homes as the Culbertson Mansion and Farmington. But if you wish to remember Louisville by the taste of its home cooking, you can try the traditional Derby Pie, whose recipe is secret, or the Hot Brown turkey sandwich, washed down with local bourbon-based drinks such as the lively mint julep.

Memphis TENNESSEE

Birthplace of the Blues

If by chance you had been strolling by 706 Union Avenue, a one-story building in downtown Memphis, Tennessee, one day 30 years ago, you might have caught a glimpse of a fresh-faced youth of 18 as he emerged after having cut his first records at the Sun Record studio. Not surprising, perhaps, in a city renowned as the birthplace of the blues. Yet that young man put his hometown more firmly on the international map than did perhaps anyone else, and today thousands of people make the trip to the lovely suburban mansion, Graceland, where he now lies buried after his death at the early age of 42. His name was Elvis Presley, the "King of Rock 'n' Roll."

If Memphis had been quick to embrace new fashions in music and make them its own, it has been more resistant to the blandishments of the drastic cosmetic surgery that is now dramatically transforming the faces of so many other American cities. An essentially conservative city with a southern pedigree, Memphis has a more cautious pace of life that at least ensures that its citizens survive the hot, steamy summers.

The location of the little community, established at the beginning of the nineteenth century on the bluffs where the Wolf River runs into the mighty Mississippi, seems to have conjured up in Andrew Jackson's mind a vision of ancient Egypt, so he called the place Memphis. The riverside site soon turned the growing community into a thriving port, a bustling commercial depot handling the South's cotton crop, and a busy market for the slave trade. Although the Civil War brought an end to the slave business, cotton has remained a major source of wealth for the city, as is hardwood timber. With a population now numbering over 646,000, Memphis ranks fifteenth among the nation's largest cities. Its tree-lined streets, ablaze with pink and white blossoms in spring, its lovely parks, its fine restaurants and lively night life, its colorful festivals, and its all-pervading southern atmosphere combine to create the city's special charm and fascination.

A cruise on one of the white sternwheelers that ply up and down the Mississippi is a good way to get an impression of the city as the high-rise towers and hotels of the downtown business area glide by above the bluffs on the east bank between the Hernando de Soto and Memphis–Arkansas bridges. Here, a 3-mile-long finger of silt, City Island, divides Ol' Man River from its smaller tributary the Wolf; the island was formed, so they say, by mud clinging to a Union gunboat sunk during the Civil War naval battle here in 1862. The southern part of the island, appropriately known as Mud Island, has been developed as a 50-acre recreation area offering a variety of attractions, with displays evoking river life, a boat marina, musical entertainment in the amphitheater, and restaurants serving Creole and southern specialties.

From Mud Island, it is a short ride on the modern monorail over the Wolf River to the downtown riverfront area, where a romantic view of sunset over the river can be enjoyed from excellent restaurants, such as the Pier on Wagner Street. Below, the river is lined with a chain of pleasant parks, while other green spaces, such as Court Square, offer places for relaxation amid the downtown bustle. On Front Street, known to Memphians as "Cotton Row," is the historic Cotton Exchange, containing the offices of the firms that have long played such an important part in the business life

An exciting ride by monorail over the Wolf River speeds visitors to the varied attractions of Mud Island, a popular recreation park devised around the theme of the Mississippi River. A five-block-long scale replica representing the course of the river between Illinois and the Gulf of Mexico winds through the park, providing an unusual and fascinating view of its interesting features.

of the city. Behind is the broad swath of Mid-America Mall, a multimillion-dollar pedestrian shopping street that represents the newer face of Memphis. Its north end opens into Civic Center Plaza, containing state- and federal-government buildings, a large ornamental pool, and, when it is turned on, an impressive 60-foot (18-m) fountain. The other end leads into Beale Street, the hub of the city's night life. On this renovated historic street, where W. C. Handy created the rhythmic, soulful sound of the blues in PeeWee's saloon, a cluster of night clubs, restaurants, fast-food stands, and shops caters to all tastes. But if the pace is too hectic, there is a place to relax by the statues of Handy and Elvis in the two little parks dedicated to the city's two best-known musicians along this fabulous street. And with a few paces more in the direction of the river, tired legs can be rested while watching a show at the renovated Orpheum Theater, one of the South's great entertainment palaces.

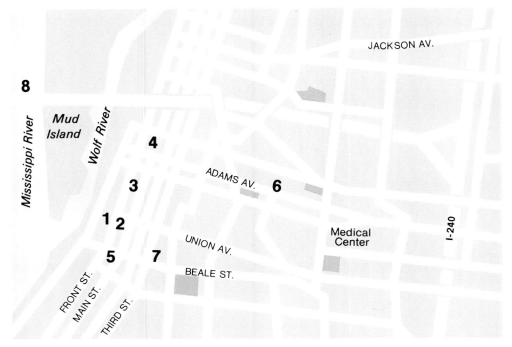

In the Victorian Village area, a few blocks east of the Civic Center along Adams Avenue, beautifully restored mansions in a variety of nineteenth-century styles provide an elegant reminder of the years when King Cotton brought prosperity to the shrewd merchants of Memphis. A tour of the lavishly furnished rooms of the Mallory–Neely House or the Fontaine House leaves a vivid impression of the comfortable life style of the rich in those days. Contrasting with the tranquil elegance of this historic district is the world-renowned Memphis Medical Center, a vast complex of hospital and research buildings some blocks to the southeast, near Forrest Park.

Scattered through the suburban areas to the east of the Martin Luther King Expressway, there are several places of interest worth taking a bus ride to visit. Children particularly enjoy a wander through Overton Park to see the many kinds of animals in the well-designed zoo and aquarium, while more culture-minded adults may prefer to take a look at the excellent collection of paintings and sculptures in the Brooks Museum of Art, also in the park. A few blocks south, an opportunity to do some shopping or to eat in pleasant surroundings presents itself at Overton Square, followed by an exciting visit to the Libertyland theme park at the Fairgrounds to enjoy a thrilling roller-coaster ride, a foot-stomping show, or an enthralling display by performing dolphins.

Also located in the eastern suburbs is the Memphis Pink Palace Museum, so named because it was built as a home in pink Georgia marble by the founder of the Piggly-Wiggly supermarket chain. With its modern extension – also pink – the museum contains comprehensive exhibits on the natural history and culture of the mid-South and also incorporates a superb planetarium. Anyone fascinated with this museum's collections will also be captivated by the wonderful Chucalissa Indian Museum and village reconstruction, which is to the southwest of the city. As well as the Brooks Museum, lovers of art can enjoy the fine collection of paintings or wander through the lovely gardens at the Dixon Gallery and Gardens on Park Avenue. But for keen gardeners and botanists, a visit to the beautiful Memphis Botanic Garden in Audubon Park is a must.

There is much to recommend in this splendid old city, not least the easy charm of the Memphians themselves. It would be particularly hard to forget the gaiety of the Memphis in May Festival and the Cotton Carnival, a superb meal at Justine's or Grisanti's incomparable restaurants, or an evening of blues or Dixieland in a Beale Street nightspot.

The Fontaine House, on Adams Street, is one of the fine nineteenth-century mansions in the Victorian Village district of Memphis. Built in 1870, the restored house is now open as a museum displaying beautiful furnishings and textiles of the period.

Miami FLORIDA

The Snowbird Resort

According to the well-known story, Miami, that bustling subtropical resort basking by the Atlantic Ocean near Florida's southern tip, came into existence through a timely gift of one spray of orange blossoms back in 1895. It was sent by a forceful widow named Julia D. Tuttle, who had bought land near the mouth of the Miami River some years earlier and wanted a railroad. After a devastating frost in the winter of 1894/95 had killed much of Florida's citrus and vegetable crop farther north, the fresh spray of flowers, untouched by frost, was handed to the railroad tycoon Henry M. Flagler. He had built a track down Florida's east coast, but only as far south as Palm Beach. Flagler got the message; he not only extended the railroad down to Miami, but also agreed to finance development there in return, of course, for a good slice of land. In July 1895, the city of Miami was incorporated, and the land boom was on.

Despite periodic devastation by hurricanes and yellow fever, buildings shot up like mushrooms, with the population following suit: 343 in 1896, 5,471 in 1910, 29,571 in 1920, and an amazing 346,931 in 1980 – and that was just in the city itself. Greater Miami, or metropolitan Dade County, now has around 1.75 million permanent residents, a number swollen even further by a staggering 11 million tourists and vacationers each year.

First explored for Spain by Juan Ponce de León in 1513, the Miami area was for centuries inhabited by only Miccosukee Indians, until a few pioneer farmers moved in during the early nineteenth century and Fort Dallas was built in 1836 – and soon abandoned – at the mouth of the Miami River. There was just a ridge of land with swamps on one side and mangrove trees and huge sand bars on the other. But the place had one important feature: its climate.

Moderated by the warm Gulf Stream, which washes the coast, temperatures here range only between 66°F (19°C) in winter and 84°F (27°C) in summer. With its superb beaches and clear blue water, Miami offered a winter escape from the snowbound industrial North and, in more recent years, from Europe too. A paradise for sun seekers, Miami is now a mecca for those who love sports and the outdoor life, many of whom come for the excellent golf and fishing. Charter boats bob on the ocean, their decks lined with fishermen eager to tussle with a marlin, dolphin, kingfish, or other game fish, while in the Port, luxurious cruise liners lie nose to tail alongside the wharves, earning for Miami the nickname "Cruise Capital of the World."

Today, however, tourism takes second place to finance and international trade in Miami's economy, but still is far more important than the city's small manufacturing industry. Miami has become a major international business center with especially strong links with Latin America. Success and affluence have produced an urban metropolis that is continually expanding and throwing up prestigious new corporate office towers and gleaming hotels.

Now covering more than 2,000 square miles, Greater Miami contains not only Miami itself, but also an assortment of other municipalities and communities, each with its own special character. Around downtown Miami, with its Cubans and culture, there are Coconut Grove, an enclave on Biscayne Bay of the chic and of artists; Coral Gables, a well-regulated

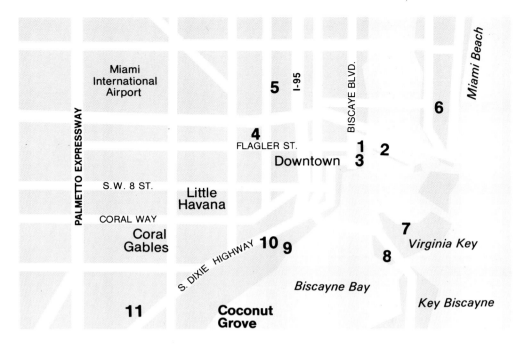

community with fine Spanish-style architecture; Miami Beach, an offshore-island bulwark of glittering hotels facing the sea; and other communities that are just part of the general urban sprawl. For some, it is the American Dream, the good life come true; for others, a vulgar parody, a nightmare of urban malaise. Undeniable, however, are its many attractions, its bewildering array of things to do and see – all in a setting of subtropical palm trees and white sandy beaches.

The heart of downtown Miami centers on the bustling activity along magnificent Biscayne Boulevard and, crossing it, Flagler Street. Behind the rows of palm trees that line Biscayne Boulevard, elegant office complexes, hotels, stores, shops, restaurants, and night clubs face Bayfront Park, 62 acres of tropical greenery enclosing the Municipal Auditorium. Flagler Street leads into the Cuban district of "Little Havana," with its lively restaurants, night clubs, and shops.

Downtown, you will also find various spectacular cultural centers where you can enjoy paintings or performances of opera, ballet, concerts, or Broadway shows. For sports fans, the highlight is the Orange Bowl stadium, home of the Dolphins football team and the famous New Year's Day football classic, preceded the day before by a stupendous parade along Biscayne Boulevard. Downtown, you can also stroll along the Miami River Walkway and ride in the cars of the Metrorail rapid-transit and Downtown People Mover monorail systems.

Greater Miami's northern districts attract many people to the Jai Alai Fronton, the Hialeah Racetrack, the Miami Wax Museum, and the Aventura Mall shopping center. Another popular attraction here is the Spanish monastery of St. Bernard, dating from 1141 and shipped from Spain for William Randolph Hearst – although for quarantine reasons, it never reached his California estate.

Along Miami's waterfront, forests of charter boats and pleasure craft clutter the sparkling Miamarina near the bustling Port. To the north, several causeways link the city with the island of Miami Beach, where fabulous hotels and night clubs line Colliers Avenue. Apart from its superb beach, the island has many other attractions, including the Center for the Performing Arts, the Bass Museum of Art, and the atmospheric Art Deco District, with its echoes of 1930s movies. South of Miami Beach are the two smaller islands of Virginia Key and Key Biscayne, linked by the Ricken-backer Causeway, along which you will find the world-famous Seaquarium, the fascinating exhibition center of Planet Ocean, and the Miami Marine Stadium.

Previous pages: Fronting the sandy beaches lining the Atlantic Ocean, miles of luxurious hotels stretch along the island of Miami Beach, providing air-conditioned comforts and entertainment for the year-round visitors to America's subtropical paradise resort.

South of downtown Miami, the road to Coconut Grove passes the luxurious Villa Vizcaya, an Italian-style palace with beautiful gardens on Biscayne Bay near the Science Museum and Space Planetarium. Among other things, Coconut Grove is noted for its acclaimed Playhouse theater, Mayfair mall, February Arts Festival – and teenage roller-skaters. Inland, Coral Gables has the outstanding Lowe Art Museum, on the University of Miami campus. But a whole cluster of interesting places of family appeal is to be found in the southernmost parts of the city, among them the Fairchild Tropical Gardens, Parrot Jungle, Serpentarium, Metrozoo, Monkey Jungle, Orchid Jungle, and the astonishing Coral Castle built by a jilted immigrant lover over 50 years ago.

If the barrage of twentieth-century attractions at last begins to pall, then it is time to take a ride into southern Florida's uncrowded countryside, where you can sample, for instance, age-old Indian culture at the Miccosukee Indian Village. Absolute musts are visits to the fascinating wildlife wilderness enclosed in Everglades National Park, one of the world's most enchanting special places, and to John Pennekamp Coral Reef State Park, an underwater paradise off the isle of Key Largo.

Against the backdrop of a replica Cambodian temple, white Bengal tigers roam comparatively freely in their open-air moated enclosure in Miami's 260-acre Metrozoo. The well-planned zoo is arranged according to world regions, with appropriate vegetation, landscapes, and architecture creating suitable habitats for the animals on display.

Milwaukee WISCONSIN

America's Beer Capital

Opposite, top: The 175-foot Victorian Gothic water tower in Watertower Park is a famous landmark in the North Point Historical District on Milwaukee's East Side. The surrounding streets in this pleasant neighborhood are lined with lovely houses built mostly between 1890 and 1915.

Opposite, bottom: The magnificent Pabst Theater, built in 1895 and beautifully restored in the 1970s after being threatened with demolition, is a beloved landmark of downtown Milwaukee. Noted for its opulent interior and fine acoustics, the 1,388-seat theater was designed for the beer baron Frederick Pabst by a brewery architect named Otto Strack, who had never had any experience of building theaters.

Over an arch in Charles Mader's famous German restaurant in Milwaukee, Wisconsin, there is a sign in gold letters that reads in translation: "God bless hops and malt." This little prayer – or, perhaps, expression of gratitude – could almost be the city's motto, for three of the nation's top four beer-making companies – Miller, Schlitz, and Pabst – have their breweries here. In this most German of all American cities, however, not only beer, but also great quantities of schnitzel, sauerbraten, and wurst of every kind are consumed with gusto daily in such fine eating houses as Mader's and Karl Ratzsch's, where that indefinable feeling of well-being, geniality, and enjoyment that the Germans lump together as *Gemütlichkeit* reigns supreme.

But if the ethnic flavor of Milwaukee is predominantly German, it is also liberally enriched with the additional spice brought by immigrants from Poland, Russia, Ireland, Greece, Italy, and countless other places. The resulting cultural mix shows up in a variety of ways, most noticeably in the bewildering range of ethnic restaurants and craft shops scattered throughout the city and in the exhilarating festivals that sparkle through the summer months, justifying Milwaukee's claim to be the "City of Fabulous Festivals." For apart from the big, spectacular celebrations – the Lakefront Festival of the Arts, the Summerfest, the City of Festivals Parade, and the Wisconsin State Fair – each ethnic group has its own special show. There is even a French get-together to celebrate Bastille Day.

It was, in fact, French fur traders and missionaries who, in the seventeenth century, first explored the area where Milwaukee now stands, a swamp where three rivers flowed into Lake Michigan, which the Indians called Millioki, or "gathering place by the waters." The city of Milwaukee was not founded officially, however, until 1846, when rival communities on each side of the Milwaukee River were amalgamated. By then, east-coast and European immigrants, mostly German, had begun to arrive, and the city rapidly benefited from the skills and wealth they brought with them. Now grown to a city of more than 636,000 people, Milwaukee ranks

Downtown Milwaukee

1. *First Wisconsin Center*
2. *Pfister Hotel*
3. *City Hall*
4. *Pabst Theater*
5. *Performing Arts Center*
6. *Milwaukee Art Museum*
7. *Milwaukee County Historical Museum*
8. *Old World Third Street*
9. *Milwaukee Exposition and Convention Center and Arena (MECCA)*
10. *Public Museum*
11. *Pabst Brewery*

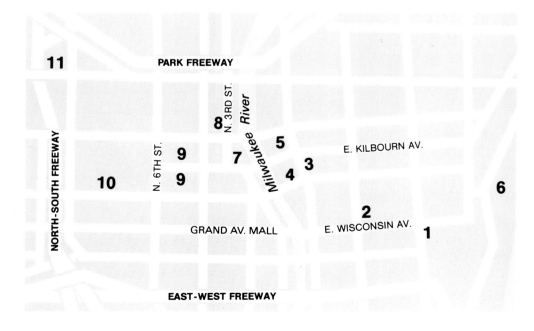

eighteenth largest in the country, a major manufacturing center producing a wide range of machines, engines, other industrial equipment – and, of course, beer.

The German influence remains. Milwaukee is one of America's safest and most law-abiding cities; its streets are clean; and, curiously, it has probably more clocks on its buildings than does any other city in the country. It is also a place of enjoyment, a lively cultural and recreational center that offers a varied selection of activities and places of interest.

Divided into three main sections – the West and East Sides of downtown and the industrial South Side – by the Milwaukee and Menomonee rivers, the city is easy and convenient to explore, especially if you first take an overall look from the observation deck on its tallest building, the elegant 41-story First Wisconsin Center, on the East Side. This notable landmark rises at the Lake Michigan end of Milwaukee's famous shopping street, Wisconsin Avenue, which is known to locals simply as "The Avenue." Here the bellboys at the gracious old Pfister Hotel may once have been rewarded with the mellifluous tones of the tenor Enrico Caruso – or the more raucous grunts of several United States presidents.

The distinctive ornate bell-tower of Milwaukee's City Hall, completed in 1895, overlooks downtown East Side, contrasting in style with the stark white shape of the Performing Arts Center built in 1969. The Center provides a focal point for symphony concerts, opera, and ballet in its 2,329-seat concert hall and 526-seat theater.

Apart from the fine shops on The Avenue, there are many smart places among the "Shops on Jefferson" and in the hurly-burly of the Milwaukee Antique Center. But for a special experience, you can walk across the bridge over the Milwaukee River into the magnificent Grand Avenue shopping center, a maze of elegant stores, shops, and restaurants created along West Wisconsin Avenue. One of the new walkways built into this development to give protection against Milwaukee's bitter winters leads to the impressive Hyatt Regency Hotel, from where you can proceed north several blocks to sample the charming atmosphere of Old World Third Street, a restored two-block shopping area where Mader's German restaurant is located and where Usinger's world-famous retail store still makes and sells its famous sausages.

A walk through Milwaukee's streets also uncovers many architectural gems, both old and new. On the East Side, rubbing shoulders with starkly modern glass structures, is the city's best-known landmark, the ornate City Hall of 1895, crowned by its 393-foot (120-m) bell tower. Nearby is the beloved Pabst Theater, whose opulent interior, now lavishly restored, has echoed for nearly a century to the sound of theatrical events ranging from Shakespeare to Broadway musicals. From here, it is but a few steps to the modern Performing Arts Center, the venue for symphony concerts and performances of opera and ballet.

Many of the East Side's special places of interest are located along the shore of Lake Michigan. Of particular appeal is the North Point Historical District, a collection of lovely old homes overlooked by a 175-foot (53-m) Victorian Gothic water tower and lit by quaint street lamps. In this area, too, are the charming Italian-style Villa Terrace house and the Charles Allis Art Museum. The East Side's most important museum, however, is farther south: the impressive Milwaukee Art Museum, designed on the lakefront by Eero Saarinen in 1957 and now greatly enlarged.

Milwaukee's other major museum, the Public Museum, is to be found in the downtown West Side, where its superb exhibits range over natural history, ethnic cultures, and earth sciences. Also not to be missed on a stroll through the West Side are the informative Milwaukee County Historical Museum; the splendid home built in 1895 for Joseph Kalvelage, popularly known as the "Castle on Kilbourn;" and the equally opulent Frederick Pabst Mansion, built for the wealthy brewer and now a National Historic Landmark. His West Side brewery is one of the many fine old buildings in Milwaukee that were built with the pale-yellow bricks that gave the city its nickname of "The Cream City."

For sports fans, Milwaukee has the County Stadium, home of the baseball Brewers and football Green Bay Packers, and the Milwaukee Arena, where the Bucks play basketball and the Admirals, ice hockey. But for family entertainment, a ride to the outstanding Milwaukee County Zoo is a

must. Other outdoor places providing quieter relaxation are the Boerner Botanical Gardens, in Whitnall Park, and the Mitchell Park Horticultural Conservatory, where the three unique glass domes packed with wonderful floral displays provide a favorite setting for photographs of Milwaukee's newlyweds.

A visit to Milwaukee would not be complete, however, without a cruise on the lake that has played such an important role in the history and life of this great port city. With Prohibition imminent after World War I, another use for its waters was even suggested to his thirsty customers by Charles Mader when he put up an exasperated poster in his restaurant window that cried: "Stock up now! Today and tomorrow there's beer. Soon there'll be only the lake!" Fortunately, Milwaukee survived, and its beer still flows freely.

The three 87-foot-high domes of the Mitchell Park Horticultural Conservatory, known to Milwaukeans simply as "the Domes," are packed with exotic plants from around the world: lush greenery in the tropical dome, desert plants in the arid dome, and six different seasonal displays each year in the third dome. On Saturdays the domes are a popular setting for wedding photographs.

Minneapolis/ St. Paul MINNESOTA

The Twin Cities

If Father Louis Hennepin, a Franciscan missionary, could return today to the spot by the falls on the Mississippi River where in 1683 he carved the arms of France on a tree, he would surely be astonished. For, looking about him, he would see an impressive cityscape of towering buildings indicating a vast modern metropolis – and not just one city but two, Minnesota's "Twin Cities" of Minneapolis and St. Paul. And if he could get to know the twins, he would soon realize that each has its own distinctive character, with Minneapolis the more extrovert and flamboyant of the two.

Much praise has been showered on the Twin Cities in recent years by surveys assessing the quality of life enjoyed by the inhabitants of America's urban areas, and Minneapolis has three times won the coveted All-American City Award. The reasons are easy to find. Minneapolis is a clean, safe, and progressive city with a tolerant, socially aware, and responsible population, and with a city government that has a good working partnership not only with neighboring St. Paul, but also with local business. Through the "5 percent club," many companies donate that proportion of their gross profits to charities and the arts in the city. This remarkable financial support has helped Minneapolis to become one of the nation's top cultural centers, boasting 136 art galleries, 15 museums, more than 90 repertory and dinner theaters, 21 music companies, and nine dance companies. With its 153 parks and 22 lakes, the "City of Lakes" is also blessed with abundant sports and recreational amenities and with a pleasant urban environment that is constantly being improved to make life better for the city's inhabitants.

One of these development projects is now in progress, ringing the downtown shopping area with seven huge parking ramps linked to the con-

Downtown Minneapolis
 1 IDS Center
 2 City Center
 3 Butler Square
 4 City Hall
 5 Hubert H. Humphrey Metrodome
 6 Foshay Tower
 7 Orchestra Hall
 8 Tyrone Guthrie Theater
 9 Walker Art Center
10 St. Anthony Main

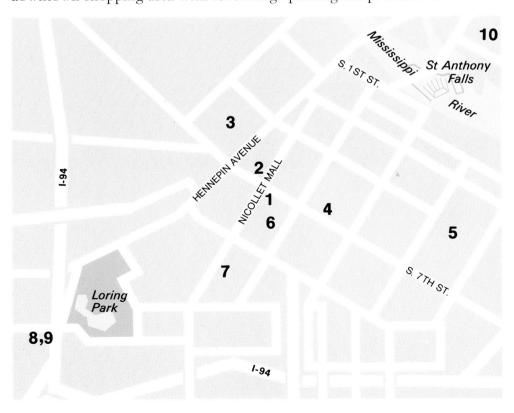

tinually expanding skyway, the elevated-walkway system designed to provide protection from Minnesota's winter cold and summer heat. Inside this area, exciting high-rise towers are rising above the old familiar landmarks, one of them, the Norwest Building, vying with the famous 57-story IDS (Investors Diversified Services) Building for the title of the city's tallest building.

The observation deck on the fifty-first floor of the IDS Building offers a magnificent panoramic view over this changing downtown scene and for 35 miles around. Below, through the cluster of glass and concrete buildings, is the little riverside community of St. Anthony, where it really all began in 1838, over 150 years after Father Hennepin's visit. In that year, Franklin Steele built a log cabin close to the sawmill and flour mill erected at the falls some years earlier by soldiers to supply Fort Snelling downstream. By 1855, the small village of St. Anthony that sprang up here had grown sufficiently to be designated a city, its progress being echoed by another settlement planned in 1854 across the Mississippi River by Colonel John H. Stevens. This was named Minneapolis, from a contraction of the Ojibway Indian word *minnehaha* ("falling water") and the Greek word *polis* ("city").

With the arrival of the railroads in the 1860s and an influx of German and Scandinavian immigrants, the two communities prospered and, in 1872, five years after Minneapolis had been chartered a city, were united under the name of Minneapolis. Throughout these early years, lumber and flour milling provided the basis for the two communities' economic progress.

The high-rise buildings of downtown St. Paul stand beside the Mississippi River east of Minneapolis. Although its skyline is less excitingly dramatic than that of its twin, St. Paul earned the nickname of the "Landmark City" as the site of the impressive State Capitol, located on a hill a few blocks to the north.

In more recent years, however, Minneapolis has diversified its manufacturing industries into electronics, computers, machinery, apparel, and food. Now a city of some 370,000 people, it is a major industrial and distribution center for the whole northern Midwest region and the site of the huge University of Minnesota campus.

Many of the warehouses along the riverfront that played a part in this story are being restored to re-create the old mill-town atmosphere of St. Anthony. A former mattress factory already has been renovated to house specialty shops and restaurants on St. Anthony Main. An earlier revitalization scheme across the river created the shoppers' paradise of Nicollet Mall in the heart of downtown. This pedestrian-oriented street of shops, restaurants, fountains, and trees is linked to the network of weatherproof walkways that crosses the downtown blocks and provides a second level of shops above street level. Also connected to the system is the new indoor City Center mall, where shoppers can find 100 stores ready to serve them until late in the evening and on Sunday. Other focal points for shopping include the restored warehouses of Butler Square and, farther out, the specialty shops and boutiques of the Cedar–Riverside and Hennepin–Lake intersections.

For evening relaxation, Minneapolis offers a wide choice of things to do. You can, for instance, wander along the entertainment "strip" of Hennepin Avenue, dine in one of the many restaurants or dinner theaters that provide a mouth-watering range of ethnic specialties, or enjoy a play, ballet, or concert at one of the city's first-class theaters or auditoriums. Among these is the internationally acclaimed Tyrone Guthrie Theater, which stages a superb repertory of modern and classical plays just southwest of downtown's Loring Park. There is also Orchestra Hall, where you can hear concerts by the renowned Minnesota Orchestra – and others – in the acoustically superb auditorium. But if you like your music on a lighter note, there are countless places in town where you can hear rock, jazz, or folk music.

Fine museums and art galleries abound in Minneapolis, the most notable being the Walker Art Center, with its fine collection of contemporary art; the wide-ranging Minneapolis Institute of Arts; the Hennepin County Historical Society and the American Swedish Institute, with their fascinating exhibits of local history; and the Bell Museum of Natural History. There are also the marvelous displays that capture the attention of young visitors to the famous Children's Museum.

For those who prefer sports and outdoor activities, there are major-league baseball and football games featuring the Twins and the Vikings at the magnificent 55,000-seat Hubert H. Humphrey Metrodome, with the North Stars ice-hockey team providing the thrills at Bloomington's Metropolitan Sports Center. Facilities for every kind of sport are available throughout the city for people who like to take part rather than watch, while Minneapolis's many parks provide opportunities for more gentle relaxation. A visit to Lake Harriet and the other lakes on the western side of town is especially delightful.

If you wish to venture farther afield, Minneapolis has Minnehaha Falls and Park, the Minnesota Zoo, the Valleyfair amusement park, and the Elizabethan-style Renaissance Festival. But for a real celebration, it is advisable to be in Minneapolis in July for the annual ten-day Aquatennial festivities, when the city sparkles with colorful parades, boat races, concerts, and an assortment of other events. There is so much going on in this lively city all the time that it comes as no surprise when you hear classical music wafting out of the bus shelters on Nicollet Mall.

Downstream from Minneapolis, the Mississippi River swings to the east to make a long northward loop before turning southward again on its long journey to the Gulf of Mexico. Here, the city of St. Paul has spread over the hills behind the north bank of the river, its downtown business districts

Downtown St. Paul
1 State Capitol
2 Minnesota Historical Society
3 Arts and Science Center
4 Town Square
5 Landmark Center
6 Civic Center
7 St. Paul Cathedral
8 City Hall and Courthouse
9 Alexander Ramsey House
10 James J. Hill House

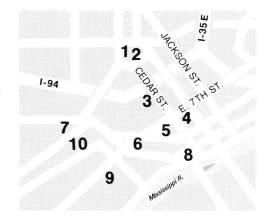

bristling with high-rise buildings that are not so spectacular as those of Minneapolis and hint at the city's more reserved and conservative character. Older than its twin and predominantly Catholic, St. Paul became home to Irish and German immigrants in the 1850s soon after the original community founded by settlers from Fort Snelling had become the capital of the new Minnesota Territory. Over the years, tycoons like James J. Hill, the railroad engineer, harnessed the skills of the inhabitants, founded new industries, and steered the blossoming city to prosperity. Although, like many other aging industrial centers, St. Paul has seen a decline in its central-city population in recent years – the 1980 census recorded 270,230 residents – it remains a vibrant community that boasts numerous attractions. With Minneapolis, it forms an outstanding cultural and recreational center that has a thriving theater life second only to that of New York City.

Standing proudly on its landscaped hill just north of downtown, the majestic Minnesota State Capitol, completed in 1904, is an appropriate grand focal point for the "Landmark City." In its construction, the celebrated architect Cass Gilbert used a rich assortment of decorative stone to embellish the interior and topped it with one of the world's largest self-supporting marble domes. From nearby Cass Gilbert Memorial Park, you can get a superb overview of the city laid out below, while the exhibits in the adjacent Minnesota Historical Society building provide a fascinating survey of the state's colorful history.

Walking south on Cedar Street from the Capitol, you enter the checker-board of streets that crisscrosses the downtown district by the Mississippi River, lined with office towers, banks, hotels, big stores, and shops, and

The Minnesota State Capitol, completed in 1902 from designs by the celebrated architect Cass Gilbert, is the third and most magnificent statehouse to be constructed in St. Paul. Among its notable features are the huge marble dome, the gold sculptured group of horses above the main door, and the lavish interior decoration, which includes many paintings and statues.

dotted with open spaces created by small green parks, modern plazas, and parking lots. Older buildings stand shoulder to shoulder with newer structures, many of which are linked to the climate-controlled walkway system above street level. At the intersection of Cedar and Tenth streets is the impressive Arts and Science Center, where you can enjoy stage musicals and plays at the excellent Chimera Theater and explore the wonders of science at the remarkable Science Museum of Minnesota. The museum's most outstanding attraction, however, is the William L. McKnight–3M Omnitheater, a scientific-film auditorium with a wrap-around screen that gives viewers the sensation of being involved in the action.

Farther along Cedar, two blocks have been transformed into the spectacular Town Square complex, in which two office towers soar above a luxury hotel and a number of shops and restaurants clustered around a four-story, glass-enclosed park filled with trees, flowers, and trickling waterfalls. Another fine shopping center in the vicinity is the Norwest Crossing, where the storefronts are painted to resemble Victorian-style buildings.

One of the most important downtown developments to appear in recent years, the ultramodern Civic Center complex, has excellent facilities for entertainments, sports, trade shows, and conventions. Older structures of special interest include the domed Renaissance-style St. Paul Cathedral, the twin-spired Assumption Church of 1873, and the beautiful Federal Courthouse, now restored as the Landmark Center and used for civic activities and performing- and visual-arts events. Nearer the river are the fine Public Library, the Minnesota Museum of Art, and the Art Deco-style City Hall and Courthouse, with its huge revolving onyx statue, *The Indian God of Peace*, by Carl Milles. From here, it is a short walk to the river, where you can catch the *Josiah Snelling* or *Jonathan Padelford* from Harriet Island for a pleasant riverboat cruise.

Many of St. Paul's other major attractions are scattered throughout the districts on the west side of the city. Quite close to downtown are the furnished Victorian home of Alexander Ramsey, the first territorial governor, in the attractive historic residential area around Irvine Park; the imposing sandstone house of the railroad magnate James J. Hill; and, farther west, the present-day Governor's Mansion.

From here, the broad thoroughfare of Grand Avenue runs west for over 4 miles, a fascinating boulevard lined with a colorful assortment of shops and boutiques, fine ethnic restaurants, and elegant homes. In this part of town, you can also hear concerts by the renowned St. Paul Chamber Orchestra and the Minnesota Orchestra at the impressive O'Shaughnessy Auditorium, a superb building that has been highly praised for both its design and its excellent acoustics.

To the south, at the junction of the Mississippi and Minnesota rivers, you can step back in time to the days before the birth of the Twin Cities among the army buildings that have been reconstructed at Historic Fort Snelling. Nearby, in Mendota, you can visit the oldest church in the state, St. Peter's, constructed in 1853, and the home of Minnesota's first state governor, the charming stone-built Sibley House of 1835.

In the city's northwestern districts, the vast green expanse of Como Park, the largest of the Twin Cities' many parks, encloses a huge lake, a golf course, an amusement park, and a magnificent conservatory. Many other outdoor attractions and activities are concentrated at the nearby State Fairgrounds, which attracts over 1 million people to the colossal 12-day State Fair in late August. People interested in the championship livestock and agricultural exhibits at the fair will also be fascinated by the reconstruction of nineteenth-century farm life at the nearby Gibbs Farm Museum.

Apart from the State Fair, the people of St. Paul enjoy year-round festivals, even in the deep snows of winter, when the citywide Winter Ca nival brings a tingle of excitement with its sports competitions, novelty contests, and delightful King Boreas Treasure Hunt.

Speaking of treasures, the entire state of Minnesota abounds in places of interest and scenic attractions just waiting to be discovered by visitors. The Twin Cities are well located at the hub of transportation networks for journeys far afield to the wild northern forests and lakes of Voyageurs National Park; Paul Bunyan country around Bemidji and Brainerd; and Itasca State Park, where the Mississippi River begins as a trickle. Shorter drives bring you to the beaches and fishing spots of White Bear Lake and to many attractive communities along the beautiful St. Croix River to the east, such as the lovely historic lumber town of Stillwater, Marine-on-St. Croix, and Taylors Falls.

The Crystal Court is a spacious glass-enclosed atrium providing a pleasant atmosphere for shoppers and sightseers in the famous IDS tower on Nicollet Mall in downtown Minneapolis.

Nashville TENNESSEE

Music City, U.S.A.

One Saturday night in 1927, George D. Hay took the microphone at Nashville's WSM radio station to present its regular country-music show, called "Barn Dance," following the nationwide broadcast of opera and classical music from New York City. In his introduction, he referred to the grand-opera content of the previous program and, contrasting it with homely Tennessee country music, added "from now on we will present 'The Grand Ole Opry.'" The name stuck to the show and quickly became known around the world. With its growing popularity, the Opry had to move to bigger and bigger studios over the years in order to accommodate the crowds who wished to see the show, and in 1974, it moved to its present 4,400-seat studio in the 120-acre entertainment and music park called Opryland, 6 miles northeast of downtown.

The Grand Ole Opry now presents the oldest continually running radio show in the world, and thousands still flock into Nashville every year to see the performances, especially during the June Fan Fair, a five-day extravaganza of spectacular shows featuring the big country-music stars. They also sample the fun of the Opryland showground; see the homes of stars such as Minnie Pearl, Johnny Cash, and Conway Twitty scattered throughout Nashville; and wander around the busy downtown district of recording studios, agents, and music publishers known as Music Row, where over half the nation's records are produced.

Not unexpectedly in a city dubbed "Music City, U.S.A.," music is big business here, although surprisingly, it takes only third place in the city's

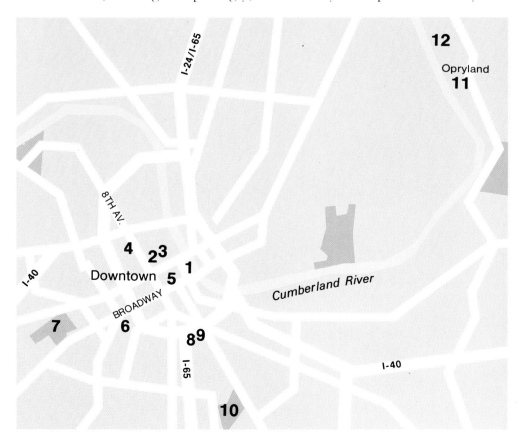

economy after publishing and insurance. As the capital of Tennessee, Nashville is also involved with government and the administration of state business, and is a major educational and commercial center. A spreading metropolis of 456,000 people, it stands at the hub of a network of interstate highways where the Cumberland River flows in sweeping loops through the center of the state. The site was settled in 1779 by frontier pioneers, who named their 1-acre plot Fort Nashborough after the Revolutionary War hero General Francis Nash. A few years later, the name was changed to Nashville, and in 1843 the town became the state capital. Occupied by Union forces for most of the Civil War, Nashville was the scene of much bloody fighting in 1864, and several historic sites record the momentous events of those days.

Today, a partial reconstruction of Fort Nashborough sits by the Cumberland River, engulfed by the glass and steel towers of the modern business districts. On the river, the sternwheelers *Music City Queen* and *Captain Ann* glide by with their cargoes of sightseers, offering constantly changing views of the city's skyline. A more spectacular viewpoint, however, is the observation deck on the thirty-first story of the Life & Casualty Building in the heart of downtown, from where you can see, on the north side, the gleaming new skyscrapers between Union Street and Charlotte Avenue and several other buildings of special interest. Standing out prominently is the beautiful white State Capitol, a Greek Revival building topped with a cupola that was designed by William Strickland and completed in 1859. Beyond it is a mecca for smokers, the Museum of Tobacco Art and History, while nearer the river gleams the unmistakable

Above: The Tennessee State Capitol stands in majestic splendor overlooking the spacious expanse of Memorial Plaza in downtown Nashville. Designed by William Strickland in the Greek Revival style, the imposing building was completed in 1859.

Overleaf: Scattered among the music publishers' offices, talent agencies, and recording studios clustered in the colorful square-mile district of Music Row a few blocks from downtown Nashville are several museums housing memorabilia of the great country music stars. The fascinating exhibits in the Car Collectors Hall of Fame, on Demonbreun Street, include Elvis Presley's Eldorado Cadillac and many other historic automobiles.

An outdoor performance of country music attracts foot-stomping crowds to the Juke Box Theater, one of many live shows featured at Nashville's celebrated Opryland musical entertainment park. Elsewhere in the park the magnificent 4,400-seat Opry House hosts the Grand Ole Opry, the nation's oldest continuous radio show.

shallow dome of the Municipal Auditorium, which vibrates with excitement every August during the Longhorn World Championship Rodeo. Much closer, on Deaderick Street, rises the elegant James K. Polk Building, part of the landscaped complex that includes the Tennessee State Museum, with its exhibits highlighting the state's history, and the Performing Arts Center, which has three theaters that regularly host concerts, musicals, and dance spectacles.

Among the stores and shops that line the downtown streets is the distinctive Arcade, a popular glass-covered shopping mall between Fourth and Fifth avenues. People flock into this part of downtown in the evening to dine and to enjoy the bubbling night life along Printer's Alley or to taste the sleazier attractions along lower Broadway. Nearby is the famous old Ryman Auditorium, which has had a colorful history first as a religious tabernacle, then a legitimate theater, and from 1943 to 1974 the home of the Grand Ole Opry; it now stands as an honored monument to those early days.

If you go southwest along Broadway past the highway that encircles the downtown area, you arrive at the unique district of Music Row, which is always a hive of activity. Wandering through its fascinating streets, you come upon several special museums related to the country-music world, among them the Car Collectors Hall of Fame – featuring the automobiles of the stars – the Country Music Wax Museum, and, the most visited of all, the Country Music Hall of Fame and Museum.

West of here, Nashville boasts a unique landmark. Appropriately for a city known as the "Athens of the South," it is a magnificent full-size replica of the Parthenon, built in 1931 in Centennial Park. It now serves as an art museum, while the park hosts the big Tennessee Crafts Fair every May and the Tennessee Grass Roots Days celebration of state life each September.

Southeast of downtown, along Interstate 65, are the Cumberland Museum and Science Center, a showcase of scientific exhibits with a fine planetarium, and the Herschel Greer Stadium, where baseball fans gather to cheer on the minor-league Nashville Sounds. Others make their way farther out of town to the Tennessee State Fairgrounds to enjoy the thrills of stock-car racing at the Nashville International Raceway, or, if it is September, to take part in the fun at the annual Tennessee State Fair.

In Nashville's outskirts and the surrounding Davidson County area, there are numerous other places of special interest. The most notable include the Cheekwood Botanical Gardens and Fine Art Center, which occupy part of the estate created in the 1930s by a former coffee magnate on a hilltop to the southwest of town. Elsewhere are sites of historic significance, such as the "Queen of Tennessee Plantations," the stately Belle Meade Mansion of 1825; the delightful Traveler's Rest, a beautiful house completed in 1820 that served as the Confederate headquarters in the Civil War struggle for Nashville; and The Hermitage, President Andrew Jackson's elegant 1819 home across the road from the lovely Tulip Grove mansion, northeast of downtown. Civil War battle sites are commemorated in nearby Franklin, at old Fort Donelson to the west of Dover, and in the area of Murfreesboro to the southeast.

Excellent recreational facilities abound in the Nashville area, particularly for golf and tennis, with opportunities for all kinds of water activities available on Hickory and Percy Priest lakes. There are also several state parks offering an escape into the natural beauty of Tennessee's countryside. But the most popular attraction of all remains, of course, Nashville's Opryland, that unique family-entertainment center and showcase of American country music where the Grand Ole Opry still draws thousands of visitors to "Music City, U.S.A."

The Hermitage, President Andrew Jackson's gracious plantation home, stands amid beautiful landscaped gardens 12 miles east of Nashville. Built in 1819 and enlarged in 1834, the house, now a National Historic Landmark, contains many fine furnishings and personal items that once belonged to the Jackson family.

New Orleans LOUISIANA

The Birthplace of Jazz

New Orleans is one of those wonderful cities that evoke special feelings and memories in people who come under their irresistible spell. Colorful and romantic, it possesses a unique atmosphere that derives from its rich French, Spanish, and Crèole heritage and from its role as a flourishing world port. Moss-draped live oaks by the steamy bayous, gracious old homes embellished with cast-iron balconies, echoes of jazz from a French Quarter club – these are just some of the images that live on in your mind, jostling with memories of the unrestrained gaiety of Mardi Gras or of Cajun cooking, with jambalaya, gumbo, or shrimp creole to set the taste buds tingling.

The character of this enthralling city has been forged by the cultural interaction among the various peoples who have come to live here and by the city's unique location on the flat, marshy delta where the mighty Mississippi River at last glides into the Gulf of Mexico. In 1718, the Sieur de Bienville founded a settlement on a "beautiful crescent of the river" and named it after the duke of Orléans, the regent of France. The grid of streets that Bienville laid out stands out on today's city plan as the Vieux Carré, or "old square," better known as the French Quarter, for elsewhere the streets radiate from the bends in the river. First handed over to Spanish rule in 1763 and then back to French control in 1801, New Orleans finally came

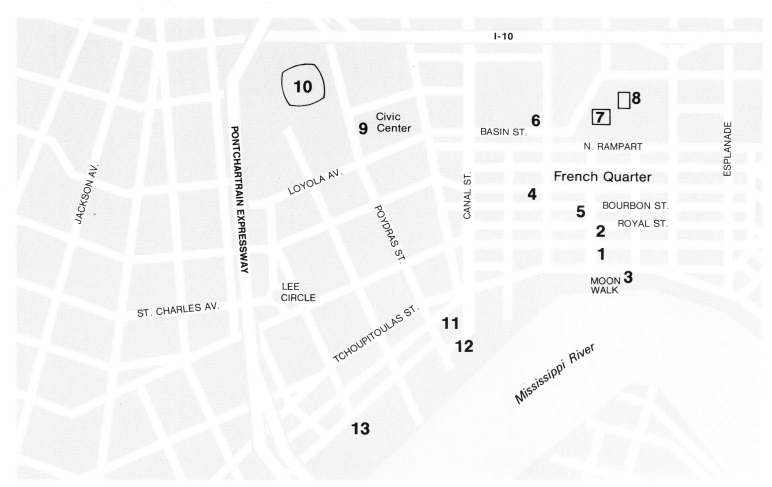

Above: Mississippi riverboats offering interesting sightseeing cruises line the New Orleans riverfront at the end of Canal Street. Here the tower of the International Trade Mart (right) is a well-known landmark not far from the bulky outline of the Hilton and Towers Hotel. The Trade Mart houses shipping and consular offices and a maritime museum in its 33 stories, and at the top there is an observation deck providing stunning views of the city.

Left: Along the atmospheric streets of New Orleans's French Quarter, historic houses embellished with lacy ironwork balconies front directly on to the sidewalks, adding much to the charm and beauty of this lovely old city. Among them are the three adjoining houses that widowed Mrs. Miltenberger built for her three sons on Royal Street in 1838.

under the American flag in 1803, when Napoleon sold the vast French territories in North America to the United States for $15 million – the celebrated Louisiana Purchase. After General Andrew Jackson's forces beat off the British in a belated encounter following the War of 1812, New Orleans, now secure, began to flourish as a port handling cotton, sugar cane, and indigo grown on nearby plantations. Today, with its improved and developing facilities, the port ranks number one in the country in tonnage handled, with ships trading all over the world, and ship building, petroleum refining, and metal smelting, together with a wide diversity of manufacturing industries, form the basis of the city's economy. The metropolitan area has grown rapidly in population in recent years, although there has been a fall in the city itself to around 558,000 in 1980.

Summer temperatures in New Orleans are comparable with those elsewhere in the South, but here they are accompanied by high humidity, which causes condensation to form – curiously, if you are not used to it – on the outside of air-conditioned automobile windows. Nevertheless, it is best to walk around the central parts of the city, which are packed with countless interesting sights. From the cocktail lounge or observation deck atop the 33-story International Trade Mart by the riverfront, there are stunning views over the city, which is sandwiched between the Mississippi River and the salt-water expanse of Lake Pontchartrain to the north.

Below is the huge bend in the river that gave New Orleans its nickname "Crescent City." Beside it, the straight, narrow streets of the Vieux Carré, the original city, are lined with one- and two-story buildings, adorned with lacy iron balconies, which front directly on to the sidewalk, with many a quiet old courtyard enclosing a trickling fountain and lush green foliage to catch the eye as you pass. Jackson Square, once a parade ground, is the heart of this intriguing historic district, whose street names bear witness to its multinational heritage. Facing the square, St. Louis Cathedral, built in 1794 on the site of an earlier church and named after King Louis IX of France, stands between the Cabildo, seat of the Spanish colonial government, and the Presbytère, built on the site of an older monastery but not completed until 1813. Also bordering the square are the twin Pontalba apartment buildings, the first in America, built by a Spanish baroness in 1852; the revitalized Jackson Brewery, now bustling with restaurants and boutiques; and Pirates Alley, now frequented by artists.

As you walk through the Vieux Carré, you can drink in the history, dine in fine restaurants, browse through the boutiques and antique shops of Royal Street – where a streetcar named Desire really did run years ago – and sample the excellent café au lait and the French doughnuts called *beignets* at the Café du Monde near the fruit and vegetable sheds of the bustling French Market. By night, the scene changes when the bars and clubs along Bourbon Street come to life, the drinks flow, and music – above all, the unmistakable sound of jazz – permeates the mild air.

New Orleans, the acknowledged birthplace of jazz, boasts the excellent Jazz Museum on Conti Street, and at Preservation Hall on St. Peter Street, where all the greats have played, you can still hear the real thing without frills. In May, the city vibrates when all kinds of bands – from Dixieland to ragtime, from folk to blues – strike up for the New Orleans Jazz and Heritage Festival. It is still a tradition for a band to turn out for a funeral, playing somber dirges on the way to the cemetery and more jaunty numbers on the way back, much to the delight of the now cavorting mourners. It was also customary in the early days to bury the dead in above-ground tombs because of the swampy terrain, as a visit to the fascinating St. Louis Cemetery No. 1 on Basin Street reveals.

To prove that New Orleans can offer symphony concerts and opera in addition to jazz, there is the prestigious new Cultural Center, just outside the French Quarter, which has been developed around the refurbished

Above: In the steamy heat of summer a horse-drawn carriage offers a gentle and cool way to explore the many fascinating sights of the French Quarter in New Orleans. Among the historic treasures here are the two Pontalba Buildings that flank Jackson Square. They were planned as apartments and shops in the mid-nineteenth century by wealthy Micaela Almonester de Pontalba, who wished to revive the French Quarter's then declining prosperity.

Opposite: Behind the house fronts lining the streets of the French Quarter are hidden many old courtyards filled with lush greenery that offer a cool escape from the humid heat of summer.

Overleaf: Every year during February or March the streets of New Orleans vibrate with the unrestrained celebrations of Mardi Gras, a succession of extravagant parades, featuring elaborate floats and marching jazz bands, and of grand balls and all kinds of festivities. Thousands of visitors flock into the city for the event, the greatest extravaganza of merrymaking in the New Orleans calendar.

The foot-stomping rhythm of jazz, the traditional music of New Orleans, still vibrates in the clubs of Bourbon Street and other honkytonks throughout the city.

9,100-seat Municipal Auditorium and 2,200-seat Theater of the Performing Arts.

The boundary between the French Quarter and the downtown business district is sharply marked by Canal Street, a broad boulevard lined with big stores, hotels, and offices that sweeps away from the lofty International Trade Mart down by the river. From the waterfront here, you can board the *Mark Twain*, the *President*, or other riverboats for cruises past the bustling wharves of the port and the new Convention and Exhibition Center, the site of the 1984 Louisiana World Exposition. Away from the river are the impressive Civic Center Complex, which includes the fine new City Hall, and the colossal Louisiana Superdome, the largest enclosed arena in the world with seating for up to 97,000 spectators. Among many other events, the Superdome hosts the home football games of the Saints and the annual Sugar Bowl classic.

From Canal Street, you can take a pleasant ride by streetcar through the attractive nineteenth-century residential area known as the Garden District, with its beautiful iron-balconied mansions set back among lush gardens. Farther on is lovely Audubon Park, with its huge zoo and fine views of the Mississippi near the campuses of Tulane and Loyola universities. The largest park in New Orleans, however, is the 1,500-acre City Park, farther north, which contains the excellent Museum of Art. Boating, swimming, and fishing attract many people to huge Lake Pontchartrain, where yacht clubs, an amusement park, and the University of New Orleans lie along the beautiful lakeside drive.

Steeped in history, yet bubbling with life, New Orleans offers such an endless stream of sensations and delights to the eye that at times it is good to drive into the peaceful Louisiana countryside, where you can contemplate the Old South's rich heritage at such exquisite plantations as Houmas House, one of those beautiful reminders of yesteryear that abound in this part of America.

New York NEW YORK

The Big Apple

Known the world over as the symbol of America, the Statue of Liberty has stood for 100 years on its island at the entrance to New York harbor, welcoming travelers by sea to America's shores. Many of the immigrants who, earlier this century, sailed in beneath its gaze to seek a better future in the New World went no farther than New York City itself, and to its rich cosmopolitan tapestry they have added the colorful threads of their own cultural heritages. A pulsating, dynamic metropolis, where the fast pace of life continues around the clock, New York is the ultimate experience in big-city living – many would say it is the most exciting city in the world. To aspiring people in show business and sports during the 1920s and 1930s, to make good in New York was to reach the giddy pinnacle of success; to them, New York was, and still is, the shiny "Big Apple" at the top of the tree.

With a population of over 7 million, New York is the largest city in the United States, a great seaport and the heart of the country's financial and business activity. At the same time, it is the nation's thriving cultural center, justifiably claiming to be the "Theater Capital of the World" and boasting some of the world's most outstanding museums.

"Give me your tired, your poor, Your huddled masses yearning to breathe free, The wretched refuse of your teeming shore." A symbol of freedom known around the world, the Statue of Liberty holds her torch aloft to guide travelers by sea into the harbor of the great city of New York. The 152-foot figure, on its 150-foot pedestal, stands on top of an abandoned fort now housing the American Museum of Immigration. Created by the sculptor Auguste Bartholdi and erected in 1886, the statue was a gift from France to the United States to commemorate their alliance in the War of Independence.

New York: the Five Boroughs

Beneath the glittering skyscrapers that puncture the Manhattan skyline – to many people, the most thrilling city spectacle anywhere – a whole world of sights, sounds, and experiences gives New York its electric appeal. The shops on Fifth Avenue, the world-famous museums, the gourmet restaurants, the views from the Empire State Building, the dazzling theater-land of Broadway, the brightest lights of Times Square, the glories contained in Lincoln Center, the bustle of Greenwich Village, the elegance of the Waldorf-Astoria – New York is an endless cornucopia of delights to excite even the most sophisticated of travelers. It is perhaps easy to forget, when enjoying the city's many attractions, that off the tourist track are areas, like the Bowery, that draw your attention only through newspaper stories about slums, social deprivation, or crime. Like any other great metropolis, New York has its seamier side and its problems. Yet some years ago, when bankruptcy threatened, civic pride suddenly reawakened and determined efforts began, under the "I Love New York" slogan and the

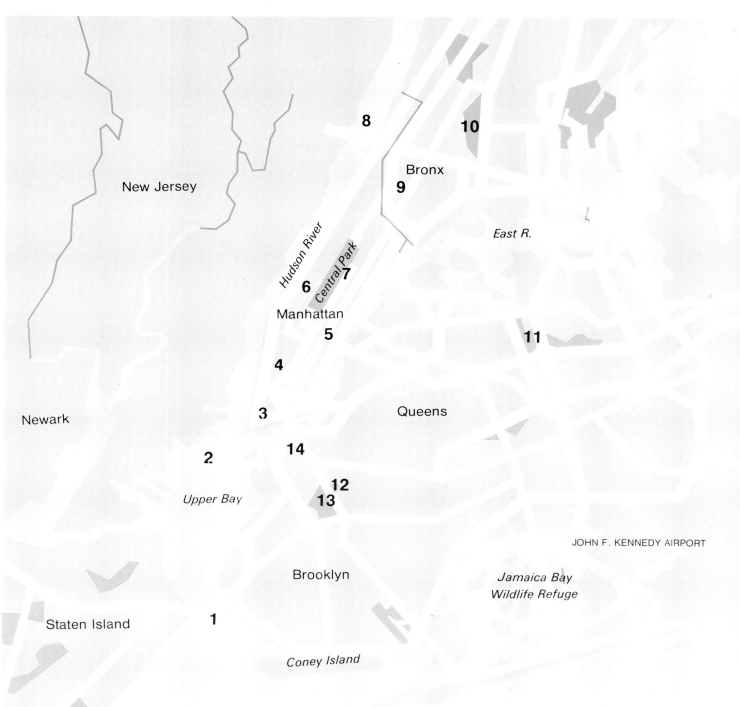

"Big Apple" campaign, to spruce up the city's decaying image. That such schemes have had some effect can be judged by the fact that in the past few years, visitors to New York have totaled around 17 million a year, their annual spending in the city exceeding $2 billion.

With so much money boosting the city's economy, the Manhattan cityscape is in a constant state of change or renewal, with office towers and hotels sprouting as worn-out buildings come down under the swing of the wrecker's ball. The result is a city of great architectural interest, with turn-of-the-century brownstone houses contrasting with soaring skyscrapers that represent a diversity of twentieth-century styles – from Art Deco to sleek, mirrored glass – the most recent additions including the magnificent Trump Tower complex and the huge Marriott Marquis hotel.

Everyone who visits New York takes back his or her own memories and experiences, for this city, with its constantly changing face, is impossible to characterize in generalizations. One reason is its tremendous

Overleaf: The majestic span of Brooklyn Bridge sweeps across the East River linking the borough of Brooklyn with the throbbing districts of Lower Manhattan and offering unforgettable views of the world's most famous skyline. Opened in 1883, the bridge was one of the greatest engineering feats of the nineteenth century.

Below: At the intersection of Broadway and Seventh Avenue is gaudy, neon-lit Times Square, the "Great White Way" in the heart of New York City's theaterland. Its jostling movie houses, night clubs, playhouses, and shops form a colorful potpourri of big city sights.

159

As befits the city that hosts the United Nations Organization, New York is a place where you can find representatives of every nation and ethnic group on earth.

ethnic diversity, which has given it not only a large Jewish community, black Harlem, Chinatown, and Little Italy in Manhattan, but also a whole range of international enclaves in the four other boroughs, or counties, that make up the city: the Bronx, Queens, Brooklyn, and Staten Island. Each borough has its own special character and points of interest worth making a trip to discover, once you get your bearings in this huge, geographically complex city. A fascinating introduction to New York is the spectacular multimedia show presented in the McGraw-Hill Building on the Avenue of the Americas (Sixth Avenue).

New York City is clustered around the mouth of the Hudson River at the southern tip of New York State. Of the five boroughs, only the Bronx is attached to the mainland; the rest occupy islands. Manhattan is a 12.5-mile narrow finger of land separated from the Bronx to the north by the Harlem River, and from Queens and Brooklyn on Long Island to the east by the East River, which is really a strait. In the Upper Bay to the south of Manhattan are three small islands – Ellis, Liberty (with its famous statue), and Governor's – and farther south, the much larger expanse of Staten Island.

When you look down on this colossal modern metropolis as you fly into John F. Kennedy or LaGuardia airports in Queens, it is astonishing to think that in 1626 the local Indians sold Manhattan to the Dutch for trinkets worth, it is said, 60 guilders – in today's money, less than $100. Prior to that, the waters of the area had been explored for France in 1524 by the Florentine Giovanni da Verrazano and for the Netherlands in 1609 by the English navigator Henry Hudson, for whom the river is named. Encouraged by Hudson's favorable report, the Dutch established a trading settlement at the southern tip of Manhattan, an Indian name meaning "Heavenly Land," which they soon named New Amsterdam, and other small villages in present-day Harlem and Brooklyn. By 1664, under its celebrated governor, Peter Stuyvesant, New Amsterdam was a flourishing city of over 1,000 people; in that year, English forces led by the Duke of York captured it and renamed it New York. The British also occupied the city during most of the Revolutionary War, after which New York served briefly as the capital of the new United States. Throughout the nineteenth century, the city grew dramatically as vast numbers of immigrants then entering the country stayed to make it their home.

To explore and to know the whole of New York is a lifetime's adventure, and most visitors do not step outside Manhattan. Certainly, this vibrant heart of the city contains so many things to see and do that many people manage to take in only the highlights. The original Dutch settlement of New Amsterdam has long vanished under the jumble of soaring skyscrapers that now rises above the financial districts around Wall Street at Manhattan's southern tip. Yet many later historic buildings do survive here, among them Trinity Church, St. Paul's Chapel, and Federal Hall – the site of the nation's first capitol – all dwarfed by the towering masonry cliffs that surround them. The newest and tallest buildings in Lower Manhattan, the twin 110-story towers of the World Trade Center, provide marvelous views over the city from an open-air rooftop observation deck 1,377 feet (420 m) above the ground.

From Battery Park, a 21-acre oasis of greenery at the tip of Manhattan, you can take a pleasant ferry trip to Liberty Island to see the Statue of Liberty and Immigration Museum and to nearby Ellis Island, where, between 1892 and 1924, around 17 million immigrants were held as they anxiously awaited entry to the country or deportation if refused. Among the piers that bristle along Manhattan's waterfront is the South Street Seaport, an historic district where restored warehouses, counting-houses and old ships re-create the atmosphere of New York's early sea-faring days. Walk a few blocks north, and you can stroll across the impressive engineering marvel of the Brooklyn Bridge before returning to see historic City

Hall and to explore the fascinating streets that make up the ethnic potpourri of Chinatown, Little Italy, SoHo, and the Lower East Side. Not to be missed is a nighttime walk in nearby Greenwich Village, a bubbling neighborhood of arts and crafts shops, coffee houses, restaurants, and Off-Broadway theaters. Not far away, the lively focal point of Washington Square, with its famous arch, marks the southern end of Fifth Avenue, the glamorous, long boulevard that divides the East and West Side of Manhattan.

North of Washington Square, Manhattan's streets form a grid pattern that reflects the city's growth northward from Lower Manhattan, its oldest section. Numbered streets run from east to west, and avenues – some of them named, such as Lexington, and Madison – from north to south. This part of the city as far as Central Park is known as Midtown Manhattan, a busy area packed with notable sightseeing landmarks and crowded streets. Here you will find the famous old Chelsea Hotel, once frequented by colorful literary figures; Madison Square Garden, a magnificent entertainment, sports, and office complex close to busy Pennsylvania Station; the 102-story Empire State Building, completed in 1931; and the colossal Grand Central Station on East 42nd Street, near the unmistakable Art Deco Chrysler Building, with its unique shining spire – just one of many architectural gems in this part of the city. And by the East River is the United Nations Headquarters, housed in an elegant complex that is appropriate to this important world organization.

Places of entertainment to suit every taste abound in Midtown Manhattan. Among them is Rockefeller Center, a business and entertainment complex of skyscrapers just west of Fifth Avenue where the Art Deco Radio City Music Hall stages first-rate concerts and spectacular shows and the popular sunken Rockefeller Plaza is always bustling with activity. Along Broadway, which cuts diagonally across Midtown, the glittering lights of Times Square mark the center of New York's famous theater district, although by day, the "Great White Way" has a somewhat less glamorous appearance. Among Midtown's cultural attractions are Carnegie Hall, the famous concert auditorium, and the world-renowned Museum of Modern Art. Farther north, on Broadway, the prestigious Lincoln Center for the

A focal point of New York City's cultural life, the prestigious Lincoln Center for the Performing Arts is a complex of fine modern buildings that include the Metropolitan Opera House, Avery Fisher Hall (home of the New York Philharmonic), and New York State Theater (home of the New York City Ballet and Opera).

Performing Arts, a fine complex of modern halls on three sides of a plaza, presents opera, concerts, dance, and drama by such world-class companies as the New York Philharmonic, the Metropolitan Opera, and the New York City Ballet.

Lincoln Center lies west of beloved Central Park, an 840-acre patch of landscaped parkland and lakes between 59th and 110th streets that was designed by the celebrated nineteenth-century landscape architect Frederick Law Olmsted. This huge green oasis provides New Yorkers with the opportunity to escape from the noise and fumes of the city streets and to enjoy all kinds of recreational activities in the heart of the city. It divides Upper Manhattan into the Upper East and Upper West Sides, which differ in character from each other. The Upper East Side is Manhattan's fashionable residential quarter and the location of such world-famous art museums as the Metropolitan Museum of Art, the Frick Collection, the Guggenheim Museum, and the Whitney Museum of American Art. On the less-affluent Upper West Side are the American Museum of Natural History and the Hayden Planetarium.

North of Central Park stretches the black neighborhood of Harlem, with its booming night life and such sightseeing attractions as the historic district of Strivers Row, comprising a collection of fine brownstone houses. The streets near the Hudson River also contain many points of interest, including the world's largest Gothic-style cathedral, St. John the Divine; Grant's Tomb; the fascinating Museum of the American Indian; The Cloisters, a delightful medieval-art museum in Fort Tryon Park; and Dyckman House, a Dutch colonial farmhouse of 1783. And spanning the Hudson River, linking New York to New Jersey, is the majestic George Washington Bridge, one of the world's most elegant suspension bridges.

Despite its poor reputation as a dangerous area for outsiders, the Bronx, north of Manhattan, has many places of interest to make a trip there worthwhile. Among its pleasant residential neighborhoods and tree-shaded parks are such highlights as the renowned Bronx Zoo, the New York Botanical Gardens, several fine museums, educational institutions, and numerous historic houses, among them the eighteenth-century Dutch Van Cortlandt Mansion and the Edgar Allan Poe Cottage. But probably the best known of all its attractions is the 70,000-seat Yankee Stadium, where baseball fans gather to roar for the famous New York Yankees.

Across the East River on Long Island, the residential borough of

Above: Coney Island, New York City's famous seaside resort, has a crowded public beach that stretches for more than 3 miles along Brooklyn's Atlantic shoreline. Along the boardwalk a host of garish penny arcades, roller coasters, honkytonk bars, "Nathan's Famous" hotdog stands, and other attractions compete for the attention (and dollars) of visitors.

Left: One of the finest Gothic churches in the United States, St. Patrick's Cathedral was completed on New York City's Fifth Avenue in 1874. Overshadowed by the skyscrapers of today's thrusting city, this famous Manhattan landmark offers a haven of peaceful tranquillity from the noisy bustle of traffic and shoppers along the stylish thoroughfare.

Opposite: The unusual architectural design of the Guggenheim Museum, the creation of Frank Lloyd Wright, contains spiraling ramps lined with works of modern art. The museum is a familiar sight on Fifth Avenue facing Central Park.

New Yorkers take advantage of the vast open space of Central Park to indulge in their particular recreational interest, whether jogging alone or taking part in team football practise. The park also provides many popular entertainment facilities, including a zoo, a theater, and a carrousel.

Queens is home to a whole range of ethnic communities. A borough of rich contrasts, Queens contains many historic buildings, New York's two principal airports (John F. Kennedy and LaGuardia), motion-picture studios, fine parks, and excellent sports facilities. Among these are Shea Stadium – the home of the Mets baseball and Jets football teams – Aqueduct and Belmont horse-racing tracks, and the National Tennis Center in Flushing Meadows–Corona Park, site of the 1939 and 1964 World's Fairs. And across Jamaica Bay, with its wildlife refuge, is Rockaway Beach, a favorite summer playground for New Yorkers.

The 3 million people who live in the borough of Brooklyn, next door to Queens, can argue that theirs is the fourth largest city in America, an astonishing thought when you remember that only Chicago, Los Angeles, and New York itself have bigger populations. The borough has a rich ethnic mix of various European, West Indian, and Puerto Rican communities, and an architectural legacy of historic buildings that includes many fine brownstone houses. Apart from Nathan's hot dogs and the bridge over the East River, Brooklyn boasts many attractions, not least the famous Brooklyn Museum, the Brooklyn Heights Historic District, such green spaces as Prospect Park and the magnificent Brooklyn Botanic Garden, and the garish amusement area of Coney Island. The borough is also the home of the famous Brooklyn Academy of Music, active since 1859.

Drive south through Brooklyn and across the magnificent Verrazano Narrows Bridge on the edge of the Atlantic Ocean, and you enter a totally different world in the comparatively sparsely populated, almost rural borough of Staten Island. Rich in historic associations and with a legacy of Dutch place names, the island has preserved many of its old buildings in such outstanding ventures as the Snug Harbor Cultural Center and the Richmondtown Restoration. There are also several fine museums – including the unusual Jacques Marchais Center of Tibetan Art – a small zoo famous for its reptiles, and many recreational facilities.

With its quieter pace of life, Staten Island offers a welcome change from the bustle of Manhattan, whose breath-taking skyline beckons across the Upper Bay. As you return on the Staten Island Ferry to enjoy more of Manhattan's attractions, you can imagine the thoughts and feelings of the immigrants long ago as they caught their first glimpse of the Statue of Liberty, the symbol of welcome to a new land of hope.

Oklahoma City OKLAHOMA

Oke City

One of the strangest events in the history of the West took place on April 22, 1889, in what is now central Oklahoma. At noon that day, the shrill sound of bugles rang out to signal the start of a remarkable race in which thousands of pioneer settlers charged off like Roman charioteers into the virgin prairies to stake claims in the newly opened up "Unassigned Lands," part of the former Indian Territory once reserved for the Indians. The "Run of '89" settled the entire area and created 15 towns, including what was to become Oklahoma City, where by nightfall that day some 10,000 people had laid out their markers. It was a glorious new chapter in the winning of the West. The Indians, however, would justifiably have claimed that it was yet another cynical betrayal of the so-called Five Civilized Tribes, who earlier in the century had been forcibly removed from their traditional homelands in the southeastern states and promised possession of Indian Territory "as long as grass shall grow and rivers run."

So Indian Territory became Oklahoma, the state with the largest Indian population in the Union. Not confined to reservation life, the Indians regularly celebrate their cultural heritage in traditional pow-wows, or gatherings, in Oklahoma City during the summer months. Their beautiful crafts are widely displayed in the city's shops and museums and at the replica village of Indian City in Anadarko.

White settlers made their own contributions to the cultural potpourri of Oklahoma City, which, with its many religious colleges and churches of all denominations, lies firmly in the heart of America's "Bible Belt." That the city is conscious of its roots in the Old West is evidenced by its still operating stockyards and "Cowtown," its numerous stores selling western-style gear, its year-round horse shows and rodeos – none more spectacular than the annual National Finals Rodeo – and its prestigious National Cowboy Hall of Fame and Western Heritage Center, a supreme celebration of the golden age of the cowboy.

Named from two Choctaw Indian words meaning "Land of the Red People," Oklahoma City grew from two adjacent town sites along the Santa Fe Railroad near the North Canadian River. In 1910, three years after Oklahoma became a state, the city, by then a community of 56,000 people, won the battle with nearby Guthrie to become the state capital. At first, its prosperity depended largely on agriculture, livestock, and a local automobile industry. But in 1928 came the first gush of oil from beneath the prairies that transformed the city's economy and planted wells even on the grounds of the State Capitol. World War II brought Tinker Air Force Base and the aircraft industry, followed by the development of electronics and computer industries.

Now a vast five-county metropolis encompassing 13 cities, Oklahoma City spreads across 622 square miles on both sides of the North Canadian River. Although one of America's largest cities in area, it has a very low population density, with only 872,000 people living in the metropolitan area, 403,000 of them in the city itself. There is thus a feeling of spaciousness about Oklahoma City that is reinforced by its pleasant tree-shaded residential districts, interspersed with parks and four huge lakes that stretch for miles into the surrounding ranching and farming country.

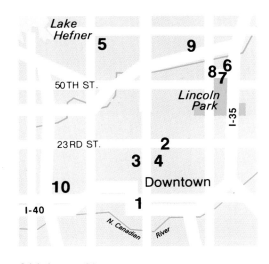

Oklahoma City
1 *Myriad Convention Center*
2 *State Capitol*
3 *Oklahoma Heritage Center*
4 *William Fremont Harn Homestead*
5 *Oklahoma Museum of Art*
6 *National Softball Hall of Fame*
7 *Oklahoma City Zoo*
8 *Kirkpatrick Center*
9 *National Cowboy Hall of Fame and Western Heritage Center*
10 *Oklahoma State Fair Park*

In preparation for the Centennial marking its foundation in 1889, downtown Oklahoma City is undergoing an extensive program of renewal that is creating many attractive plazas and parks amid the prestigious new buildings. One of these is Robert S. Kerr Park, a beautifully landscaped plaza close to the new Myriad Convention Center and Gardens and linked to the underground shopping tunnels of the Metro Concourse.

During the past 20 years, a massive urban-renewal program, based on a plan by the celebrated architect I. M. Pei, has transformed much of the center-city area and created magnificent buildings, plazas, and parks among the older high-rise towers, a beautiful setting for the city's annual Festival of the Arts. Standing out amid the new developments is the superb Myriad Convention Center, which provides 1 million square feet of space for meetings, entertainments, and sports events across the street from the spectacular Myriad Gardens. Nearby are the new Galleria retail complex and the Oklahoma Theater Center, an award-winning building in which plays and musicals are staged during the winter season. Another downtown landmark is the city's main performing-arts center, the Civic Center Music Hall, home of the Oklahoma Symphony and Ballet Oklahoma. Some blocks east of here, Robert S. Kerr Park, a pleasant small plaza, provides a focal-point entrance to the Metro Conncourse, an underground network of tunnels lined with shops and restaurants.

In contrast to the new downtown developments, two beautiful, furnished turn-of-the-century houses, the Overholser Mansion and the stately building now called the Oklahoma Heritage Center, provide a glimpse of past life styles in the lovely old residential district of Heritage Hills, just north of downtown. Not far away, an even older gem, the William Fremont Harn Homestead, has been preserved as a relic of the Run of '89, while another fine mansion, farther out of town in the attractive residential area of Nichols Hills, houses the wide-ranging collections of the Oklahoma Museum of Art.

Northeast of the downtown district are the domeless Oklahoma State Capitol, completed in 1917 and now accompanied by oil wells, and the State Museum of Oklahoma, which traces the state's history to the present day. Farther out of town, many of the city's major attractions are concentrated in the Lincoln Park area close to the outstanding zoo. Among the high-

lights here are the 45th Infantry Division Museum; the Oklahoma Firefighters Museum; the National Softball Hall of Fame; the superb Kirkpatrick Center, which houses several excellent museums and educational entertainment facilities under one roof; and, a short distance away, the famous National Cowboy Hall of Fame and Western Heritage Center, not far from the celebrated Haunted House restaurant. For more light-hearted fun, there is also the Springlake Amusement Park, with the Frontier City Amusement Park a few miles away along the Northeast Expressway. North of the city, too, is Enterprise Square, a fascinating showcase of American business.

Another family-entertainment center, White Water, offers all kinds of aquatic fun and excitement on West Reno Avenue, west of downtown. Also in this area is the huge Oklahoma State Fair Park, with buildings and facilities for shows, exhibitions, and sports and entertainment events. The park's All Sports Stadium hosts baseball games of the minor-league Oklahoma 89ers, while the covered State Fair Arena is used for home games of the Blazers ice-hockey team and for various other events. The highlight of the year at the park is the State Fair in September, a spectacular celebration that includes a rodeo, stock-car races, an ice show, and other lively entertainments.

Opportunities for recreation and sports abound throughout the city area, with Lakes Hefner, Overholser, Draper, and Thunderbird offering boating and fishing, the last two also permitting water skiing. For evening entertainment, there is a choice of night clubs, piano bars, restaurants of all kinds (many serving the famous local steaks), and theater and other cultural events. And if you keep an eye on the unpredictable weather, you can take a day trip to such interesting places around Oklahoma City as Guthrie, Stillwater, Shawnee, and, of course, Indian City, that fascinating evocation of Indian life in Anadarko.

Above: The National Cowboy Hall of Fame, in the northern districts of Oklahoma City, commemorates the romantic era of the Old West and is sponsored by 17 states. Among its extensive collections are many paintings by such celebrated western artists as Frederic Remington and Charles Russell.

Top: Unique among the nation's statehouses, the Oklahoma State Capitol has working oil wells on its grounds in Oklahoma City. It is also one of the few capitol buildings without a dome.

Omaha NEBRASKA

Cornhusker Metropolis

When you look around today at the sprawling metropolis of Omaha, Nebraska's largest city, it is perhaps difficult to appreciate that its history goes back only 130 years. Before 1854, this was part of the vast prairie stretching beyond the horizon on either side of the great Missouri River, a rich hunting ground of the Omaha Indians, who gave the future city their name. White people came and went without settling: the explorers Lewis and Clark in 1804, the occasional fur trapper, soldiers from nearby Fort Atkinson, and the Mormons on their great trek west in 1846. It was only in 1854 that Omaha was founded – by a ferryman from Council Bluffs, Iowa, across the Missouri River.

Eight years later, in 1862, two events secured the little community's future. First, it was chosen to be the eastern terminus of the new transcontinental Union Pacific Railroad, which was planned to link up with California. Second, the federal government proclaimed the famous Homestead Act, which brought a deluge of settlers into Nebraska in response to grants of free land. As a jumping-off point, Omaha was soon swarming with the riffraff seen in every frontier town in those days, the gamblers and gunfighters who hoped to gain easy money at the expense of any innocent immigrant.

Despite the harsh conditions and extremes of weather in the virgin territories, a place "where it rains grasshoppers, fire, and destruction" according to one disillusioned pioneer farmer, the land was coaxed into becoming rich cattle-raising and wheat-growing country. Omaha began to blossom as the market center and distribution point for the region's produce. Entering the city from the south today, you can still see the vast stockyards that continue to supply its important livestock and meat-producing industry and, on the Missouri, barges laden with agricultural machinery, grain, and other farm crops. As well as its interest in agriculture, however, Omaha has acquired over the years a thriving insurance business and the headquarters of the Air Force Strategic Air Command.

Now a city of around 314,000 people, Omaha retains strong links with its pioneering past, while claiming big-city status. It has the easy-going, friendly pace of a much smaller town where the cuisine specializes in beef and huge steaks, but it can boast all the appropriate attributes of a sophisticated modern metropolis: fine downtown stores and showcase suburban shopping centers, spacious parks, lavish sports and recreational facilities, university campuses, museums, and theaters that offer a wide range of music and entertainment.

In recent years, a program of renewal has been bringing life back to the downtown area after a period of slow decline had seen a general move of people out to the suburban areas. In one of these schemes, the Old Market, once a wholesale fruit and vegetable depot, has been transformed into a brick-paved maze of lively alleys lined with boutiques and craft shops, restaurants and bars – and even a puppet museum. A more recent project has created the Central Park Mall from a rundown warehouse district between Douglas and Farnam streets. Here, an artificial stream meanders through a pleasant urban park complete with waterfall and pool, an attractive setting for outdoor concerts and city festivals.

Among the downtown streets, you can also find such outstanding

Opposite, top: As a major livestock market and meat-packing center — and one of the best places in America to find a good steak — Omaha still has busy stockyards operating just south of downtown.

Opposite, bottom: The industrial center of the Great Plains region, the city of Omaha sits on the bluffs on the Nebraska side of the Missouri River opposite Council Bluffs, Iowa, its once-declining downtown district now being revitalized by imaginative construction projects.

cultural attractions as the fascinating Pacific Railroad Museum, the Western Heritage Museum, and the captivating Children's Museum; here, too, are the Omaha Magic Theater and the renowned Orpheum Theater, a restored vaudeville hall with a magnificent Wurlitzer organ now offering opera, ballet, symphony concerts, and occasional Broadway shows. But top of the list must be the renowned Joslyn Art Museum, a beautiful, modern pink-marble structure that houses an excellent collection of paintings of the American West and other art treasures.

Venturing west along Dodge Street past the landmark of the Mutual of Omaha Dome, you will find several interesting places in the sprawling district of West Omaha. Apart from the campus of the University of Nebraska and its acclaimed Medical School, there are places of entertainment like the excellent Omaha Community Playhouse and the Emmy Gifford Children's Theater; Peony Park, a magnificent amusement center providing fun for all the family; and the Ak-Sar-Ben race track, where you can experience not only the excitement of horse racing, but also the thrills of the rodeo and other sporting events. Here, too, is the birthplace of President Gerald Ford, with its delightful rose garden. Ten miles west of downtown is one of Omaha's most celebrated places, the internationally famous Boys Town, which was founded for homeless youngsters by Father Flanagan in 1917. Run by a teenage mayor, this forward-looking institution, affectionately known as the "City of Little Men", offers a warm welcome to visitors to its huge campus.

South of downtown, you can wander through the grounds of the admirable Henry Doorly Zoo, where many of the animals – including a

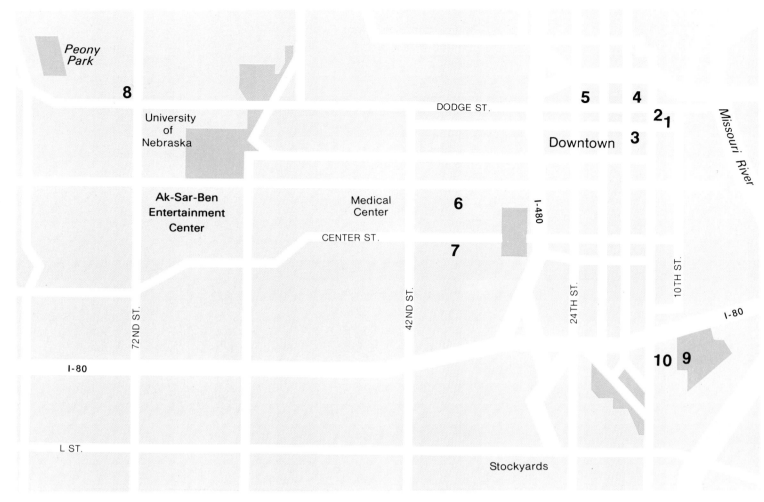

Omaha

marvelous collection of tigers and other large cats – enjoy the freedom of spacious outdoor pens. Roars of a different kind, however, can be heard echoing from the nearby Rosenblatt Stadium, especially when baseball fans crowd in to yell for Omaha's Royals. From here, a drive south along the Missouri River bluffs takes you to lovely Mount Vernon Gardens and Fontenelle Forest on the edge of Bellevue, Nebraska's oldest community. Once a fur-trading post founded in 1823, Bellevue is now better known as the headquarters of the Strategic Air Command, where there is an awesome museum displaying aircraft and missiles. From Bellevue, you can take a leisurely cruise on the river for a more peaceful prospect on life.

Tucked away in the districts north of downtown is the house used during the Indian Wars by the eccentric General George Crook, whom General William Sherman himself acknowledged to be "the greatest Indian fighter and manager the army of the United States ever had." Other places of historic interest are located farther north in the community of Florence, where you can imagine life in days gone by at Nebraska's oldest bank and mill, the old tollhouse, and the railroad-depot museum. Here, too, you can muse on the sufferings of the Mormon migrants who died during the bitter winter of 1846/47 and are now laid to rest in the famous Mormon Cemetery. Farther north, you can see how soldiers lived at Fort Atkinson, the first military fort west of the Missouri, built in 1820.

Along this northern stretch of the Missouri River, there are also several attractive parks for pleasant outdoor relaxation, including N. P. Dodge Park and Freedom Park, with its marina where several former sea-going warships are now moored.

"You should see us now," urges the slogan promoting tourism to Omaha today, and although history definitely lives on in this old frontier cow town, twentieth-century attractions and amenities are now much in evidence.

Philadelphia PENNSYLVANIA

City of Brotherly Love

High above the streets of Philadelphia, Pennsylvania, a 37-foot (11-m) statue of William Penn, the noble old city's seventeenth-century Quaker founder, stands atop the tall, slender tower of the ornate City Hall. Because no building here is permitted to obstruct Penn's view – which means that nothing is higher than 548 feet (167 m) – Philadelphia has no soaring sky-scrapers like those that have mushroomed in other cities in the wake of the wrecker's ball. Many new buildings have, of course, been constructed in the course of renovating decayed parts of the city in recent years, but they were designed to blend in scale, if not in style, with older structures. Occasion-ally, however, an odd juxtaposition between old and new might cause a visual jolt, perhaps none so dramatic as the siting of Claes Oldenburg's giant modern sculpture representing a wooden clothes pin in front of the majestic City Hall – although, it must be said, discreetly out of sight of Penn's statue high above. Yet the overall impression is of a cityscape of great visual excitement.

The capital of the United States for a quarter of a century following the Revolutionary War against British rule, Philadelphia is the proud guardian of some of the nation's most revered historic treasures. It was here that the two Continental Congresses met during the two years preceding the

In a section of downtown Philadelphia, the birthplace of the United States, is "America's most historic square mile," the pleasant tree-shaded area of Independence National Historical Park, where the city preserves some of the nation's most revered historic treasures. Among the sights that lure millions of visitors to the park every year are the beloved Liberty Bell, Independence Hall, and Congress Hall. Along the Delaware riverfront are the spot where the city's founder, William Penn, landed in 1682, now called Penn's Landing, and the oldest section of Philadelphia, known as Old City, at the foot of Benjamin Franklin Bridge (left).

Philadelphia's elaborately ornamented City Hall stands in the heart of the central business district at the intersection of Broad and Market streets. Its impressive tower, topped with the famous statue of William Penn, is an inescapable city landmark that dominates the downtown skyline.

struggle, that Thomas Jefferson, John Adams, and Benjamin Franklin drafted the Declaration of Independence, and that the Founding Fathers drew up the Constitution of the new nation. The buildings in which these momentous events were enacted are respectfully preserved as a National Historical Park, one of several quiet pockets of history amid the bustling commerce and industry of today's city.

A century before the Revolutionary War, in 1682, Penn founded his "faire countrie towne" on 1,280 acres of flat, fertile land just above the junction of the Delaware and Schuylkill rivers and coined the name Philadelphia from Greek words meaning "City of Brotherly Love." The grid of streets that he planned, with four squares symmetrically placed around one central square, remains today in the heart of the city, its hub the present City Hall. Over its 300-year history, Philadelphia has grown considerably beyond the original plan, swallowing up the neighboring German settlement of Germantown, founded in 1683, and spreading suburbs into the surrounding county areas. Today, Philadelphia is America's fourth largest city, with a population of around 1.7 million, a modern manufacturing center producing textiles, pharmaceuticals, and other goods, with excellent transportation networks linking it to other cities on the east coast. It is also a city that is conscious of its past, much of which remains to delight and captivate both visitors and residents.

Several well-defined areas of Philadelphia are of particular interest to the sightseer, starting appropriately by the Delaware River at Penn's Landing.

Among the attractions here are the riverside park, with its sculpture garden and outdoor entertainments, its shops and restaurants, and its collection of historic sea-going ships. Nearby, at the foot of Benjamin Franklin Bridge, is the Old City, now a commercial district containing a number of historic treasures. Among these are the charming cobblestone Elfreth's Alley, with its early-eighteenth-century houses; the Arch Street house of Betsy Ross, who, according to tradition, sewed the first Stars and Stripes for George Washington; and Christ Church, where the first president, Ben Franklin, and other Revolutionary War leaders once worshiped.

A few blocks away, between 5th and 6th streets, you can relive the gripping events of the Revolutionary period among the original buildings now preserved in Independence National Historical Park. The monuments here include Independence Hall, where the Declaration of Independence and the United States Constitution were adopted, and the revered Liberty Bell, housed in its special pavilion. Just south of here is the fashionable Society Hill district, a model of urban revitalization, with restored town houses, elegant boutiques, fine restaurants, old churches, museums, and the sophisticated New Market shopping complex in Head House Square.

The city's principal shopping areas include Market, Chestnut, and Walnut streets, which run parallel to one another through the Center City district and are lined with elegant stores such as John Wanamaker (with its unique organ concerts), and shopping centers like the superb Bourse, the Gallery at Market East, and the Olde Chestnut Street Mall. There are also the exotic shops of Chinatown along Race Street and Antique Row along Pine.

Many of Philadelphia's major cultural institutions are concentrated to the northwest of the central area along the Benjamin Franklin Parkway, a diagonal tree-lined boulevard that slices through Logan Circle. The Academy of Natural Sciences, the science-oriented Franklin Institute, the Free Library, the superb Rodin Museum, and the outstanding Philadelphia Museum of Art are all along the route of the quaint Fairmount Park Trolley Bus, which also tours Fairmount Park and calls at its many attractions, including the zoo and a number of beautiful historic mansions.

A favorite recreation area for city residents, Fairmount Park, the country's largest city park, comprises 8,700 acres of landscaped gardens and

Downtown Philadelphia

1 *Penn's Landing*
2 *Elfreth's Alley*
3 *Betsy Ross House*
4 *Independence Hall*
5 *Liberty Bell*
6 *Head House Square*
7 *New Market Complex*
8 *Academy of Music*
9 *Academy of Natural Sciences*
10 *Franklin Institute*
11 *Rodin Museum*
12 *Philadelphia Museum of Art*

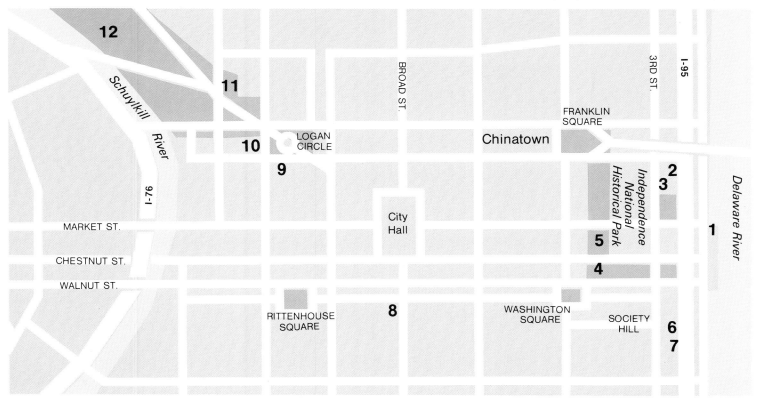

meadows bordering the Schuylkill River and Wissahickon Creek in the northern part of Philadelphia. On the park's northernmost fringes, several miles from the Center City, are the old community of Germantown, with its fine mansions and estates – now designated a National Historical Landmark – and the nearby beautiful residential and shopping district of Chestnut Hill.

Sports fans in Philadelphia gather for big events at the three stadiums around the intersection of Broad Street and Pattison Avenue at the far end of South Philadelphia. At Veterans Stadium, excitement is always high for home games of the Eagles football and Phillies baseball teams, while at the Spectrum, different kinds of crowds flock in for a wide range of events, including 76ers basketball, Flyers ice hockey, boxing matches, and the U.S. Professional Indoor Tennis Championships.

When the sun goes down, Philadelphia comes to life with nighttime entertainment to suit all tastes and with a bewildering selection of restaurants that serve the best in American and international cuisine. In addition to night clubs and cabarets, piano bars and discos, there are hotels, dinner theaters, and restaurants offering live entertainment. Theaters that are active year round stage all kinds of productions, including serious drama, musicals, opera, and dance. Among the leading houses are the Forrest, Shubert, Burgundy, and Walnut Street theaters; the Society Hill Play-

Below: Standing serenely like a classical Greek temple overlooking the placid waters of the Schuylkill River, the magnificent Philadelphia Museum of Art (top left), the third largest in the United States, contains more than half a million priceless works of art of all kinds. The museum is one of many cultural institutions on the route of the quaint Fairmount Park trolley that passes along Benjamin Franklin Parkway northwest of downtown.

house; and the Annenberg Center at the University of Pennsylvania in West Philadelphia. The downtown Academy of Music, a major magnet for music lovers, hosts the celebrated Philly Pops concerts and performances by the famed Philadelphia Orchestra and Opera Company, while the Spectrum and the Robin Hood Dell East auditoriums offer popular music in a lighter vein.

Throughout the year, a succession of colorful events and festivals enlivens the daily routine and adds to the considerable charm and appeal of this cosmopolitan city. But pride of place goes to the world-famous Mummers Parade, Philadelphia's answer to New Orleans's Mardi Gras, which fills Broad Street with colorful gaiety on New Year's Day.

Philadelphia is well placed for sightseeing tours into the Pennsylvania countryside to such pleasant spots as the Brandywine Valley, the Delaware Water Gap, and the Pocono Mountains. That this is George Washington country is evidenced by the many historic sites in the area, none so famous as Washington's heroic winter-camp site at Valley Forge, not far from the city. And across the Delaware River is New Jersey and the Atlantic coastline, where the glittering casinos of Atlantic City offer a different kind of relaxation, worlds apart in time from the historic city of Philadelphia, the shrine of American liberty.

Below right: The quaint old Philadelphia district of Society Hill around 2nd and Pine streets, once a tract of land owned by the seventeenth-century Free Society of Traders, has atmospheric cobblestone streets lined with lovely brick town houses, many now restored. The district has been revitalized in recent years with the opening of fine restaurants and boutiques and is now a fashionable residential area.

Phoenix ARIZONA

Sun Valley City

It was an English adventurer, apparently more cultured than the usual rough mining prospector or pioneer settler, who gave Phoenix, Arizona, its curious name when he became one of its first residents over a century ago. He maintained that, like the legendary phoenix bird reborn from its own ashes, a great city would one day rise from the ruins of the ancient Hohokam Indian culture, which had thrived in this region more than 500 years earlier. His prediction was astonishingly close to the mark, for the little military-supply camp established in 1860 near the Hohokam ruins by the Salt River is now the fastest-growing city east of California, ranking ninth largest in the country with a population surging past 790,000 in 1980.

Located amid the spectacular desert and mountain country of south-central Arizona, Phoenix lies in the broad, scenic region within Maricopa County known as the Valley of the Sun. With its ring of satellite communities – Sun City and Glendale to the west, and Paradise Valley, Scottsdale, Tempe, Mesa, and Chandler to the east – the city spreads for some 50 miles in all directions toward the surrounding backdrop of mountains. The checkerboard of streets that makes up the urban sprawl is interrupted on the northeast by the distinctive red-rock outline of Camelback Mountain and by the broad east–west gash cut through it by the Salt River. High-rise buildings reveal the location of the downtown district, and here and there, patches of green parkland contrast with the surrounding dry, brown country. The whole spectacular panorama spreads out before you from the top of South Mountain Park, on the southern edge of the city.

Over the years, several major events were influential in the development of Phoenix. The most significant were the arrival in 1887 of the first railroad, which brought in many settlers from other parts of the country; the designation of the city two years later as territorial (then state) capital; the building in 1911 of the Theodore Roosevelt Dam on the Salt River, which boosted the city's growth and provided irrigation water for the area's citrus and cotton crops; and the emergence since World War II of thriving electronics and aerospace industries, which now form a major element in the city's manufacturing economy.

With temperatures that range on average between 51°F (11°C) in winter and 91°F (33°C) in summer, the certainty of sunshine on around 300 days of the year, and an annual rainfall of only 7.5 inches, Phoenix enjoys an attractive climate. This has been both a considerable magnet for people moving into the Sun Belt states from other parts of the country in recent years and a crucial factor in the growth of the now flourishing tourist industry in the Valley of the Sun. Spacious hotel resorts are continually springing up to provide accommodation for the increasing numbers of people who take winter vacations in the area.

For vacationers, the staggering beauty of Arizona's varied landscapes is a special attraction, and there are numerous reminders of the region's Indian, Spanish, and Mexican heritage, as well as echoes of more recent American pioneer history. Opportunities abound for outdoor recreational activities, the wide range of choices including golf, tennis, horseback riding, mountain climbing, hiking, fishing, hang gliding, hot-air ballooning, and even skiing. For hot, sunny days, there are also plenty of facilities for water activities at the area's man-made lakes, and even a chance to ride artificially

Opposite: Adventurous spirits who climb up the slopes of the 15,000-acre South Mountain Park on the south side of Phoenix are rewarded with spectacular panoramas of the sprawling metropolis, whose suburbs extend across the broad Valley of the Sun as far as the distant mountains.

Standing out prominently in the northeastern section of Phoenix, Camelback Mountain is the city's most distinctive natural landmark, a red rock outcrop that glows in the sunset on the boundary with the fashionable suburb of Scottsdale.

produced 5-foot (2-m) waves at the Big Surf lake in Tempe. One of the oddest and most popular water sports in Phoenix, however, is river tubing, which simply involves floating lazily down the Salt River in a truck inner tube, suitably equipped with iced drinks and a broad-brimmed hat for shade. For the not too energetic, there are various spectator sports, which, in addition to baseball and basketball, include horse- and dog-racing and numerous lively rodeos, none more spectacular than the Phoenix Jaycees' Rodeo of Rodeos in March.

Phoenix contains many places of interest within its downtown business and shopping district, the area around the intersection of Central Avenue and Van Buren Road, just north of the Salt River. Among the highlights here are the impressive granite State Capitol, set in a large pleasant park; the Victorian district of Heritage Square, with the lovely Rossen House of 1894; the Phoenix Art Museum, with its specialist collection of art of the American Southwest; and the excellent Heard Museum, a showcase of the anthropology, history, and culture of the Southwest. In this area, too, are the green expanse of Encanto Park and the State Fairgrounds, which hosts the State Fair every fall. On the fairgrounds is the 14,000-seat Veterans

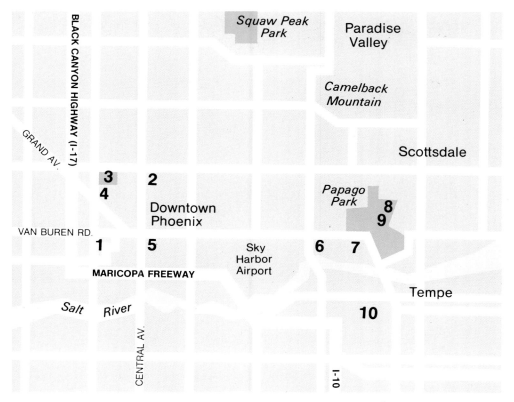

Memorial Coliseum, a multipurpose arena that is often filled with basketball fans supporting the Suns.

On the east side of the city, the excavated ruins of dwellings deserted by the Hohokam Indians around A.D. 1400 are preserved at the Pueblo Grande Museum. Beyond are Municipal Stadium, which hosts home games of the minor-league Giants baseball team, and the huge Legend City amusement park. Here the red-sandstone hills of Papago Park overlook the city spread out to the west; this vast park contains the 125-acre Phoenix Zoo, with its 1,000 animals, and the fascinating Desert Botanical Garden, where a large proportion of the world's species of cacti are on display.

North of the park and behind Camelback Mountain, the Old West community of Scottsdale is both a fine shopping district and a treasure trove for arts and crafts lovers. Students of architecture also find much of interest here, not only the beautiful houses that line many of the streets but also the exhibits of modern architecture at the Cosanti Foundation and at Frank Lloyd Wright's former home, Taliesin West.

A wide range of cultural events – including theater, symphony and chamber concerts, opera, and dance – is always available at theaters and performing-arts centers throughout the Phoenix area, with the Celebrity Theater in Phoenix and the Grady Gammage Auditorium at the University of Arizona in Tempe also staging pop and other light-music concerts. Many of the restaurants in the Valley of the Sun also provide entertainment, particularly those in the plush resort hotels and the informal western-style restaurants scattered throughout the mountains to the northeast.

Despite all the attractions within Phoenix, no visit would be complete without venturing into the breath-taking country on all sides, where many spectacular sights are within a day's drive of the city. To the north, for example, are the ghost town of Jerome; the art lover's mecca of Sedona; the former territorial capital of Prescott; Arcosanti, the experimental "City of the Future;" scenic Oak Creek Canyon; the ancient Indian dwelling at the Montezuma Castle National Monument; and the dramatic rock face of the Mogollon Rim. To the east, you can take the wild Apache Trail through the desert scenery past the eerie Lost Dutchman Mine and the Superstition Mountains. Phoenix truly stands at the gateway to a vacationers' paradise.

Pittsburgh PENNSYLVANIA

The Once Smoky City

Mention to a friend that you are about to spend a few days in Pittsburgh, and chances are you will get a response that somehow conveys horror, sympathy, and ironic amusement all at the same time. If so, it is a sure sign that your friend has not visited Pennsylvania's second city for some years and is relying on the traditional image of Pittsburgh as the "Smoky City." For this great industrial center, the steel capital of America – whose skies, it is true, were once darkened with the smoke and grime of its blast furnaces, rolling mills, and factories – has been considerably cleaned up in recent years.

The view from the restaurant atop the towering United States Steel building, which dominates the downtown "Golden Triangle" business district, or from an observation deck on nearby Mount Washington reveals the attractive profile of the great city laid out below. Spread out over the hills where the Allegheny and Monongahela rivers unite to form the mighty Ohio River, Pittsburgh is divided into distinct areas linked by more bridges than there are in any other city in the United States. From the air, the rivers take the form of a giant silvery wishbone lying on its side, with its apex, the Ohio River, on the left (the west). Its arms, the Allegheny and the Monongahela, embrace the compact downtown district between the North Side suburbs, known as Old Allegheny, and the steep wooded slopes of Duquesne Heights and Mount Washington on the South Side.

As early as the 1750s, the strategic importance of this site for controlling communications and trade down the Ohio and Mississippi rivers to the Gulf of Mexico was recognized and bitterly contested by French and British forces during the French and Indian War. The point of land where the Allegheny and the Monongahela converge saw a succession of military forts built by both sides during the seesaw struggle for possession: Fort Prince George, Fort Duquesne, and formidable Fort Pitt, named after William Pitt, Britain's young, new prime minister. Evidence of these early fortifications can still be seen in present-day Point State Park and its museums and Blockhouse. A more recent addition to this historic site is the impressive 200-foot (61-m) fountain, fed by an underground river, that is now a well-known landmark at the tip of the Point.

With the discovery of coal on Mount Washington in the 1760s, Pittsburgh emerged as an industrial giant. Named after the old British fort, it earned distinction as the "Arsenal of the North" during the Civil War. Later, such enterprising magnates as Andrew Carnegie, Thomas Mellon, Henry Clay Frick, and Henry Heinz made fortunes out of the city's hotchpotch of factories and mills, and thousands of immigrant workers arrived to shape the rich ethnic diversity of its population.

Clustered into the Golden Triangle behind Point State Park are the gleaming high-rise towers that house the headquarters of many of the giant industrial corporations that grew up in those early days. Here, too, are big hotels, department stores, and shopping complexes like the elegant Bank Center, among which oases of green can be found in Mellon Square, Market Square, with its colorful food stalls, and Equitable Plaza, where the Three Rivers Arts Festival enlivens the scene every spring. For the culturally minded, there are the graceful Heinz Hall for the Performing Arts, which offers opera, ballet, and concerts by the renowned Pittsburgh

Overleaf: One of the finest views of the Golden Triangle, Pittsburgh's compact central business district, is from the top of Duquesne Heights on the south side of the Monongahela River. A cluster of towering offices and hotels, dominated by the dark outline of the United States Steel building, forms a magnificent backdrop for the green expanse of historic Point State Park, flanked by the graceful curves of the city's many river bridges.

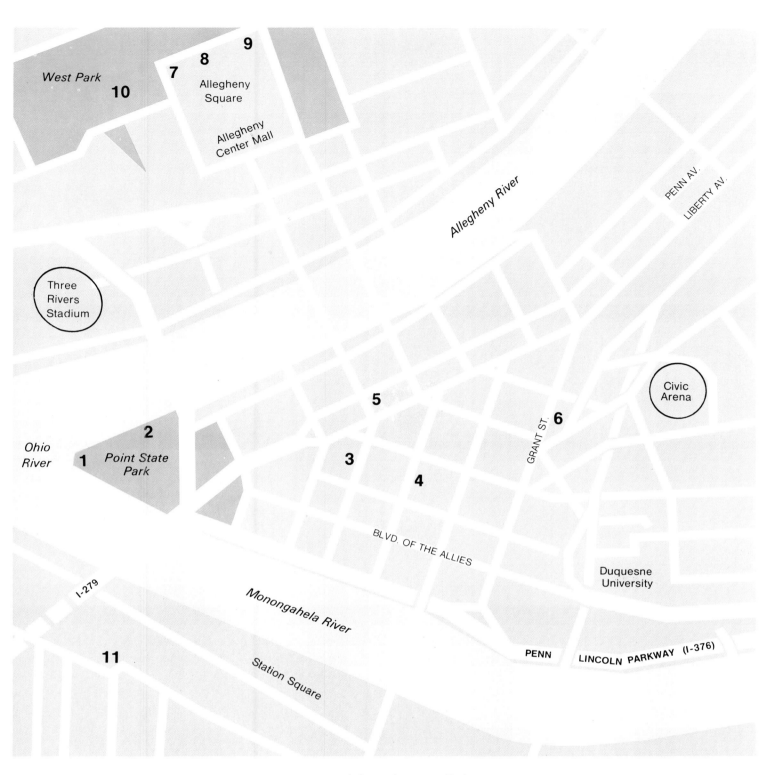

Symphony; outdoor concerts by the American Wind Symphony at Point State Park; and performances by theater groups, jazz bands, and puppeteers in the city parks. On the eastern edge of the downtown district, the shallow-domed Civic Arena and Exhibit Hall squats by the towering United States Steel building, hosting sporting events, industrial expositions, musical performances, ice shows, circuses, and the annual international Folk Festival.

East of downtown, the Oakland district encompasses many cultural and educational institutions donated to the city by its great industrial magnates. Here is the renowned Carnegie Institute, contributed by the founder of United States Steel to illustrate his maxim that "the man who dies rich dies thus disgraced." It comprises art and natural-history collections, a fine library, and a music hall that houses a huge pipe organ. Schenley Park has another steelman's donation, the Phipps Conservatory, a popular botanical

Pittsburgh: the Golden Triangle and North and South Sides
1 *Point State Park Fountain*
2 *American Wind Symphony*
3 *Market Square*
4 *Bank Center*
5 *Heinz Hall for the Performing Arts*
6 *United States Steel Building*
7 *Old Post Office Museum*
8 *Buhl Planetarium*
9 *Hazlett Theater*
10 *West Park Aviary and Conservatory*
11 *Mount Washington Overlook*

Above: One of Pittsburgh's best-known old landmarks is the imposing 42-story, Gothic-style tower of the University of Pittsburgh, known to local people as the "Cathedral of Learning." It stands in spacious parkland surroundings among other educational and cultural institutions — and close to the impressively ornate Frick-Schenley Fountain — in the eastern suburb of Oakland.

Above right: The charming red cars of two nineteenth-century cable railways, known as the Duquesne and Monongahela Inclines, carry visitors up 600-foot wooded hillsides to the excellent observation points and restaurants on Grandview Avenue that overlook downtown Pittsburgh.

garden with dazzling flower displays all year round, and the Henry Clay Frick Fine Arts Building, which boasts a fine collection of Renaissance art. Also bearing the Frick name is the internationally famous Frick Art Museum at Point Breeze. A well-known landmark in Oakland is the 42-story Gothic-style tower known as the "Cathedral of Learning" at the University of Pittsburgh, with its first-floor display representing the city's ethnic communities.

Across the Allegheny River facing Point State Park, the historic residential district of Old Allegheny rises gently on the North Side behind colossal Three Rivers Stadium, where football and baseball fans gather to roar support for the Steelers and the Pirates. Apart from its beautiful old homes, the area has many notable attractions, including the Aviary of tropical birds in West Park and, in Allegheny Square, the Buhl Planetarium, Hazlett Theater, Old Post Office Museum, and Allegheny Center, a modern complex of offices, shops, and town dwellings. Farther north, Riverview Park has the famous Allegheny Observatory.

Over the bridges spanning the Monongahela River south of the Golden Triangle, you can ride up the 600-foot (183-m) slopes of Duquesne Heights and Mount Washington in the old, picturesque red and yellow cable cars known as the Incline. Down by the river, you can spend a pleasant hour or so browsing through the shops in the Station Square complex, created by revitalizing the site of the former Pittsburgh and Lake Erie Railroad station. To round off a visit to the South Side, you can then board one of the paddleboats of the Gateway Clipper Fleet, moored at an adjoining wharf, and enjoy a delightful river tour past the gleaming skyline of the Golden Triangle.

Portland OREGON

The City of Roses

At dinner in Oregon City one evening in 1845, Francis W. Pettygrove, a businessman from Maine, flipped a coin with his partner, William Overton, to decide the name of the settlement they had founded on their 64-acre claim by Oregon's Willamette River. If Overton had won, the United States would now have two Bostons, one at each northern corner of the country. But fate decreed that Pettygrove's choice should prevail, and the new town was named after Portland, Maine.

Now a major seaport and business center of the Northwest, with a city population of around 336,000, Portland lies at the northern end of the broad, fertile Willamette Valley between Oregon's Coast Range and Cascade Mountains, the end of the road for the nineteenth-century pioneers who made their way here along the fabled Oregon Trail. The city spreads across a four-county area on both sides of the northward-flowing

Seen from the higher parkland to the west of the city, the beautiful, progressive metropolis of Portland extends across the Willamette River into the hilly suburbs to the east. Beyond, the towering, snow-capped peak of Mount Hood forms a majestic backdrop on the distant horizon, a recreational playground for both city residents and tourists in the breath-taking Cascade Range.

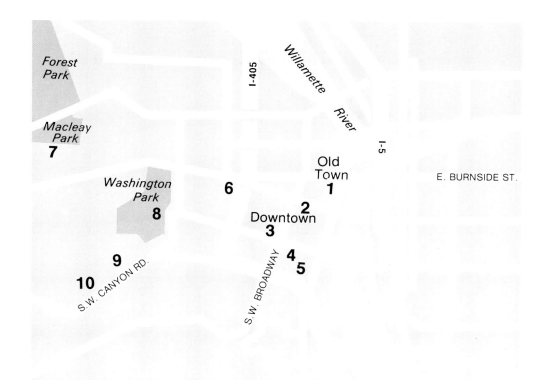

Willamette, just above its junction with the mighty Columbia River, the state boundary with Washington. Neatly divided by the Willamette into east and west sides, each with its distinctive character, Portland rises behind the downtown district bordering the west bank of the river into the residential districts and parks of the West Hills. On the east bank, the urban sprawl is broken by higher ridges of land clothed in suburban development, with the snow-covered outline of 11,235-foot (3,427-m) Mount Hood forming a majestic backdrop on the distant horizon.

It is a scene that is often partly hidden in winter, when veils of thin drizzle, which make up much of the city's annual 34 inches of rain, sweep in from the west, to be followed by stiff breezes that uncover breath-taking vistas in the clear, sparkling air. With temperatures that range between averages of 42°F (6°C) in December and 72°F (22°C) in August, the climate is never extreme, although the drier, warm summer months are the best time to visit.

Acclaimed as one of the most livable cities in America, Portland is undisputably beautiful. The enlightened attitudes of its citizens and government have helped to create an environment conducive to a high quality of life. Great strides have been made, for example, to remove industrial mess; anglers and sailboats have returned to the once polluted river; and the clean downtown streets attest to strong civic pride. Here, treasured nineteenth-century cast-iron architecture, Prohibition-era drinking fountains, and ornate iron lamp standards mingle with exciting futuristic building projects. As proof of their respect for anything old, Portlanders have even designated as an historic landmark an aged tree named Farrell's Sycamore in the center of downtown.

Known as the "City of Roses," Portland is also a city of parks – from the vast to the pocket-sized – of tree-lined avenues embellished with flower planters, and of beautiful gushing fountains and spacious plazas that invite you to relax in the pleasant surroundings. Portland offers exciting cultural activities, a wide range of evening entertainment (including excellent jazz clubs), top-rate restaurants to suit every taste, abundant outdoor leisure amenities, and spectator sports at the Memorial Coliseum, Civic Stadium, Meadows Racetrack, and other venues.

On the west bank of the Willamette, where sea-going ships often tie up among the seven bridges that link the two sides of the city, the gleaming

Ira's Fountain, also known as the Forecourt Fountain, is a famous Portland landmark in the New Town district. Constructed in 1970 in a landscaped park across from the Civic Auditorium, it features a series of waterfalls 18 feet high and 80 feet wide over which plunge 13,000 gallons of water a minute.

skyscrapers of the downtown business and shopping district soar above a kaleidoscope of interesting sights. A bird's-eye view of the scene spreads out before you from the twenty-first-floor restaurant in the 40-story First Interstate Bank Tower. Several blocks near the river on either side of West Burnside Street are known as the Old Town, a district of decorated Victorian cast-iron architecture and of streets with cobblestone corners lined with boutiques, craft and antique shops, restaurants, and atmospheric bars. Here you can experience the exotic scents of the small Chinatown district or the mouth-watering cuisine of fine restaurants like the Dan and Louis Oyster Bar in the old Bickel Building. You can drink in the atmosphere, if not the water, at the charming Skidmore Fountain, shop in the boutiques in the renovated New Market Theater, and browse among the potpourri of stalls at the open-air Saturday Market beneath Burnside Bridge.

South of the Old Town, the business and shopping district successfully mingles the old with the new, although the bold, modern Portland Building has caused some raised eyebrows. Among the highlights for the sightseer and shopper is a busy 22-block transit mall used by the city's orange-and-white buses where the fine stores, shady trees, flower tubs, kiosks, and statues create a pleasant atmosphere for strolling and browsing. Here you will also find the 12-block oasis of greenery known as the South Park Blocks, the Portland Art Museum, with its delightful Sculpture Mall, and the Oregon Historical Society Museum. Other places of interest are the superbly restored Yamhill Place and the majestic Pioneer Courthouse, with its magnificent new plaza.

Some 20 years ago, a run-down 54-block neighborhood in the southern part of downtown was demolished to make way for the construction of the impressive New Town district, or Portland Center, a highly praised complex of high-rise apartments, offices, shops, and restaurants with landscaped plazas and fountains and underground parking. Well-known city landmarks here are the two spectacular fountains, the Lovejoy and the Forecourt. Also known as Ira's Fountain, the Forecourt is a favorite for splashing around in during summer hot spells.

Ira's Fountain dominates a square that has been praised as "perhaps the greatest open space since the Renaissance," a suitable setting for Portland's outstanding cultural center, the Civic Auditorium. The remodeled 3,000-seat hall hosts performances by the Oregon Symphony, the Portland Opera,

Almost on Portland's doorstep to the northeast is the awesome forested scenery of the Columbia River Gorge, where breath-taking panoramas of plunging cliffs and feathery waterfalls can be seen from such spectacular viewpoints as Crown Point.

and various theater and dance companies. Elsewhere in the city, the Portland Civic Theater and a dozen or so other playhouses offer varying programs of plays and musicals throughout the year. Outdoor concerts and other entertainments are also great favorites at various places around the city. In addition, there are numerous annual festivals, among which the celebrated Rose Festival in June, with its colorful parade, sporting contests, and many other events, is the high point.

Some of Portland's major attractions are to be found in the beautiful West Hills districts, which overlook the city. Here you can wander through 5,000 acres of forested wilderness in Forest and Macleay parks and visit the nearby French Renaissance-style Pittock Mansion of 1914, with its spectacular panoramic views. You can also spend days enjoying the attractions of Washington Park, a little way to the south, where you will find the famous International Rose Test Garden, the beautiful Japanese Garden, and – a miniature-train ride away – the zoo and its renowned herd of elephants, the Western Forestry Center, and the Oregon Museum of Science and Industry (known here as the "OMSI").

In the heart of a vast scenic and recreational playground, Portland is a fine starting point for out-of-town drives to such outstanding attractions as the forested Mount Hood area, with its excellent skiing facilities; the spectacular Columbia River Gorge and beautiful Multnomah Falls; the superb Oregon coastline south of historic Astoria; and the awesome, devastated country around Mount St. Helens volcano in neighboring Washington State.

Providence RHODE ISLAND

Little Rhody's Capital

Found guilty in 1635 of "new and dangerous opinions against the authorities," after having demanded the right of religious liberty and freedom of conscience, the young minister Roger Williams found himself banished from his home in the Massachusetts Bay Colony. With a band of followers and helped by friendly Indians, he made his way to the head of Narragansett Bay, in what is now the state of Rhode Island; the following year, he founded a settlement there that he named "in commemoration of God's merciful Providence." To honor his memory, a statue of Williams now stands at his burial site on a hillside at Prospect Terrace, overlooking the fine city that has grown around his original settlement.

The capital of Rhode Island and the state's main industrial center and seaport, Providence is the largest city in New England after Boston, with a metropolitan-area population of over 500,000, of whom some 156,000 live in the city. Its varied manufactures include the jewelry for which it is famous, while its deep-water harbor handles huge oil tankers and ships carrying coal, cement, lumber, and other cargoes.

In the midst of these activities, Providence has succeeded in preserving many of its historic buildings, although nothing remains of the original farming village, a haven for religious dissenters of the time, which was almost totally destroyed in 1676 during the Indian uprising known as King Philip's War. The earliest surviving buildings in the city date from the eighteenth century, when Providence was a thriving seaport whose prosperous shipowners and merchants built prestigious mansions with the wealth they accrued. The town was then actively involved in the struggle against British colonial rule, which led to the burning of the British schooner *Gaspée* and the signing in Providence of Rhode Island's own Independence Act on May 4, 1776, two months before the Declaration of Independence was proclaimed in Philadelphia. After the Revolution, Providence entered a period of industrial growth, during which, in 1832, it was incorporated as a city. Thousands of immigrants, mostly from Sweden, Portugal, and Italy, streamed in during those years in response to the demand for labor, and between 1850 and 1890, the population quadrupled – from 41,000 to 175,000.

Downtown Providence centers on the point where the Moshassuck and the Woonasquatucket rivers, both now largely covered over, join to form the southward-flowing Providence River, about 1 mile above its entry into Narragansett Bay. The city's downtown streets clamber over several hills above the flatlands around the river junction, which were prone to flooding until the Fox Point Hurricane Barrier was constructed downstream across the Providence River. On the east bank of the river is the city's main historic district, which contains many splendid buildings of the colonial period, lovingly restored and preserved by their present owners. On the west bank is the compact business district, with its modern high-rise offices and hotels, government and public buildings, shopping streets, and theaters.

To the north, somewhat separate, the beautiful white-marble State House, completed in 1900, stands majestically in its park on Smith Hill, overlooking the city. A repository of many of Rhode Island's historic treasures, it is also noted for its huge self-supporting marble dome, the

A statue of Roger Williams, the seventeenth-century founder of Providence, looks out over the city from the fine viewpoint at Prospect Terrace, where part of his remains now lie buried.

world's largest after that of St. Peter's Basilica in Rome.

Because distances are short in the center-city area, many of the major places of interest can be seen by walking around its streets. Just east of the State House is the site of the original 1636 settlement by a spring near the Moshassuck River, a 4.5-acre park that has been designated the Roger Williams National Memorial. At the north end of Main Street, originally called Towne Street, which borders the east side of the Providence River, is the beautiful steepled First Baptist Meeting House of 1775, and at the south end, where ships once unloaded their cargoes, old waterfront buildings have been restored to house smart boutiques, restaurants, and art galleries.

Behind and running parallel to Main Street is Benefit Street, the city's proud "Mile of History," lined with grand mansions and charming artisans' homes, many of which are open to visitors during the Festival of Historic Houses in May. Here, too, are the Old State House of 1762, where Rhode Island's independence was proclaimed; the Doric-style Providence Athenaeum of 1838, which houses a fine private library founded in 1753; and the

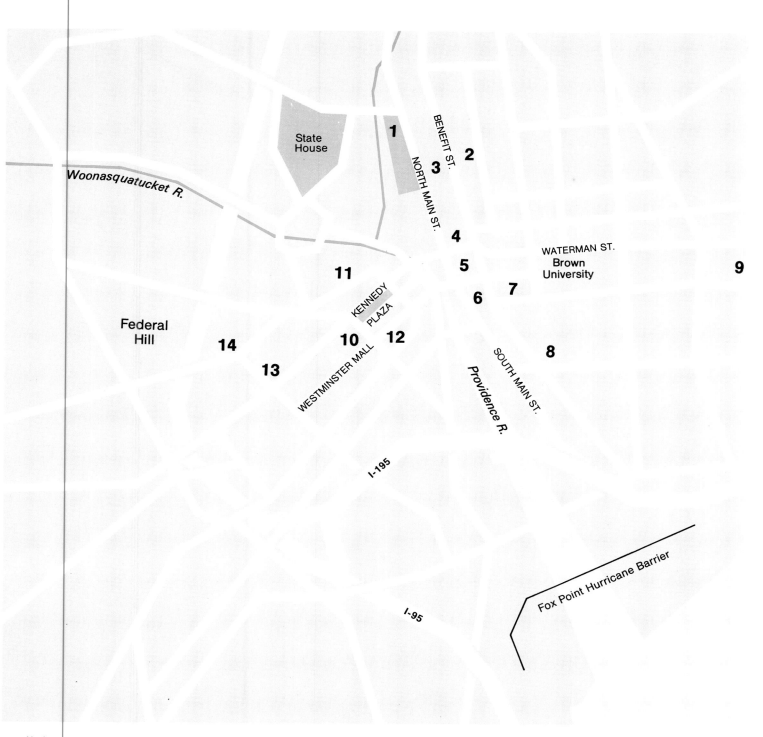

small, but outstanding Museum of Art of the celebrated Rhode Island School of Design. In adjacent side streets are such notable city landmarks as the 1707 residence of Governor Stephen Hopkins, where George Washington really did sleep – twice – and the imposing John Brown House of 1786, which John Quincy Adams called "the most magnificent and elegant private mansion that I have ever seen on this continent." Other highlights in this part of the city are the picturesque campus of Brown University, founded on College Hill in 1764; the Woods–Gerry Gallery of the Rhode Island School of Design; and the beautiful Museum of Rhode Island History.

Across the Providence River, the Bajnotti Fountain in Kennedy Plaza, the city's central square, is a good starting point for a tour of the interesting business district. Close by are the City Hall, built in 1878 in the style of the Louvre in Paris and lavishly decorated inside; Union Station, a splendid gateway to the city for railroad travelers that was constructed in 1898; and the delightful Arcade, a shopping mall designed like a Greek temple in 1828

Downtown Providence

1 *Roger Williams National Memorial*
2 *Prospect Terrace*
3 *Old State House*
4 *First Baptist Meeting House*
5 *Museum of Art, Rhode Island School of Design*
6 *Governor Stephen Hopkins House*
7 *Providence Athenaeum*
8 *John Brown House*
9 *Museum of Rhode Island History*
10 *City Hall*
11 *Union Station*
12 *The Arcade*
13 *Majestic Theater, Trinity Square Repertory Company*
14 *Civic Center*

Right: Rhode Island's impressive State House, located in beautiful parkland some blocks north of downtown Providence, is crowned with a 10-foot bronze statue called Independent Man, a symbol of the state's heritage of freedom. Among the many historic items preserved inside the building is the original parchment charter given to Rhode Island by King Charles II in 1663 granting "full liberty of religious concernments."

Below: Beautiful steeples of centuries-old churches rise above old timbered houses in the gracious historic district of Providence on the east bank of the Providence River. In addition to the celebrated First Baptist Meeting House, founded by Roger Williams in 1638, this fascinating part of the city contains the First Unitarian Church of 1816, in the steeple of which hang the largest and heaviest bells ever cast by the foundry of Paul Revere and Son.

that now buzzes with specialty shops and restaurants on three levels. A step away are more shopping delights along Westminster Mall, a smart pedestrian walkway bustling with activity.

In nearby streets, you will find the famous Majestic Theater, now the Lederer, home of the celebrated Trinity Square Repertory Company, and the sumptuous Providence Performing Arts Center in the restored Loew's State Theater, which hosts performances by the Rhode Island Philharmonic, Providence Opera Theater, and Festival Ballet. One highlight not to be missed, after seeing the fine Public Library and modern Civic Center, is the Italian neighborhood of Federal Hill, beyond whose gateway arch you enter a delightful world of outdoor cafés, specialty shops, and fine restaurants centered on a pleasant Italian piazza and fountain.

For a change of pace, Providence offers a variety of spectator sports and a succession of festivals and other events throughout the year. There is also a chance to escape from city streets in the wonderful 450-acre Roger Williams Park, on the south side of town. You can also relax in one of the city's great seafood restaurants and sample the delights of a Rhode Island lobster, a clam bake, or one of the famous local johnnycakes.

Although a host of sightseeing attractions awaits the visitor in the cluster of communities around Providence, it is only a short drive to two special places of outstanding interest: fabulous Newport, famous for yachting events and for its stately mansions built by nineteenth-century millionaires in various grand styles as summer "cottages"; and Mystic Seaport, a restored whaling village in neighboring Connecticut.

Transporting the visitor back to an earlier age, the streets of old Providence are lined with charming historic houses, many of them beautifully preserved by their present owners.

Richmond VIRGINIA

The Confederate Capital

When you stand in the wilderness park bordering the James River and look back at the uncompromisingly modern skyline of Virginia's capital, Richmond, you have to remind yourself that there are few cities in the United States with stronger historic associations than this one. For this is the place where, for instance, that firebrand orator Patrick Henry stood in St. John's Church just before the Revolutionary War and roared at his questioning compatriots: "I know not what course others may take but, as for me, give me liberty or give me death." This, too, is the city that served as the Confederate capital during the cataclysm of the Civil War, from which it emerged in defeat and in ruins. The whole place is steeped in history, its streets trod by such national figures as Thomas Jefferson, Benedict Arnold, Jefferson Davis, Robert E. Lee, and the writer Edgar Allan Poe, their memory preserved in the city's many museums and historic sites. And outside the city, in the beautiful green countryside bordering the James River, are graceful old plantation homes that stand as reminders of Virginia's colonial heritage.

As early as 1607, shortly after America's first settlement was founded at Jamestown, Captains John Smith and Christopher Newport sailed up the James River to the falls, planted a cross, and claimed for England the whole area then ruled by the Indian chief Powhatan. But it was not until 1679 that William Byrd began a settlement that was later named for Richmond-upon-Thames in England. As a thriving tobacco market and flour-milling center, the town became Virginia's capital during the Revolutionary War, during which it suffered pillage by forces led by the traitor Benedict Arnold. Chosen as the Confederate capital in 1861, Richmond was successfully defended by General Robert E. Lee in several major Civil War battles, a struggle that ended with the burning of the business district and bitter surrender.

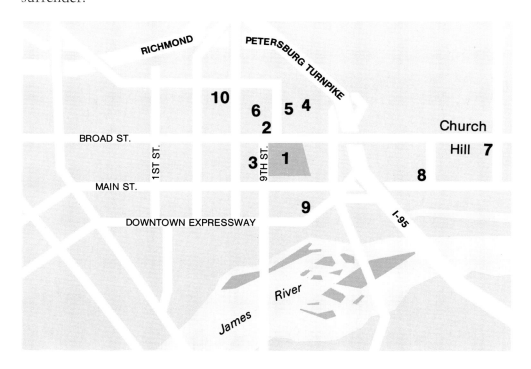

Rebuilt after the war, Richmond is today a study in contrasts, a bustling modern city of nearly 220,000 people with the charm and grace of a much smaller town, a city whose historic heritage blends easily with the commerce of twentieth-century life. A major financial and government center, Richmond is also an important industrial city and river port, involved in the manufacture and distribution of a wide range of products, among them, of course, tobacco.

A panoramic view over nearly four centuries of history thus awaits the visitor who ascends to the Sky Deck atop the 22-story City Hall on downtown Broad Street. Below, the downtown streets and neighborhoods teem with interesting places. South of City Hall is one of Richmond's gems, the beautiful white State Capitol, designed like a Roman temple by Thomas Jefferson in 1785 and containing the famous statue of George Washington sculpted by Jean-Antoine Houdon. A short walk away is St. Paul's Church, where on Palm Sunday in 1865, Jefferson Davis, the Confederate president, received the fateful news that Richmond was in dire peril as the Union armies approached. On East Franklin Street is the beautiful antebellum house that the man who sent the message, General Robert E. Lee, rented with his family after the Civil War ended. Lee's uniform and sword are preserved, along with other Civil War exhibits, in the Museum of the Con-

The capital of Virginia since 1779 and of the Confederacy during the Civil War, the historic city of Richmond stands on the James River, where the foaming white water that marks the fall line provides thrills for today's rubber rafters.

Overleaf: Set on 12 acres of pleasant tree-shaded grounds in the heart of downtown Richmond, the beautiful Virginia State Capitol has been the seat of state government since 1788. Its central portion, with its elegant classical portico, was designed by Thomas Jefferson while serving as ambassador to France, and was inspired by a Roman temple he saw there.

In the restored Heritage Square area, the excellent Valentine Museum has displays tracing Richmond's history since early Indian times, and you can get a glimpse of the elegant life style of the well-to-do in the eighteenth century by visiting the nearby mansion where Chief Justice John Marshall lived on the street that bears his name.

Many renovated nineteenth-century homes decorated with elaborate ironwork line the streets of the neighborhood of Church Hill, southeast of downtown, where Patrick Henry made his famous speech in St. John's Church. This area also contains the charming Old Stone House, built in 1737 and reputedly Richmond's oldest home, which is now filled with memorabilia of Edgar Allan Poe, who once lived in the district. The dark days of the Civil War are commemorated in Chimborazo Park, south of here, where the Visitor Center presents dramatic displays and talks on the battles that took place to the south and east of the city.

Another of the city's old neighborhoods, the eighteenth-century commercial area close to the river known as the Shockoe Slip, has recently undergone revitalization, and its cobblestone streets now sparkle with nightspots, restaurants, and shops. Similar renovation has given new life to turn-of-the-century houses in the self-contained community known as the Fan district, where many restaurants have sprung up along the long streets that fan out northwest of downtown. Along the northeastern edge of the Fan district runs one of America's most beautiful streets, Monument Avenue, a tree-shaded boulevard lined with majestic old houses and statues of Confederate heroes. While looking at these monuments, you might be stimulated to visit the nearby Battle Abbey Museum, on Boulevard, which houses an excellent collection of historic portraits and Confederate firearms. And, while in the area, you should not miss the outstanding Virginia Museum of Fine Arts, where you can spend hours gazing at the fabulous Fabergé jewelry and Art Nouveau exhibits.

When tired of museums and historic sites, you can drive southwest along Boulevard for a cruise on the James River or a leisurely stroll through the spacious grounds of Byrd and Maymont parks, just two of the many pleasant open spaces among Richmond's streets. In the opposite direction, you can enjoy the fun of the colossal Kings Dominion theme park, 17 miles out of town, or visit Scotchtown, the plantation home of Patrick Henry. West of Richmond, there is the superb Tuckahoe Plantation, and along the James River, a selection of fine historic homes to visit, among them the Berkeley, Shirley, and Wilton plantations. But the most memorable experience of all is a visit to the place where the United States began, the historic triangle of Jamestown, Williamsburg, and Yorktown, some 50 miles southeast of Richmond.

There is never enough time to experience Richmond's countless attractions. Even if you are not a keen history buff or student of architecture, the city can offer all the amenities you expect in a place of this size: excellent stores and specialty shops, first-class restaurants, outdoor recreation, and night life. The City Stadium and the Coliseum host a continuous program of sporting events, while the city's theaters and dinner theaters provide evening entertainment to suit all tastes. One of the finest of these is the Barksdale Dinner Theater in the 250-year-old Hanover Tavern, north of the city. Even here you cannot escape history, for they say that at one time the bartender of the tavern was none other than – Patrick Henry.

Far right: The Old Stone House on East Main Street is now furnished as a mid-eighteenth-century home and contains touching objects that once belonged to the writer Edgar Allan Poe.

Right: Memories of the tragic events of the Civil War abound in the many museums and battlefield sites scattered around Richmond, once the focal point of the struggle as the Confederate capital.

St. Louis MISSOURI

Gateway to the West

In the concourse area of Lambert International Airport in St. Louis,
Missouri, there is a long mural that depicts the history of mankind's conquest of the air; the painting sets the tone for this great city, the hometown
of the celebrated pioneer aviator Charles A. Lindbergh. For St. Louis has
always been concerned with travel and enterprise; it is a major center of
communications located in the heart of America, whose energy, industry,
and determination in the quest for progress have combined to create the
unique "Spirit of St. Louis."

The importance of the location where St. Louis now stands was recognized as long ago as 1763, when Pierre Laclede marked out the site of a
French settlement just below the junction of the Mississippi and Missouri
rivers that would serve as a market center for the wide-ranging fur trade at
that time. He called it St. Louis after the pious thirteenth-century French
king Louis IX, who spent much of his life on the long journeys of the
Crusades.

After the Louisiana Purchase brought the vast French-owned Great
Plains of the West under the American flag in 1803, St. Louis was the
natural starting point for the epic journey of exploration undertaken by
Lewis and Clark up the Missouri River into the uncharted western territories. Within a few years, migrants on the long trek to settle the new lands
began to flock into St. Louis by road, river, and rail from the eastern states
and as far away as Europe. By 1870, St. Louis had become the "Gateway to
the West," the nation's third largest city, with over 300,000 people. Its
riverfront bustled with cargo vessels and elegant steamboats, and its streets
thronged with people who represented a bewildering diversity of nation-
alities and tongues. The skills that these pioneers brought to the burgeoning
riverside community molded St. Louis into what it is today: a thriving
modern city of over 450,000 inhabitants; the nation's busiest inland river
port and market, handling wool, grain, livestock, and lumber; and a major
manufacturing and research center that produces an astonishing range of
goods that includes beer, chemicals, aircraft, and shoes.

St. Louis
 1 Gateway Arch
 2 Laclede's Landing
 3 Old Cathedral
 4 Old Courthouse
 5 Busch Memorial Stadium
 6 Soulard Market
 7 Powell Hall
 8 New Cathedral
 9 St. Louis Zoo
10 Municipal Opera House
11 Missouri Botanical Garden

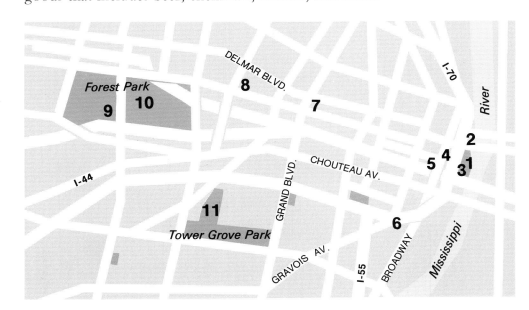

Everyone visiting St. Louis, of course, makes for the Mississippi riverfront, where the golden era of the steamboats can be relived on one of the graceful cruise riverboats moored alongside the cobblestone levee. Particularly enjoyable is an evening of old-time movies, ragtime music, hilarious vaudeville, and noisy melodrama on the wonderful old *Goldenrod Showboat*, the appropriate venue for the ragtime and jazz festival in June.

Dominating the entire riverfront area, the immense Gateway Arch, the nation's tallest monument, soars to 630 feet (192 m) at its apex above Jefferson Memorial Expansion Park and the Museum of Westward Expansion at

its foot. Designed by the eminent architect Eero Saarinen in 1948 to commemorate the epic migrations of the nineteenth-century pioneers to the West, this elegant, gleaming stainless-steel structure incorporates a specially designed capsule-train inside each leg to carry sightseers to the observation room at the top. From here, there is a breath-taking view for 30 miles around, with the city stretching away westward from the Mississippi into the distant suburbs. Below, squeezed between the graceful old Eads and Martin Luther King bridges to the north, the nine square blocks of Laclede's Landing, once a rundown remnant of delightful shops, restaurants, and offices, where lively nightspots vibrate to the sounds of Dixieland, blues, and rock music. Here, the air is filled with the aroma of spicy foods and the licorice made at a local factory.

Near the arch, two of the oldest buildings in St. Louis stand as reminders of pre-Civil War days, their elegant, classic outlines contrasting with the rectangular towers of the downtown offices, hotels, and stores behind. One is the Old Cathedral, built in 1834 and now accompanied by its

Above: Behind the Mississippi riverfront the neat checkerboard of streets in downtown St. Louis extends westward on each side of the broad thoroughfare of Market Street. Among the distinctive landmarks down by the river are the magnificent Gateway Arch and the immense Busch Memorial Stadium.

Overleaf: The spectacular stainless-steel Gateway Arch soars above the St. Louis riverfront, dwarfing the high-rise buildings of the downtown district and the riverboats moored at its feet. Framed within the elegant curve of the arch is the historic Old Courthouse where the celebrated Dred Scott case was heard and where slaves were once auctioned on the steps.

museum; the other is the historic Old Courthouse, a domed Greek-style structure of 1845, where the black slave Dred Scott brought and lost his celebrated lawsuit to win his freedom, a judgment that helped to push the nation into the tragedy of the Civil War.

In both the downtown area and the outlying county districts, St. Louis boasts many fine stores and shops, superb restaurants, theaters, concert halls, and museums – everything you expect to find in such a modern metropolis. Downtown, Gateway Mall has been planned as a broad axis of open space running westward from Gateway Arch across the city, although not all the blocks in the scheme have yet been acquired. All around, the streets contain a wide variety of attractions. Mention must be made of the ultramodern arena of Busch Memorial Stadium, home of the football and baseball Cardinals, and location of the Sports Hall of Fame; Kiel Auditorium, where audiences can enjoy anything from a celebrity concert to a spectacular Broadway show; opulent Powell Hall, once a movie house and now hosting concerts by the famed St. Louis Symphony Orchestra; and the magnificent fountain sculpted by Carl Milles in Aloe Plaza to symbolize the meeting of the Mississippi and Missouri rivers.

Throughout the St. Louis area, there are also many places of historic interest, such as the downtown Campbell House; the Eugene Field House, with its fascinating toy museum; the imposing Cupples House, the farm that belonged to General (and President) Ulysses S. Grant; and the renovated Soulard Market, in the neighborhood first settled by French

immigrants. Places like the Central West End district, location of Maryland Plaza, and, farther out, West Port Plaza and Plaza Frontenac are paradises for shoppers, where hours can be spent just browsing in the pleasant surroundings. The Central West End is also the site of the huge and impressive Cathedral of St. Louis, the so-called New Cathedral, whose interior is adorned with a dazzling display of colorful mosaics.

A little farther west, bordering the city limits, is the gem of St. Louis's attractions: Forest Park, the site of the 1904 World's Fair, which gave the United States – and the world – the first hot dog, hamburger, ice-cream cone, and iced tea. Scattered throughout this vast park, the third largest in the country, are such varied attractions as the superb St. Louis Zoo, the Art Museum, the McDonnell Planetarium, and the huge Municipal Opera House, a popular summertime venue that is affectionately known to city residents as "The Muny." Not far away is another favorite place, the Missouri Botanical Garden, nicknamed "Shaw's Garden," enclosing the renowned geodesic-dome greenhouse known as the Climatron, the Japanese Garden, and the Scented Garden for the blind.

Many varied and interesting places to visit are located within a short driving distance from St. Louis. Within the county area is the Six Flags over Mid-America entertainment center, where you can enjoy the thrills of the Screamin' Eagle roller coaster. Farther away are the Daniel Boone home at Defiance; the old Mississippi River town of Hannibal, with its memories of Mark Twain; and, downriver, the historic community of Sainte Genevieve.

St. Petersburg/ Tampa FLORIDA

Florida's Bay Area

When you gaze at the huge, exotic Moorish-style building topped with 13 onion-domed minarets that now houses the administrative offices and classrooms of the University of Tampa in Florida, you can imagine it in its heyday as the sumptuous, elegant Tampa Bay Hotel nearly a century ago. Then the world's high and mighty, including leading politicians like Theodore Roosevelt and such great international performing artists as the ballerina Pavlova and the pianist Paderewski, came to stay in its richly appointed guest rooms overlooking the Hillsborough River. The splendor of those days has been preserved for us to admire today in the south wing of the building. Here the Henry B. Plant Museum honors the farsighted businessman who built the hotel in 1891, after bringing the railroad to Tampa six years earlier as part of his plan to attract tourists to Florida's west coast.

Like his great rival, the railroad tycoon Henry Flagler, who opened up the state's east coast to development, Plant was a leading figure in setting Florida on the road to becoming America's flourishing winter vacationland. Today Tampa, with its neighbor St. Petersburg, stands at the hub of a whole string of coastal resort communities that bask by the warm blue waters of the Gulf of Mexico between Tarpon Springs and Marco Island, its superb modern airport handling the thousands of visitors who fly in each year to enjoy the area's many attractions and its enticing climate. Here average temperatures range between 60°F (16°C) in January and 82°F (28°C) in August, the prevailing sea breezes moderating extremes, while much of the annual rainfall total of 50 inches (127 cm) is concentrated in heavy summer thunderstorms that quickly pass. With its abundance of sunshine, Florida's western shoreline has become known as the Suncoast and the city of St. Petersburg nicknamed the "Sunshine City."

Both urban centers lie on the great sea inlet of Tampa Bay, a magnificent natural harbor fed by several rivers and natural springs. Located at the mouth of the Hillsborough River, Tampa has spread inland and around the Bay to become Florida's third largest city and the seat of Hillsborough County, with a 1980 population of just over 271,000. Across Tampa Bay, St. Petersburg, a rapidly growing city of about 237,000 people, faces eastward from its location at the southern tip of a long peninsula in Pinellas County that separates the Bay from the Gulf of Mexico. Long causeways carrying major highways leapfrog across the upper part of the Bay, here named Upper Tampa Bay, between the two cities, providing access from Tampa to the 30-mile ribbon of island beaches that lie offshore in the Gulf between St. Petersburg Beach and Clearwater Beach farther north. Another superb engineering feat, the dramatic 15-mile-long Sunshine Skyway, soars above ocean-going ships passing through the entrance to Tampa Bay, and links St. Petersburg with Bradenton, Sarasota, and the coastal communities to the south.

With its wonderful climate and clear blue skies, St. Petersburg became a favorite choice years ago for older people looking for a place to retire. But its growth really started when General John C. Williams came down to Florida to escape the blizzards of Detroit in 1876 and founded a small community that was soon to become known as St. Petersburg. The name was chosen to honor his own birthplace by a Russian aristocrat who liked

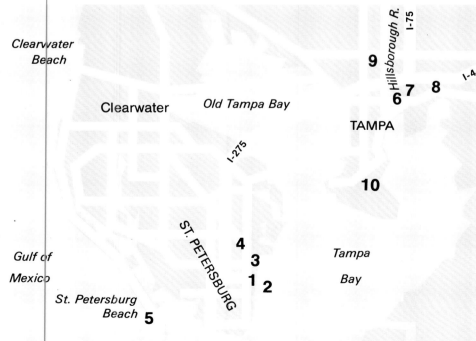

The narrow Hillsborough River flows through central Tampa between the developing downtown business district and the University of Tampa campus (bottom right). Here the old Tampa Bay Hotel, with its exotic silver minarets, is a familiar landmark, contrasting with the modern stainless-steel structure of the Tampa Museum across the river.

St. Petersburg and Tampa

1 *Bayfront Center*
2 *Pier Place*
3 *Museum of Fine Arts*
4 *Sunken Gardens*
5 *London Wax Museum*
6 *University of Tampa*
  (and old Tampa Bay Hotel)
7 *Tampa Museum and Tampa Bay*
  Performing Arts Center
8 *Ybor City*
9 *Tampa Stadium*
10 *Jai Alai Fronton*

the place and brought in a railroad, changing his own name in the process to Peter A. Demens.

The old image St. Petersburg gained as a senior citizens' retirement home is now changing as younger people are moving in with the development of the area's tourist and high-technology industries. Certainly St. Pete, as the locals affectionately call it, has much to attract the young, with its informal life style and its unequalled opportunities for outdoor recreational activities, particularly water sports, sailing, and fishing.

Yachts and other sleek craft line the moorings in the Municipal Marina on downtown St. Petersburg's splendid waterfront, where a 2,500-foot (762-m) pier, popular with anglers, stretches out into Tampa Bay. On the pier is one of the city's most striking landmarks, an inverted five-tiered pyramid structure housing shops and restaurants and known as Pier Place, not far from which is moored the sailing ship *Bounty*, specially constructed for the movie *Mutiny on the Bounty*. Nearby are the huge Bayfront Center, the focal point of St. Petersburg's entertainment and cultural life, which hosts a variety of theatrical, musical and sporting events, and other shows, and the St. Petersburg Museum of Fine Arts, with its notable collection of French nineteenth-century paintings.

Another excellent art museum in the city is the Salvador Dali Museum in Poynter Park, which contains the finest collection of paintings by the celebrated Spanish Surrealist artist. In addition, St. Petersburg boasts several other fine museums, including its well-known Historical Society Museum, while St. Petersburg Beach has its famous London Wax Museum, with its exhibits of historical and fictional characters.

Glamorous old hotels still survive to delight the eye and recall days gone by both in St. Petersburg itself and on the offshore islands. Among the most famous are the ornate Manhattan Hotel built by John Williams in 1890 and several luxury hotels of the 1920s scattered around the downtown district; the sumptuous pink Don CeSar Resort Hotel of 1928 at St. Petersburg Beach; and the magnificent Belleview Biltmore Hotel built by Henry Plant in 1897 at Belleair farther north on the road to Clearwater. Much new building is also under way, with such new development projects as the museum and shopping center called Pier Park and the Festival Market Place changing the skyline along the Bayfront. Amid these changes the delightful Sunken Gardens remain one of St. Petersburg's timeless attractions, an oasis of tropical plants, birds, and animals away from the bustle of city streets.

Across the causeways that stride over Old Tampa Bay to the east, the city of Tampa presents a more thrusting, commercial image to the world than its sedate neighbor. The financial and distribution center for Florida's west coast, Tampa is also a major port and industrial city engaged in processing local agricultural and fishing products and manufacturing a wide range of goods, including the famous cigars that earned the city its nickname "The Cigar Capital of the World." In addition, the recent growth of high technology industries in the area is bringing new prosperity to the city, which is now undergoing considerable development. Together with the rehabilitation and restoration of old buildings like City Hall, ambitious construction projects are revitalizing the central business district, the most impressive including the prestigious Tampa Bay Performing Arts Center and the 41-story Barnett Plaza office building designed to be the city's tallest structure. Another huge project is transforming 177-acre Harbor Island into a major commercial and residential complex, while several others are planned to begin in the near future. Tampa's changing skyline can be viewed from one of the pleasant cruise ships that carry sightseers round the Bay area from the Hillsborough River wharves.

Despite the magnificent natural harbor that Tampa Bay afforded, the first Europeans to visit the area, a succession of sixteenth-century Spanish explorers – Ponce de León, Pánfilo de Narváez, and Hernando de Soto – failed to establish a permanent settlement here because of hostile Calusa

Indians. It was not until 1823 that a community was founded by the Hillsborough River, protected by the building of the military post of Fort Brooke, and soon it came to be known as Tampa, the Indian name for the site, which some say means "stick of fire." Years later, just after Henry Plant built his railroad to the town in 1885, Cuban cigar-makers founded new factories in the area and helped to boost Tampa's growth. One of them, Vicente Martínez Ybor, gave his name to the district where the factories were located, Ybor City, now Tampa's Latin Quarter. It is a fascinating historic district of plazas, sidewalk cafés, and buildings with ironwork balconies where you can tour the original cigar factories and savor the romantic Cuban atmosphere. Ybor City's colorful past, including its links with the Cuban patriot José Martí and the Spanish-American War of 1898, is captured and preserved in the exhibits displayed at the Ybor City State Museum housed in the delightful old Ferlita Bakery building.

Among the other outstanding museums in Tampa are the fascinating Museum of Science and Industry, the Tampa Museum, housing a wide-ranging art collection, and three galleries displaying exhibits of contemporary art at the University of South Florida campus. The city's other cultural attractions include the Florida Gulf Coast Symphony, the San Carlo Opera, three ballet companies and various theaters, outstanding among which is the renovated old Tampa Theater.

Tampa Stadium, northwest of downtown, is the setting for the Bay area's major spectator sports events, the home games of the two football teams, the Tampa Bay Bandits and Buccaneers, and of the Rowdies soccer team. Elsewhere around Tampa there are horse- and greyhound-racing events, spectacular games at the Jai Alai Fronton and spring training sessions held by several United States city baseball teams. In addition to sporting attractions, an assortment of other events and shows entices

The beautiful sandy beaches and abundant sunshine of Florida's west coast have helped to turn the "Sunshine City" of St. Petersburg into a major vacation center. Luxurious hotels and resorts, facilities for outdoor recreaction, and other attractions abound along the entire Suncoast area.

Sailing is a major leisure activity in the Tampa Bay area, and excellent facilities are provided in marinas in both St. Petersburg and Tampa.

visitors throughout the year to the Florida State Fairgrounds and ExpoPark 7 miles northeast of downtown, the location of the huge Florida State Fair held every February. Another major February event in the city is the entertaining Gasparilla Pirate Invasion of the city, followed by a big parade, just one of the many colorful celebrations that enliven the Bay area's year.

There is also fun for the whole family at Tampa's Lowry Park, at the water-activities park of Adventure Island, and at the city's leading attraction, Busch Gardens/The Dark Continent, a not-to-be-missed adventureland based on seven exotic African themes. A short drive northeast of the city are two of Florida's most outstanding attractions: the landscaped paradise of Cypress Gardens and Walt Disney World, another wonderland theme park "imagineered" by the great cartoonist genius, which conjures up visions of romantic, far-away places.

No longer sleepy small towns, St. Petersburg and Tampa together form a rapidly growing business, residential, and vacation area that is now attracting more and more people with its amenities and attractions.

Salt Lake City UTAH

"This Is the Place!"

"This is the place!" With awesome authority, the story goes, Brigham Young looked out from his pioneer wagon on that historic July day in 1847, uttered these few simple words, and brought the great westward trek of 148 Mormons to a halt by the Great Salt Lake in what is now Utah. As their former leader, Joseph Smith, had foretold before his murder, freedom for the Mormons from religious persecution would come only when they reached their promised land of Deseret "up in the mountains where the Devil cannot dig us out." It would, in fact, have been difficult to find a more inhospitable place than this arid, uninhabited mountain wilderness where sagebrush and fetid mud flats bordered a lake whose water was so salty that it was unfit to drink. Yet the pioneer families persevered, surviving through faith, the sweat of their brows, and a certain amount of timely divine providence, evidenced when a flock of hungry sea gulls swung in from the lake to save their first crop from the ravages of a grasshopper plague.

Over the years, irrigation, using springs and melt water from the mountain snows, brought agricultural prosperity to the growing community. Mining and the refining of local ores, followed in more recent times by the extraction of oil and natural gas, also helped the economy and laid the foundations for a wide range of manufacturing industries. Today, almost 1 million people, more than half Utah's entire population, live in the metropolitan area, over 163,000 of them in Salt Lake City itself, the state capital.

The city is still the world headquarters of the Mormon religion, the Church of Jesus Christ of Latter-day Saints, to which, it is estimated, over 60 percent of the city's population subscribes. The Mormon heritage is cer-

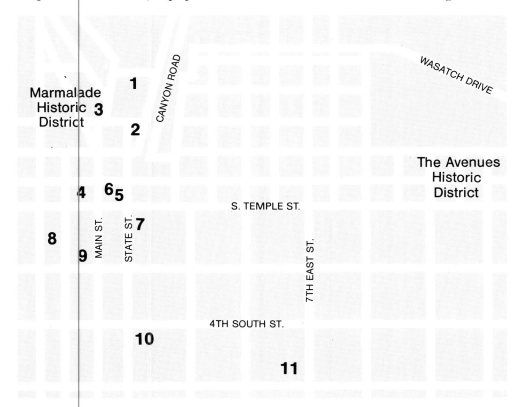

Downtown Salt Lake City
1 State Capitol
2 Council Hall
3 Pioneer Memorial Museum
4 Temple Square
5 Beehive House and Eagle Gate
6 Mormon Church Office Building
7 Hansen Planetarium
8 Salt Palace Center
9 Capitol Theater
10 City and County Building
11 Trolley Square

Overleaf: Overlooked by the snow-covered peaks of the Wasatch Front to the east, Salt Lake City extends across the flat valley in a neat checkerboard of streets laid out by Brigham Young. In the heart of the city is Temple Square (bottom left), where the six-spired Mormon Temple and the domed Tabernacle are unmistakable landmarks not far from the starkly modern structures of the Salt Palace Center (bottom).

Salt Lake City's majestic gray-granite Temple, with its distinctive Gothic-style spires, is the symbolic heart of the Church of Jesus Christ of Latter-day Saints, the Mormons. Built over a 40-year period from 1853 to 1893 from stone quarried in nearby Little Cottonwood Canyon, the Temple stands amid beautiful, flower-filled gardens in the walled enclosure of Temple Square.

tainly a visible reality. The unusually broad streets and sidewalks dividing the checkerboard of 10-acre blocks are an immediate reminder of the orderly city plan laid out by Brigham Young within days of his arrival at the site. Mormon buildings, monuments, and historic sites are scattered throughout the city, and, as Mark Twain remarked even in the 1860s, there is "a grand general air of neatness, repair, thrift and comfort around and about and over the whole." Although it may be argued that the somewhat complex regulations governing the sale and consumption of alcohol in Salt Lake City may confuse the first-time visitor, and the quiet downtown streets disappoint the evening reveler, this is nevertheless a hospitable as well as unique place.

The setting of Salt Lake City is itself an impressive sight: the city nestles in a flat valley some 4,300 feet (1,312 m) above sea level between towering mountain ranges. To the east, immediately behind the city, rises the 10,000-foot (3,050-m) wall of the Wasatch Mountains, known locally as the Wasatch Front, while to the west, the 9,500-foot (2,898-m) peaks of the Oquirrh Mountains give a jagged edge to the distant horizon. And northeast of the city, the glinting shallow waters of the Great Salt Lake stretch beyond the eye's reach over an area of 1,600 square miles.

The heart of Salt Lake City is Temple Square, a 10-acre walled block in the downtown area enclosing the principal buildings of the Mormon Church. Immediately recognizable here is the gray-granite, six-spired

Above: On Thursday evenings many visitors to Temple Square sieze the opportunity to attend a rehearsal of the famous Tabernacle Choir, accompanied by the superb pipe organ which fills one end of the acoustically perfect interior.

Left: Beehive House, the official residence built in 1853-54 for the Mormon leader Brigham Young, stands at the intersection of South Temple and State streets, its gracious elegance contrasting with the uncompromisingly modern Church Office Building that towers behind it.

Just a few blocks from downtown Salt Lake City, car barns built in 1908 that once housed the city's electric trolleys have been skillfully converted into a magnificent shopping, restaurant, and entertainment complex called Trolley Square, which is always bustling with activity. A landmark on the site is the 97-foot Trolley Tower (right), which formerly contained water for indoor sprinklers.

Temple, designed in a form of Gothic style by an architect blessed with the name of Truman O. Angell. Used for special church ceremonies, the Temple is not open to the public, unlike the Tabernacle auditorium crouching beside it. Resembling an elongated, upturned bowl, the Tabernacle is a remarkable construction capped with an acoustically perfect timber roof that is held together by wooden pegs and rawhide bindings. Inside is a magnificent pipe organ, and to hear a Sunday concert, or even a Thursday-evening rehearsal, by the world-renowned Mormon Tabernacle Choir here is indeed a memorable and moving experience.

Other Mormon buildings can be seen within easy walking distance in the neighboring block to the east. Beyond the imposing, elegant Hotel Utah on South Temple Street are the Classical Greek-style Administration Building; the Lion House, built for Brigham Young's wives and children; and the beautiful Beehive House, Young's official residence. Behind these buildings and standing amid beautiful gardens filled with flowers, trees, and bubbling water, the gleaming modern tower of the Church Office Building – containing the famous genealogical library – soars above the city skyline, offering marvelous views for miles around.

Spanning State Street beside the Beehive House, the wide arch of Eagle Gate, named for the somewhat fearsome bird at its apex, once marked the boundary of Young's estate. It provides a wonderful frame, when looking north, for the beautiful copper-domed Utah State Capitol building, which is impressively sited on rising ground a few blocks away and faces the lovely old Council Hall, once used by the city and territorial government. On the west side of the Capitol is the fascinating Pioneer Memorial Museum, packed with articles and mementoes of the nineteenth century.

Apart from sightseeing, the downtown streets offer convenient oppor-

tunities for shopping, not only in the many stores and boutiques, but also in several vast enclosed shopping centers. Two of these are adjacent to the Temple Square area: Z.C.M.I. Center (a development of the Zion's Cooperative Mercantile Institution) and Crossroads Plaza. A bus ride away is Trolley Square, where a delightful collection of shops, restaurants, and theaters has been assembled in the city's former trolley barns, now beautifully restored. Also close to Temple Square are the ultramodern buildings of the Salt Palace Center complex, which provide facilities for business conventions and host a variety of cultural and sporting activities, including art exhibits, symphony concerts, and the home games of the Golden Eagles (ice hockey), Utah Jazz (basketball), and Stingers (volleyball). And, a block away, the Capitol Theater is a popular venue for lovers of opera and ballet.

As well as the first-class Hansen Planetarium, on South State Street, Salt Lake City boasts two particularly fine museums on the huge University of Utah campus, east of downtown: the Museum of Fine Arts and the Museum of Natural History. Nearby, on the edge of the Wasatch Front, are old Fort Douglas, the Hogle Zoo, and Pioneer State Park, another historic Mormon site featuring a reconstructed Mormon settlement, Young's Forest Farmhouse, and the massive "This Is the Place" Monument, which commemorates the Mormons' arrival in Utah.

Places of interest outside Salt Lake City are too numerous to mention, but the highlights must include the immense hole gouged out of the ground at Bingham Copper Mine; the Wasatch Mountains and winter ski resorts of Park City, Alta, and Snowbird; and the Great Salt Lake itself. Swimming in the warm, briny water of the lake, it is easy to be deceived into thinking, as was fur trapper Jim Bridger in 1824, "Hell, we're on the shores of the Pacific!"

One of the most beautiful and imposing of the nation's statehouses, the Utah State Capitol, completed in 1916, stands amid pleasant gardens on a hill overlooking downtown Salt Lake City. Its interior features include the impressive main hall and rotunda, decorated with murals, and the Gold Room, the state reception chamber. The building faces the smaller, but equally attractive, brick-built Council Hall, constructed in 1864-66 and used as the seat of territorial and city government for nearly 30 years. Dismantled and relocated in 1963 on its present site (right), the Council Hall now houses a visitors center.

San Antonio TEXAS

City of the Alamo

From the observation deck atop the lofty Tower of the Americas, the lights of San Antonio spread out like a glittering magic carpet ready to transport the visitor away to taste the city's many exotic delights.

"Remember the Alamo!" The heroic battle cry echoed over the Texas plain at San Jacinto early on the morning of April 21, 1836, as General Sam Houston's ragtag band of fewer than 300 Texan and American volunteers hurled themselves upon a vastly superior Mexican army led by the hated General Santa Anna. Their magnificent victory that day paved the way for the territory's independence from Mexican rule later that year. It avenged the bloody slaughter that had been carried out by 5,000 Mexican troops under Santa Anna just over six weeks earlier, on March 6, when they had overrun the 188 men, women, and children holed up in the old Spanish mission of San Antonio de Valero, now immortalized by its more familiar name, the Alamo.

The story of the massacre, in which Davy Crockett, Jim Bowie, and Colonel William Travis met their heroic deaths, is today graphically retold on film for visitors to the Alamo Theater and Museum, across the plaza facing the mission in the heart of the city of San Antonio. The Alamo itself, now honored as the "Cradle of Texas Liberty," has become one of the most famous buildings in American history and a place of pilgrimage for all visitors to San Antonio, the city that bears its name.

This part of Texas came under Spanish rule over 250 years ago when the fortress of the Presidio de Béjar was built in 1718, together with a string of five Franciscan missions, one of them the Alamo, along the sluggish, narrow, winding river that today flows through the city. Close by, a settlement known as La Villita, or "little village," soon took root as traders and craftsmen moved in. A century later, after the decline of Spanish power ended with Mexico's independence in 1821, large numbers of English-speaking, non-Catholic "Anglos" moved into Texas, and agitation for their own independence under Stephen Austin finally led to open revolt in 1835, with the city of San Antonio in the vanguard.

Following the annexation by the United States of the nine-year-old Republic of Texas in 1845, the city's population grew to around 12,000 people by 1870, its prosperity boosted by the arrival of the railroads and the development of the cattle-raising industry. In more recent years, oil, manufacturing, military bases, and tourism have been major contributors to the city's economy. Today, ranked as America's eleventh largest city with over 785,000 people, San Antonio is the financial and commercial center of southwestern Texas, a busy modern metropolis that is nonetheless proud of its colorful Spanish and Mexican heritage. A city of contrasts – blending hard-headed business with unashamed festivity, carefree opulence with back-street poverty, modern urban American life with colorful ethnic tradition – San Antonio has great fascination. Its wealth of places of interest, its beautifully restored buildings and districts, its bubbling fiestas and exciting night life, and its benevolent climate combine to create the city's unique appeal.

The best vantage points to get an overall panoramic view of the city are the revolving restaurant and observation deck high up on the 750-foot (229-m) Tower of the Americas in the downtown area. From here, the outer suburbs can be seen stretching beyond the encircling Loop 410 highway into the flat land to the south and toward the rolling Hill Country to the north. The Tower rises from the 92-acre HemisFair Plaza, created for the 1968 World's Fair and the site of a huge convention center; the Arena, home base for the Spurs, the city's basketball team; a brand-new hotel; and various exhibition halls, including the Institute of Texan Cultures and the Mexican Cultural Institute.

From the Plaza, despite the appeal of riding in one of the downtown area's horse-drawn carriages or open-air trolleys, it is but a short walk to one of America's most delightful and memorable experiences: the enchanting Paseo del Rio, or River Walk, which follows a horseshoe loop of the San Antonio River some 20 feet (6 m) below the level of the streets. Amid

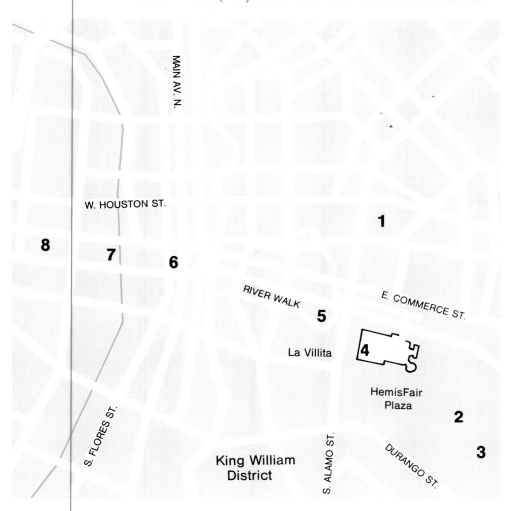

the lush tropical vegetation and tall trees that flourish down here are colorful shops and boutiques, chic night clubs, and open-air restaurants serving Mexican, Texas, Chinese, Italian, and other ethnic specialties to the throbbing sounds of Mexican mariachi music, Dixieland jazz, or country and western. There is even a theater, the Arneson River Theater, where the audience watches the action on stage from grass-covered steps on the opposite bank. And on the jade-green river itself, paddleboats for twosomes or candlelit barges for diners, complete with serenading musicians, glide by the changing sights along the banks. Throughout the year, the spectacle bubbles with even greater excitement during the city's many festivals.

A few steps from the river in this area is the original settlement of La Villita, which has been restored and landscaped to create a charming old-world setting of adobe houses, craft shops, art galleries, and restaurants bustling with activity around Juarez Plaza. And some blocks to the west, another reminder of San Antonio's Spanish past, the Governor's Palace, a beautifully preserved building that is now a historic showplace, stands in Military Plaza. Nearby, the restored Mexican market, El Mercado, throngs with people from morning until night; it provides a wonderful setting for fiestas when the night echoes to mariachi music and the warm

Now standing peacefully amid the bustle of downtown San Antonio, the old Spanish mission of San Antonio de Valero, known to everyone simply as the Alamo, is one of the most famous buildings in America history. It was here that Davy Crockett and other heroes met their deaths at the hands of the Mexicans in 1836 in the struggle for Texas independence.

air is perfumed by the spices of Mexican foods.

South of the downtown area, history buffs can find much to fascinate them in the impressive film presentation at the Heart of Texas entertainment center and in the historic King William district, with its elegant mansions built by German merchants a century ago. Not far away, a taste of old Texas awaits at the Buckhorn Hall of Horns, where the old-time Buckhorn Bar saloon, a curious collection of trophies, and the cottage of the author O. Henry have been gathered together on the grounds of the Lone Star brewery. From here, the old Mission Road leads directly to the chain of beautiful Franciscan missions founded by the Spaniards south of San Antonio in the early eighteenth century and still used as parish churches.

In the districts north of downtown are San Antonio's major museums: the Museum of Art, located in a renovated brewery; the general-interest Witte Museum; the Texas Ranger Museum; and the McNay Art Institute, a lovely Spanish-style mansion housing a fine collection of Post-Impressionist and other paintings. But for those who prefer outdoor sights and activities, there are the 343-acre Brackenridge Park, with its excellent zoo, miniature railway, and lovely oriental-style Sunken Gardens, and, farther out of town, the fascinating San Antonio Botanical Center, where all kinds of plants can be seen in superb displays.

With its festive atmosphere and innumerable attractions, San Antonio has great appeal for the visitor, offering both south-of-the-border excitement and modern American comforts.

San Diego CALIFORNIA

West Coast Paradise

One of the top entertainment states in San Diego, California, is a sleek performer named Shamu – not, as you might imagine, an exotic cabaret singer or a sensuous oriental dancer, but a killer whale whose playful antics draw crowds to the city's famous Sea World marine park in Mission Bay. Wild animals, whether trained to perform or just being themselves, are among the leading attractions in this far southwestern corner of the United States, for San Diego also boasts one of the world's finest zoos in the heart of the city and the marvelous 1,800-acre Wild Animal Park on the outskirts. On top of that, visitors to San Diego in the winter months can witness the exciting spectacle of California gray whales migrating along the Pacific coast just 1 mile or so off Point Loma.

Not only animals thrive in San Diego's warm, sunny climate; so do people. With an average annual temperature of 70°F (21°C), a year-round rainfall of only 10 inches, and constantly low humidity, San Diego is, according to meteorologists, the "only area in the United States with perfect weather." In the 1970s, during the rush to the Sun Belt, the city's population increased by 25 percent to reach 875,504 by 1980. As one of America's fastest-growing cities, San Diego ranks as California's second largest city after Los Angeles and eighth in the nation.

One of the most livable cities in the country, San Diego has a wealth of attractions to draw visitors: the beaches, the mountains, the Mexican heritage, the lively cultural life, the sea fishing and countless other leisure activities, the fascinating places for sightseeing, and much more. Tourism,

The gleaming skyline of downtown San Diego beckons along the long sweeping curve of San Diego Bay, where the harbors and marinas of Harbor and Shelter islands are crowded with white pleasure boats and yachts.

Downtown San Diego

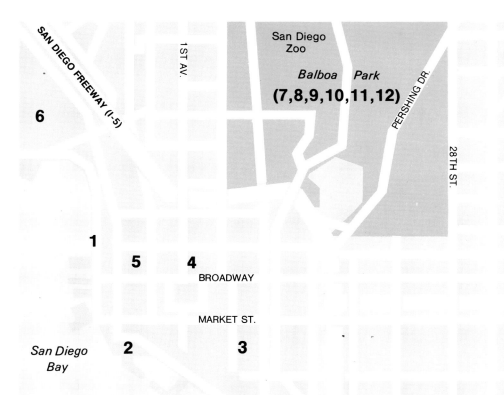

Below: The busy thoroughfare of Broadway cuts through the heart of downtown San Diego from the waterfront. This part of the city was originally laid out as a new town at the turn of the century by the sugar heir John Spreckels. Its streets are now overshadowed by many high-rise offices and hotels and contain such prestigious new developments as the Horton Plaza Center and the Convention and Performing Arts Center.

San Diego's third largest industry, brings in around 11 million visitors every year. More important to the city's economy, however, are its manufacturing activities – in such "clean" industries as aerospace, electronics, high technology, and medical research – and its military, especially naval, installations. With its excellent climate and fertile soils, San Diego County also supports a thriving agricultural industry that is the world's largest producer of avocados.

San Diego Bay, the largest naval base in America, is the home port of the U.S. Seventh Fleet, whose great ships and facilities share the magnificent 17-mile natural harbor with hundreds of small pleasure craft, cruise vessels, fishing boats, and cargo ships moored in the marinas and along the port jetties. The harbor is sheltered on the west by the 4-mile-long Point Loma peninsula and on the south by North Island – with its community of Coronado – and the long, narrow sand bar of Silver Strand.

Superb sandy beaches, spectacular cliffs, rugged inlets, and pleasant resort villages like La Jolla, with its renowned Cove, line the beautiful San Diego County shoreline for some 70 miles between the Mexican border to the south and the charming seaside resort of Del Mar to the north. Between the Pacific Ocean and the pine-covered Laguna Mountains, San Diego spreads over some 392 square miles of hills and valleys, with splashes of bright bougainvillea and geraniums and waving palm trees adding color to the glittering white cityscape. Marvelous vistas open up from the many high points, although there is an equally magnificent view of the city from the seaward side from the tip of the Point Loma peninsula. Here, the Cabrillo National Monument commemorates the landing in 1542 of the explorer Juan Rodríguez Cabrillo, who claimed the whole area for Spain.

It was not until 1769, however, that the Spaniards established the presidio garrison and mission of San Diego de Alcalá on a hill above the San Diego River just north of the bay. The mission, the first of a chain of 21 founded by Father Junípero Serra along the California coast, was soon moved to a site by the river, where it still stands. In the 1820s, a settlement known as the Pueblo de San Diego grew downhill near the presidio, surviving today as Old Town. After a brief period of Mexican rule, San Diego came under the American flag in 1848, but it remained a comparative backwater until a new town, now the downtown district, was developed along the bay waterfront at the turn of the century. Two world expositions in the city, in 1915/16 and 1935/36, helped to put San Diego on the map, its development also boosted by the establishment of military bases here.

Downtown San Diego now bristles with gleaming high-rise offices and hotels that overlook the spectacular waterfront, or Embarcadero. Among the attractions here are the picturesque sailing ship *Star of India* and other old vessels, which are berthed at the fascinating Maritime Museum, and the charming old-world shopping and restaurant complex of Seaport Village. Some blocks to the east is the atmospheric Gaslamp Quarter, once the city's business district, where many of the Victorian buildings have been restored to house shops, art galleries, and restaurants.

Just northeast of the downtown district, the beautiful landscaped 1,074 acres of Balboa Park contain, in addition to recreational and sports facilities, a collection of fine museums and other cultural amenities, most of them built in Mexican style. A 100-acre section of the park is occupied by the magnificent San Diego Zoo, which is also a lush botanical garden, where some 4,000 animals, many of them rare, live in natural outdoor enclosures.

Part of Old Town, San Diego's original settlement some 2 miles northwest of Balboa Park, is preserved as a State Historic Park. Here you can imagine the life of the first residents among such buildings as the presidio commander's spacious adobe home, the Casa de Estudillo. Nearby are the interesting Junípero Serra Museum – up the hill among the gardens, pines, and eucalyptus trees of Presidio Park – and fascinating Heritage Park,

Heritage Park, in San Diego's Old Town, is a collection of beautiful late nineteenth-century houses once belonging to prominent citizens, which have been gathered together on the present site after being threatened with demolition elsewhere in the city. Among them are, left to right, the Sherman-Gilbert House of 1887, now housing an art gallery, agency, and shop; the Bushyhead House, also of 1887, containing several specialty shops; and the Christian House of 1889, which is used as a restaurant.

where many of San Diego's fine Victorian buildings have been recon-structed after being saved from demolition.

Along the coast north of the San Diego River is Sea World marine park, where Shamu the killer whale performs, along with dolphins, and other sea animals. Sea World is part of the 4,600-acre Mission Bay Aquatic Park, developed from marshland for sailing, swimming, fishing, and other water activities. Indeed, San Diego is a sports lover's paradise, with facili-ties for golf, tennis, and countless other recreational activities scattered throughout the entire county, and spectator sports played at the San Diego Sports Arena and at the Jack Murphy Stadium. The performing arts, too, play a large role in San Diego's life style, with the Old Globe Theater standing out among the city's playhouses and the Civic Theater in the Performing Arts Center the highlight for performances of symphony concerts and opera.

But among San Diego's many attractions, its nearness to Mexico counts very highly, and no visit would be complete without taking the 16-mile ride on the red trolley from downtown to sample the exotic delights of the colorful Mexican border city of Tijuana and of other fascinating spots on the Baja California peninsula. On the United States side of the border, there are such enticing places to visit as Mount Palomar Observatory, in the mountains to the north, and Anza Borrego Desert State Park, which preserves the remote natural beauty of America's enchanting Southwest.

San Francisco   CALIFORNIA

Golden Gate City

Echoing the sentiments of the celebrated English eighteenth-century writer Dr. Samuel Johnson, who once remarked, "When a man is tired of London, he is tired of life; for there is in London all that life can afford," the California playwright and novelist William Saroyan gazed on the gem of all American west coast cities and concluded, "If you're alive, you can't be bored with San Francisco." It is an opinion that many have shared, for much has been written about the countless attractions of this exceptionally lovely metropolis, one of the best loved of all the world's great cities. Cultured, sophisticated, and cosmopolitan, San Francisco offers all the good things that urban living can provide and a life style that encourages personal fulfillment – and all in a breath-takingly beautiful natural setting.

A compact city of less than 47 square miles, San Francisco rolls over a cluster of hills at the tip of a narrow, 32-mile finger of land that separates the cool waters of the Pacific Ocean on the west from the vast inlet of San Francisco Bay on the east. Magnificent views of the glittering cityscape and the bay open up at every corner along streets that plunge down steep inclines, urging the city's beloved cable cars to clang their warning bells as they hurtle along. Many of the hills are well-known city landmarks, the highest including 938-foot (286-m) Mount Davidson, crowned with its huge cross, and the nearby Twin Peaks, which rise above 900 feet (275 m) at the city's geographical center and provide superb panoramas of the city below. Punctuating the skyline of the downtown district at the northeastern tip of the peninsula are the three much lower crests: Nob Hill, clothed in hotels and apartments; Telegraph Hill, with its famous Coit Tower; and Russian Hill, a residential area where the "Crookedest Street in the World," Lombard Street, zigzags down a precipitous slope. It is easy to understand

A favorite spot on San Francisco's busy waterfront is Fisherman's Wharf, which is both a harbor for the city's commercial fishing fleet and a tourist attraction offering a potpourri of atmospheric seafood restaurants, fish markets, and sidewalk stalls selling a colorful assortment of craft items and seafood delicacies. Tourists mingle along the walkways with outdoor entertainers to create a lively but relaxed festive atmosphere.

why a wit once observed, "When you get tired of walking around in San Francisco, you can always lean against it."

At the northern tip of the peninsula, the ocean meets the bay in a maelstrom of swirling currents through a gap in the hills, where the famous red Golden Gate Bridge, 1.7 miles long, strides across to Marin County. West of the bridge, the ocean beaches and rocks, with their lively sea lions, form part of the Golden Gate National Recreation Area, which also includes part of the bay waterfront as far east as renowned Fisherman's Wharf. Farther east, bustling piers crowded with bobbing fishing boats, ferries, and ocean-going liners cluster along the downtown waterfront beneath the glistening skyscrapers of the financial district, where the distinctive white tapering outline of the 48-story Transamerica Pyramid dominates the scene. From here the gray, two-level Bay Bridge takes an 8.5-mile hop, skip, and jump via several spans across the bay to the city of Oakland.

Banks of fog often roll in from the sea to envelop San Francisco in a cool gray blanket and start up an eerie chorus of many-toned foghorns; but

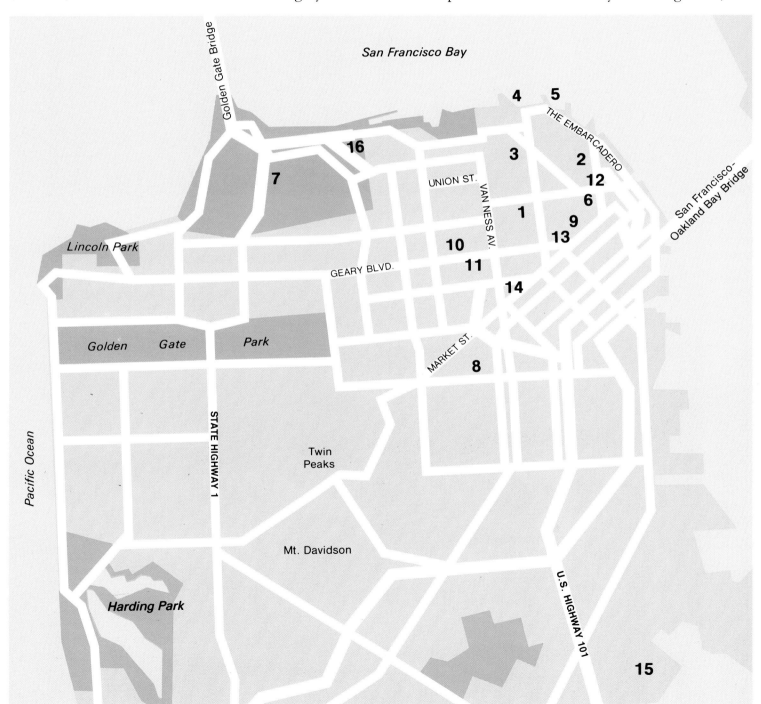

One of the world's best-known landmarks, the orange-red span of Golden Gate Bridge strides across the entrance to San Francisco Bay linking the great west coast city with the beautiful country of Marin County to the north. A walk across the 1.7-mile bridge, with the cold, swirling waters of the bay 220 feet below and with magnificent views of San Francisco's majestic skyline unfolding with each step, is an exhilarating and unforgettable experience.

Previous page: In a single block between Hyde and Leavenworth streets, Lombard Street winds down a steep slope in ten hair-raising bends flanked by pleasant houses and gardens. Known, as a result, as the "Crookedest Street in the World," this is one of San Francisco's most curious sightseeing attractions.

morning fog generally dissipates by noon, leaving the city basking in sparkling sunshine beneath clear blue skies. San Francisco is, in fact, one of America's top four sunniest cities, although temperatures remain almost constantly springlike, within the range of 70°F (21°C) in summer to 55°F (13°C) in winter. It is part of the local folklore that for every 10 miles you travel away from San Francisco, the temperature rises 10°F (5.5°C), and that if the mercury tops 70°F (21°C) in the city, local people start talking of a heat wave.

San Francisco's fogs no doubt played their part in hiding the majestic bay from European seafaring explorers, for it was not until 1776 that Spaniards traveled up from the south to found the presidio, or military garrison, of San Francisco de Asis and, in 1782, the Mission Dolores within the present-day city limits. The village of Yerba Buena ("Good Pasture"), which sprang up around the garrison, changed its name to San Francisco in 1847, after California had broken away from Mexican rule. Two years later, it was overwhelmed by a stampede of prospectors, fortune hunters, and gamblers who descended upon the "Barbary Coast" town by sea after the discovery of gold at Sutter's sawmill in the Sierra Nevada foothills to the east. Nevada's Comstock Lode gold rush of 1859 and the arrival of the transcontinental railroad ten years later also spurred San Francisco's growth, until disaster struck on April 18, 1906, when a colossal earthquake and fire killed 600 people and destroyed 28,000 buildings. It was a grim reminder that, despite its beautiful natural setting, the city lies on the awesome San Andreas Fault, which looms as an ever-present threat even today. Since 1906, however, San Francisco has recovered to become a major business center and port, constantly popular with tourists, with a population in 1980 of 678,974.

In addition to its Spanish legacy, which survives in some street names,

Left: The most distinctive building on San Francisco's skyline is the 853-foot wedge-shaped Transamerica Pyramid on Montgomery Street, which towers above nearby Jackson Square in the downtown financial district. Standing on a structural steel base, the unique 48-story building is capped by a 212-foot spire. At its foot is a pleasant half-acre park planted with redwoods.

Below: When San Francisco's 72-year-old St. Mary's Cathedral was destroyed by fire in 1962, an eye-catching ultra-modern design was adopted for the new building constructed to replace it on Cathedral Hill. Opened in 1970, the gleaming white marble new cathedral is one of the city's architectural glories.

Opposite: Flanked by marinas crowded with pleasure craft, Pier 39 juts 1,000 feet into San Francisco Bay from the Embarcadero at the foot of Beach Street. On the pier the two-level complex of timbered buildings houses a family entertainment center, specialty shops, and restaurants, a popular attraction for visitors to the waterfront area. On the southern horizon the high-rise towers of the financial district, dominated by the unmistakable Transamerica Pyramid, create one of the world's best-loved skylines.

Below: Behind the dragon-ornamented arch that spans downtown San Francisco's Grant Avenue is the fantastic 24-square-block enclave of Chinatown, the largest oriental neighborhood outside Asia. Hundreds of restaurants, and open-fronted stores selling dried snails, sharks' fins, and other exotic foods line the colorful streets.

San Francisco contains well-defined ethnic neighborhoods that enhance its international atmosphere. Chinatown, the largest Chinese quarter outside the Orient, teems with colorful shops and restaurants around Grant Avenue in the heart of downtown. Some blocks north, the Italian community has congregated around Washington Square in the North Beach district. The Japanese quarter, known as Japantown or Nihonmachi, is farther west along Post Street, not far from the superb new St. Mary's Cathedral. These districts add their own special flavor and color to San Francisco's excellent restaurant and shopping scene and contribute such delightful festivals as the Chinese New Year Celebration and the Nihonmachi Cherry Blossom Festival to the city's assortment of annual events.

San Francisco is renowned as a gourmet's paradise, with a choice of international cuisine complementing the local seafood specialties. It is also a mecca for shoppers, with elegant stores and shops lining the downtown streets around Union Square and Market Street, and fine shopping complexes at various places in the city, including the Embarcadero Center, The Anchorage, The Cannery, Ghirardelli Square, and Pier 39 in the northern waterfront area. Apart from those in the ethnic neighborhoods, there are such special shopping places as downtown Jackson Square and the charming, revitalized Cow Hollow district along Union Street.

The delightful Victorian architecture on Union Street is a special feature of San Francisco's street scene, although many nineteenth-century buildings were destroyed in the fire of 1906. Many city residents are conscious of this

architectural heritage, and beautifully restored ornate gingerbread houses brighten the districts outside the downtown area.

A different kind of nineteenth-century relic, the square-rigged steel sailing ship *Balclutha*, which once plied with cargo around the Horn, is preserved as a museum on the waterfront at Pier 43, not far from the fascinating Maritime Museum. There are many such museums with special collections throughout the city, among which the three major art museums are particularly outstanding: the M. H. de Young Memorial Museum, with the adjacent Asian Art Museum, in Golden Gate Park; the California Palace of the Legion of Honor in Lincoln Park; and the San Francisco Museum of Modern Art in the Civic Center.

The complex of buildings around the City Hall that comprises the Civic Center includes the magnificent new Performing Arts Center, which is a focal point for San Francisco's cultural life. Its component halls provide a constantly changing program of symphony concerts, opera, and ballet for the city's discerning audiences. Not surprisingly, theater thrives in this sophisticated metropolis, and several downtown playhouses offer stage plays and musicals throughout the year. Night-life entertainment is concentrated in the clubs and restaurants around Broadway in North Beach.

Although sea fishing, golf, and roller-skating occupy many sports lovers in San Francisco, there are also spectator sports and other events for the less active at Candlestick Park and at the Cow Palace on the southeastern city limits. Candlestick Park is the home of the Giants baseball and the 49ers football teams. Apart from facilities for all kinds of recreation, the city's main parks contain many special attractions. In addition to its museums, Golden Gate Park, on the west side of the city, has the renowned Japanese Tea Garden within its landscaped grounds. Harding Park, facing the ocean farther south, encloses Lake Merced, a favorite for boating and fresh-water fishing, adjoining the fine 70-acre zoo. One of the city's finest outdoor attractions, however, is the scenic walk along the 3.5-mile Golden Gate Promenade, which skirts the waterfront past the impressive Palace of Fine Arts. It offers memorable views of the magnificent Golden Gate Bridge and the bay, where the brooding outline of Alcatraz Island and its former prison looms in the distance.

Besides its delightful cable cars, San Francisco boasts an excellent system of automated trains known as the Bay Area Rapid Transit (BART), which carries passengers at speeds up to 80 miles an hour between destinations on both sides of the bay. There are also numerous cruise boats that operate from the waterfront piers and offer breath-taking views of the sparkling San Francisco skyline as they ply around the bay. Other fine views of the city can be enjoyed from the pedestrian walkway on the Golden Gate Bridge or from the road north to the lovely village of Sausalito on the bay shore. Sausalito is one of many places of interest within a day's drive north from the city; others include the Muir Woods National Monument, which preserves a magnificent stand of lofty redwoods; the dramatic Point Reyes National Seashore; and the vast vineyards of the Napa and Sonoma valleys. Across the Bay Bridge is Oakland, a city of 339,000 people, and the immense University of California campus in Berkeley. On the peninsula to the south of San Francisco are family fun parks like Marine World/Africa USA and Marriott's Great America, as well as the campus at Stanford University.

Not to be missed are trips farther afield to beautiful Lake Tahoe and Yosemite National Park, both of which are in the eastern part of the state. There is also the magnificent drive south along the Pacific Ocean to old Monterey and Carmel, set among pines and cypresses on the road to the scenic Big Sur coast, where William Randolph Hearst's castle of San Simeon stands in majestic grandeur overlooking the ocean.

"No city invites the heart to come to life as San Francisco does," wrote William Saroyan. "Arrival in San Francisco is an experience in living. . . ."

Left: San Francisco's beloved old cable cars clang up and down the city's hills offering breath-taking views of the city from every street corner, none more dramatic than the sight of the brooding island of Alcatraz far out in the bay.

Below: Despite the great destruction caused by fire after the great earthquake of 1906, thousands of beautifully ornamented Victorian houses survive in San Francisco, mostly in the districts west of Van Ness Avenue, such as the Cow Hollow neighborhood around Union Street. Behind the lovely clapboard houses on Steiner Street, the starkly contrasting high-rise office towers of the financial district are a dramatic reminder that San Francisco is also a vibrant twentieth-century city.

Savannah GEORGIA

The City of Squares

"Sir, I beg to present to you as a Christmas gift the city of Savannah, with 150 heavy guns and plenty of ammunition and also about 25,000 bales of cotton." Thus read the celebrated telegram that General William Tecumseh Sherman sent to President Abraham Lincoln shortly after having captured the South's important Atlantic port on December 22, 1864, during the Civil War. News of the burning of Atlanta by Sherman's Union forces a month earlier and of the trail of destruction they had left behind on their rapid march through Georgia to the sea had prompted the wise citizens of Savannah to surrender quickly without a fight, anxious to save their beautiful old city from the ravages of war. In doing so, these worthy people preserved one of the loveliest of all American cities for the benefit of grateful future generations.

A quintessentially southern city with a distinctive old-world atmosphere, Savannah evokes the gracious charm of a bygone age. The clip-clop of horse-drawn carriages echoes along cobblestone streets that are shaded by venerable live oak trees draped with trailing moss and are lined with elegant mansions and town houses built in the days when King Cotton reigned.

Savannah National Historic Landmark District

1 *Ships of the Sea Museum*
2 *Museum of Antique Cars*
3 *Old Cotton Exchange*
4 *City Hall*
5 *Trustees' Garden*
6 *Hampton Lillibridge House*
7 *Owens-Thomas House*
8 *Scarbrough House*
9 *Telfair Mansion*
10 *Davenport House*
11 *Juliette Gordon Low Birthplace*
12 *Green-Meldrim House*

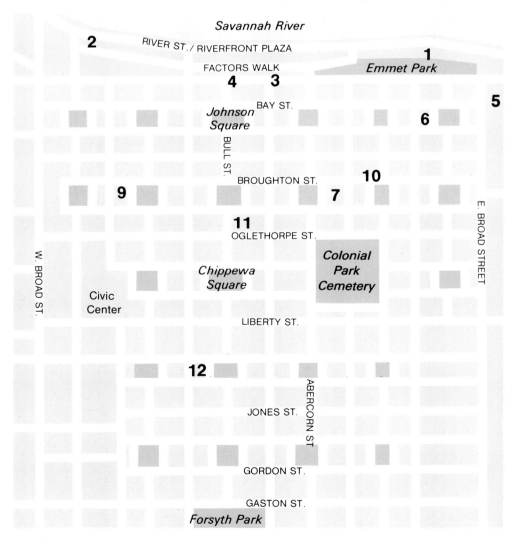

And in the many beautiful squares, blossoming azalea, dogwood, and other flowers create a riot of color to announce the spring.

Surrounded by such pleasing sights, which have helped to make tourism Savannah's second most important industry, it is perhaps hard to realize that this is also a busy modern city of more than 140,000 people; a major port – the tenth largest in the country; a manufacturing center producing . building materials, wood and paper products, chemicals, aircraft, and food; and an important military base. The prosperity that the city enjoys today is the culmination of a long, uneven story that began two-and-a-half centuries ago.

Savannah was founded on Yamacraw Bluff beside the Savannah River in 1733 when General James Oglethorpe and 120 settlers arrived from England to establish the last of the 13 English colonies in the New World, an event still commemorated in the city on February 12, Georgia Day. With military precision, Oglethorpe organized the affairs of the new community and laid out the streets in a regular pattern, with housing lots facing public squares, distinct from the conventional grid system often adopted elsewhere.

By exporting its agricultural produce, first rice and then cotton, America's "First Planned City" slowly prospered, despite occasional setbacks caused by fire and disease. But with the collapse of world cotton prices in 1895, Savannah faced economic disaster, and over the next 50 years, the once opulent mansions and town houses fell into neglect and decay. Salvation from the demolition gangs and inevitable high-rise developments seemed impossible until, in 1955, a group of farsighted and determined citizens formed the Historic Savannah Foundation and set about the daunting task of preserving the city's unique architectural heritage.

In Savannah's historic district, just a few steps from City Hall and the riverfront, is beautiful Johnson Square, the first of the squares in the plan laid out by the city's founder, James Oglethorpe. In the center of the square the monument and grave of the Revolutionary War hero Nathaniel Greene stands in tree-shaded peace.

Today, thanks to the foundation's pioneering work, 2.5 square miles of the downtown area are designated a National Historic Landmark, the largest urban-preservation district in the United States.

Perhaps the best way to see Savannah is to start where it all began, at the river, and then wander on foot through the downtown area before taking a car to explore the outlying districts. From the riverfront, too, it is possible to take a cruise around the port or along the Atlantic coast. Atmospheric Riverfront Plaza, beside the Savannah River, offers a convenient starting point for a tour. Running for nine blocks along River Street, the plaza is a lively community created by renovating cotton warehouses for use as boutiques, restaurants, discos, night clubs, and artists' studios. A sight well known to sailors from all over the world here is the *Waving Girl* statue, which stands near the river to greet passing ships. This is also the location of the famous Museum of Antique Cars and the Ships of the Sea Museum. Above River Street is Factors' Walk, with its cobbled ramps and ironwork bridges, which was once the meeting place for cotton merchants and where the Old Cotton Exchange still stands.

South of Bay Street and the impressive City Hall, the neat pattern of downtown streets and squares encloses many delights. Nearby Johnson Square is the setting every April for the colorful ethnic celebrations known as "A Night in Old Savannah," during which a taste of the traditional Chatham Artillery Punch seems to add to the enjoyment – if not sampled to excess. A more serious note is struck in this part of town by the awesome Hampton Lillibridge House on East St. Julian Street, which Savannahians claim is the city's haunted house.

For the shopper, there are the large department stores and the shops of Broughton Street and Oglethorpe Mall, while for the sightseer, a succession of interesting historic buildings and lovely squares comes into view at every street corner. Apart from the gracious homes fronting Jones, Gordon, and Gaston streets, there are many fine mansions dating from before 1820 that are open to the public. Among the most prominent are the Owens–Thomas House, the Scarborough House, the Telfair Mansion, the Isaiah Davenport House, and the birthplace at 142 Bull Street of Juliette Gordon Low, founder of the Girl Scouts of the U.S.A. Particularly interesting is the Green–Meldrim House, built in the 1850s and used by General Sherman as his headquarters during his occupation of the city.

The Victorian District, Savannah's first suburb, is also worth a visit. Located just south of Forsyth Square, this neighborhood of late nineteenth-century homes of outstanding architectural interest is undergoing restoration and boasts such gems as the lovely King–Tisdell Cottage. From here, a ride along Victory Drive, lined with palm trees and renowned for its stately mansions and blooming azaleas, offers a tempting foretaste of the beautiful country houses and plantations awaiting discovery in the rural areas outside the city. One of these is the magnificent Wormsloe plantation, a fortified house on the Isle of Hope dating from the early eighteenth century.

Among the maze of islands, marshes, and river channels on this seaward side of Savannah, there are many small picturesque communities, such as the shrimping port of Thunderbolt, to fascinate the visitor. And along the Savannah River, three old forts – Jackson, Pulaski, and Screven – remain as brooding reminders of the days when they served to defend the city and port from attack from the sea. Fort Screven, the most easterly, faces the ocean on Tybee Island, whose superb beaches provide recreation and sea breezes for Savannahians throughout the year.

Although known simply to some as the "City of Squares," Savannah, it could be argued, has so much to offer that another nickname, "The Magnetic City," seems to capture far more precisely its considerable appeal.

Above: The Waving Girl *statue on Savannah's riverfront is a tribute to Florence Martus, a local citizen who between 1887 and 1931 greeted every ship that sailed up the river to dock in Savannah, and whose friendly waves were acknowledged with the blast of the ship's horn.*

Left: A dignified reminder of the days when Savannah was the world's leading cotton port, the 1887 Cotton Exchange stands on East Bay Street close to the riverfront, linked to the former wharves by the ramps and bridges of Factors' Walk. The building now houses a masonic lodge.*

Seattle WASHINGTON

The Emerald City

To help visitors – and, no doubt, some residents – find their way around downtown Seattle, some irreverent wag coined a mnemonic from the first letters of the east–west street names that goes "Jesus Christ Made Seattle Under Protest." While this may help you to discover roughly where you are in relation to Jefferson and James streets, Cherry and Columbia, Marion and Madison, Spring and Seneca, University and Union, and Pike and Pine, it does little for Seattle's well-deserved reputation as one of America's most attractive and livable cities. In any case, for a broad overview of the city's layout, you cannot beat a ride to the top of its most famous landmark, the 607-foot (185-m) Space Needle, which towers above the center-city streets. From the observation deck or restaurants 500 feet (153 m) above ground, there are breath-taking vistas for miles around, with the great port city – its population of some 495,000 making it the largest city in Washington State – spread out below.

Hugging its seven low hills, Seattle occupies a narrow isthmus between the maze of islands and channels that make up Puget Sound on the west and the fresh-water expanse of Lake Washington on the east. North of downtown, a ship canal connecting these stretches of water cuts across the city, while Elliott Bay bulges deeply into downtown's west shoreline to form a fine natural harbor that bustles with ships of every description. On the eastern horizon, the forested slopes and snow-capped peaks of the Cascade Range raise a dramatic backdrop of magnificent scenery behind the "Emerald City," the gem of the Pacific Northwest.

Although Russian fur traders and British and Spanish explorers had passed through the area in previous centuries, it was not until 1851 that a band of settlers established a community first at Alki Point and then on Elliott Bay, where they named their cluster of huts after the local Indian chief, Sealth. The lumber that they cut from the thickly forested slopes for shipment to San Francisco was slid down the steep bluff to Henry Yesler's sawmill on the water's edge along a muddy track known as Skid Road, now Yesler Way in the heart of modern Seattle. With foresight, a civic leader named Asa Mercer shipped in unmarried women from the east as potential wives for the local lumberjacks, and the community grew. Some 20,000 people were living in the city in 1889 when it suddenly burned to the ground. Rebuilt in brick, the old downtown area survives as today's historic district of Pioneer Square.

During the 1890s, Seattle's luck changed. In 1893, the railroad finally arrived, and four years later, a ship docked in the harbor with the first cargo of gold from Alaska. During the ensuing years, Seattle boomed as the port gateway to the Alaska and Yukon gold mines, its streets filled with prospectors, fortune seekers, and the usual riffraff of raw frontier towns. But the opening of the Panama Canal in 1915 and the establishment of the Boeing aircraft factory in Seattle the following year opened up new trading and manufacturing avenues. Seattle is now a major international port handling considerable trade with Alaska, the Orient, and Europe and is the Northwest's main distribution and commercial hub and a flourishing center for tourism. Although in recent years the aircraft industry has broadened into the manufacture of space vehicles and missiles, Seattle suffered economic hardship during the Great Depression and the 1960s because of

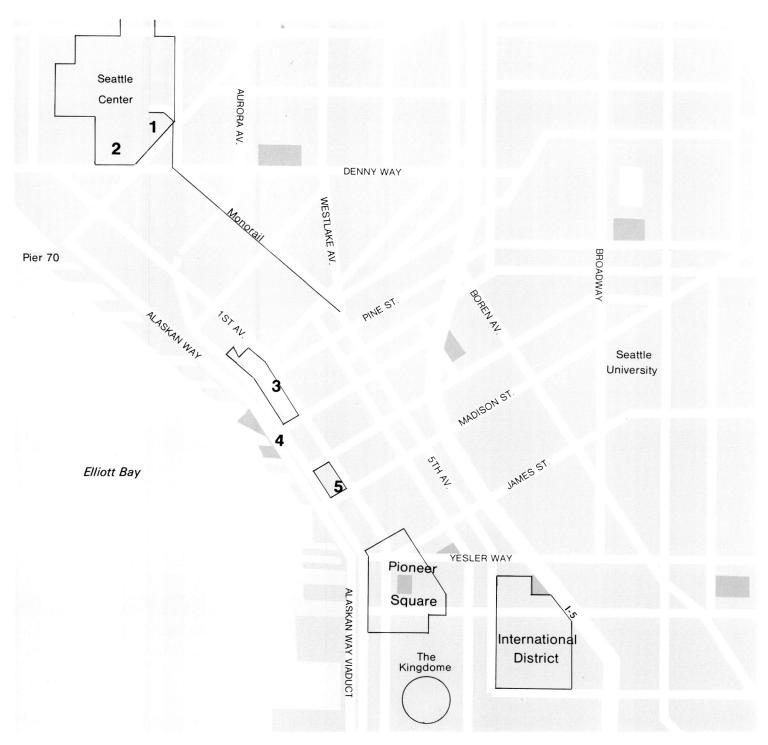

its overdependence on one major industry, and Skid Road – or, as we now say, Skid Row – became synonymous with urban deprivation.

The World's Fair held in Seattle in 1962 gave the city both a tremendous psychological boost and a legacy of cultural institutions that still thrive at the fair's site, known as Seattle Center. Its beautifully landscaped 74 acres enclose a complex of entertainment and leisure facilities beneath the shadow of the towering Space Needle. Among the highlights are the magnificent Pacific Science Center, where you can experience the latest developments in science at first hand; the Seattle Art Museum Pavilion, with its collection of paintings by northwestern artists; the Opera House, home of the city's symphony orchestra and opera and ballet companies; and the Bagley Wright Theater, where the Seattle Repertory Theater performs. The center also offers popular entertainment in the Coliseum, sports events in the Arena, shops and restaurants in Center House, thrilling rides in the amusement park, and many other attractions.

Downtown Seattle
1 Space Needle
2 Pacific Science Center
3 Pike Place Market
4 Waterfront Park
5 Waterfront Place

Overleaf: Between Seattle Center, the cultural and entertainment hub of the city, where the famous Space Needle is a prominent landmark, and the distant low rounded outline of the Kingdome sports arena, the skyscrapers of Seattle's financial and government district present an impressive skyline.

For thrilling adventures in the fascinating world of science, the hands-on exhibits in the Pacific Science Center in Seattle is an unbeatable experience. This learning-by-doing educational playground is set in beautiful landscaped grounds in Seattle Center.

From Seattle Center, a 90-second ride on the futuristic Monorail takes you to the downtown shopping, business, and government district around Westlake Mall, where modern office and hotel towers puncture the skyline. Within walking distance are the rehabilitated historic Pike Place Market – with its kaleidoscope of colorful stalls selling fresh seafood, fruit and vegetables, and jewelry and crafts – and the new neighborhood of restored buildings, offices, and shops known as Waterfront Place. Some blocks south, bordering Yesler Way, the historic district of Pioneer Square bustles with some of the city's finest bistros, jazz clubs, and boutiques in the Victorian brick buildings constructed one level above the former city center after the fire of 1889. Underground tours now provide visitors with a fascinating glimpse of the streets and shops that existed here before the fire. East of here is the fascinating International District, another busy neighborhood of craft shops and restaurants where the Chinese, Japanese, Filipino, and Indochinese communities are concentrated.

In the same area, Seattle's major sports arena, the superb Kingdome, seats up to 65,000 spectators under its immense concrete roof. The stadium hosts Seahawks football, Sounders soccer, Mariners baseball, and Super-Sonics basketball, in addition to trade shows, conventions, and other events. Other sports are held elsewhere in the city, including auto racing at the Seattle International Raceway and horse racing at Longacres Racetrack.

From Pioneer Square, you can take an enjoyable ride in a streetcar on Alaskan Way – the entire length of the busy waterfront – as far north as Pier 70, near Seattle Center. Along the way are the piers where the bobbing ferries and cruise boats load up with passengers, and Waterfront Park, between Piers 57 and 61, where the excellent Seattle Aquarium and Omnidome film theater offer fascinating glimpses of life in the sea.

Scattered throughout the city are many attractive parks, among them Volunteer Park, which contains the outstanding Seattle Art Museum; Woodland Park, with its highly acclaimed zoo; and huge Washington Park, with its arboretum and Japanese Garden, not far from the excellent Museum of History and Industry. Seattle also has several unusual features, such as the floating concrete bridges across Lake Washington and the locks and salmon ladder along the Lake Eashington Ship Canal.

Interesting places to visit abound near Seattle, which is located within easy reach of the scenic wonderland of the Cascade Range and Mounts Rainier, Baker, and St. Helens, and the mountains, coastline and eerie temperate rain forests of Olympic National Park on the Olympic Peninsula. Cruises around Puget Sound, to the San Juan Islands – between Puget Sound and Canada's Vancouver Island – and as far north as Victoria and Vancouver in Canada are also a reminder that Seattle is the gateway city to America's Pacific Northwest.

Pioneer Square, a 20-block historic district south of downtown Seattle, is a delightful area of Victorian brick and stone buildings now housing fine boutiques, excellent restaurants, and swinging jazz clubs. The area was constructed on top of the ashes of the former city center, founded in 1852, which was devastated by the great fire of 1889. Today, fascinating tours take visitors through the five-block area one level below ground, where remnants of the city's first buildings survive intact.

Washington DISTRICT OF COLUMBIA

America's Capital

In 1789, eight years after the victory over the British in the Revolutionary War, General George Washington was elected first president of the new republic of the United States. When he arrived for his inauguration in New York City, which was then the nation's capital, his majestic bearing and finery prompted one waggish senator to observe, "I fear we may have exchanged George III for George I." Despite the quip, Washington was no aloof monarch, and he was soon busily engaged in the task of planning and building a new permanent national capital, the great city that now bears his name and occupies the federal District of Columbia (D.C.). One of the most gracious and beautiful cities in the world, Washington, D.C., plays host every year to some 15 million visitors who come to admire its fine public buildings and imposing monuments and to enjoy its many other attractions.

The location of the city on the Potomac River was the result of a political compromise between the wishes of the northern and the southern states, the actual site just north of the junction of the Potomac and Anacostia rivers being chosen in 1791 by Washington himself. The new capital was to occupy a 100-square-mile area measuring 10 miles by 10 miles, with its corners aligned to face north, south, east, and west. About 69 square miles for the plan were acquired from Maryland on the east bank of the Potomac, including the river port of Georgetown, and the

Washington D.C.
1 *United States Capitol*
2 *Supreme Court*
3 *Library of Congress*
4 *Washington Monument*
5 *White House*
6 *Lincoln Memorial*
7 *Jefferson Memorial*
8 *Smithsonian Institution*
9 *National Air and Space Museum*
10 *National Museum of History and Technology*
11 *National Museum of Natural History*
12 *National Gallery of Art*
13 *Ford's Theater*
14 *Department of State*
15 *John F. Kennedy Center*
16 *Vietnam Veterans Memorial*

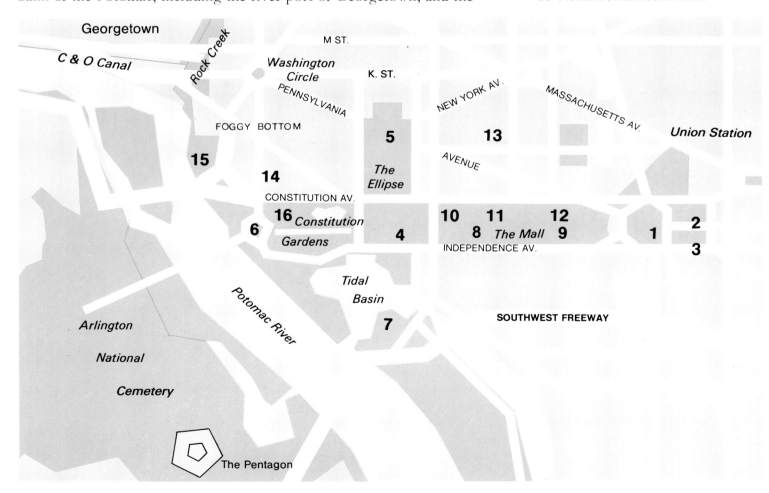

remaining 31 from Virginia on the west bank.

At the invitation of the president, the French engineer Major Pierre Charles L'Enfant devised an impressive plan for the city covering a central area of some 10 square miles. It incorporated a rectangular grid of streets, overlaid with a pattern of broad avenues radiating diagonally from evenly spaced squares and circles. Unfortunately, L'Enfant was fired within the year, after some controversy over the sale of building lots, and during the following decades, the work progressed slowly and some changes were made to his plan. To make matters worse, the British attacked and burned much of the new city during the War of 1812, and although many improvements were made after the Civil War, it was not until the turn of the century that L'Enfant's scheme was revised and used as the basis for the elegant city we see today.

Although without towering skyscrapers – city ordinances limit buildings to 13 stories – Washington is packed with impressive government buildings, cultural institutions, monuments, and statues that give it an air of majestic dignity and sophistication appropriate to a great capital city. It is perhaps easy to forget that behind this glamorous facade, Washington is just like any other American city, with its elegant shops, its restaurants and theaters, its recreational and sports facilities, its green parks and city squares, and, of course, its poorer districts and urban problems. Yet perhaps more than any other American city, Washington is particularly well equipped, with its broad boulevards and numerous squares, for the succession of lively, colorful festivals and parades that enliven it throughout the year, such varied spectacles as the Chinese New Year and Cherry Blossom festivals, the impressive Fourth of July Parade, and the Christmastime Pageant of Peace.

At the east end of the Mall in Washington, D.C., impressive bronze monuments and statues stand before the majestic United States Capitol, one of the world's best-known buildings. Constructed between 1793 and 1827 according to a basic plan by D. William Thornton of the West Indies, the building was considerably added to over the years, with the present cast-iron-framed dome designed by Thomas U. Walter completed in 1865. Fascinating tours through the huge building guide visitors through the impressive Rotunda, Statuary Hall, House of Representatives, Senate, and Crypt.

Government is, of course, Washington's main business, although some "clean" high-technology and light industries and research establishments have recently been set up in the surrounding areas. Tourism, too, is of major importance, bringing in millions of visitors to swell the resident population, which in 1980 numbered around 637,000, with some 3 million in the metropolitan area.

Locating addresses and places of interest in Washington becomes simpler when you realize that the city is divided into geographical quadrants – N.W., N.E., S.W., and S.E. – centered on the unmistakable Capitol, around which the north–south streets are designated by numbers and the east–west streets by letters (C to V, with no J, in the central area). Most of the diagonal avenues, which interconnect at the circles, are named after states in the Union. Although the city is best enjoyed by strolling around it, there is a new Metro subway system for easy journeys to the more distant attractions.

The focal point for sightseeing in Washington is the cluster of impressive buildings and monuments around the broad sweep of grassy parkland in the form of a cross that lies between the Potomac River and the Capitol. At its center, on a knoll, rises the elegant Washington Monument, a 555-foot (169-m) marble obelisk with an observation deck at the top that affords breath-taking panoramas of the city. More than 1 mile to the east, the imposing white Capitol, crowned with its huge dome, stands on a low hill at the end of the wide grassy Mall – the staff of the cross – presiding over the magnificent cityscape before it. The balancing wings on each side of the central Rotunda house the Senate and the House of Representatives. Behind the Capitol, in separate buildings, stand the Supreme Court and the Library of Congress.

On the northern arm of the cross, between lovely Lafayette Square and the grassy expanse of the Ellipse, is the stately White House, the official residence of the president of the United States and one of the world's best-known and most beautiful mansions. Completed in 1800 after a contest to find a suitable design, it was burned down by the British in 1814, and then restored and decorated in white paint to hide the smoke marks – hence its name. Five of the rooms in its elegant interior, including the magnificent East Room, are open to the public.

West of the Washington Monument, beyond Constitution Gardens and the new Vietnam Veterans Memorial, the long Reflecting Pool mirrors the austere shape of the eloquently moving Lincoln Memorial, an impressive Greek-style temple near the Potomac River that houses a massive seated figure of the sixteenth president. Across the waters of the Tidal Basin, where the celebrated cherry trees burst into a dazzling display of pink blossoms every spring, the beautiful Jefferson Memorial echoes the domed classical circular design that Thomas Jefferson favoured in his own architectural work.

Flanking the Mall between the Washington Monument and the Capitol are many of the city's great cultural institutions. On the south side, the unmistakable red building popularly known as "The Castle" houses part of the world-famous Smithsonian Institution, which administers many of Washington's museums, art galleries, and research institutes, including the adjacent Hirshhorn Museum, with its art collections; the National Air and Space Museum; and, across the Mall, the National Museum of History and Technology, and the National Museum of Natural History. Also on the north side of the Mall is the world-renowned National Gallery of Art, with its stunning East Building designed by I. M. Pei.

Behind these famous institutions, along Pennsylvania and Constitution avenues to the north of the Mall and Independence Avenue to the south, are many impressive government buildings that are worth seeing on a walk around the area. Among them is the Old Post Office building and clock tower on Pennsylvania Avenue, now renovated to contain shops, res-

taurants, and a performing-arts center in its 10-story atrium, known as the Pavilion. A walk north of Pennsylvania Avenue reveals other interesting places in the downtown business and shopping district. Here, for example, you will find the famous Ford's Theater, where Abraham Lincoln was shot, and, across the street, the house where he died; the artists' quarter known as the Tricorne; and the colorful Chinatown neighborhood, next to the prestigious new Convention Center.

Northwest along Massachusetts Avenue, the hub of streets formed by Dupont Circle leads to the many sightseeing attractions that are concen-

Standing on beautiful grounds between the Ellipse and the landscaped gardens of Lafayette Square, the lovely White House has been the official residence of every president of the United States except George Washington. Designed by the Irish-American architect James Hoban, the house has undergone many additions and changes since the foundations were laid in 1792. Today, visitors may tour the impressive interior.

Every spring hundreds of Japanese cherry
trees, donated to Washington by the city of
Tokyo in 1912, burst into clouds of soft pink
blossom around the Tidal Basin, seemingly
pierced by the gleaming white shaft of the
Washington Monument that rises from the
Mall beyond. Dedicated to the memory of the
nation's first president in 1885, the elegant,
marble-clad structure was built over a period
of stops and starts between 1848 and 1884.

trated in the city's northwestern districts. Among them, Connecticut
Avenue is renowned for its fine stores, specialty shops, and art galleries. On
Massachusetts Avenue are the famous Embassy Row – where many of the
foreign embassies are located – the Islamic Center, and the magnificent
Washington National Cathedral. New Hampshire Avenue leads from
Dupont Circle to the Foggy Bottom district by the Potomac, among whose
streets you will find George Washington University and, on the river, the
famous Watergate apartment and shopping complex and the superb John F.
Kennedy Center, the city's major performing-arts complex and home of the
National Symphony Orchestra and the Washington Opera.

Winding through its wooded ravine to the Potomac, lovely Rock Creek
Park cuts across the northwestern districts on the edge of the beautiful old

Right: The lovely Jefferson Memorial stands in solitary, majestic splendor beside the Tidal Basin, a domed and colonnaded structure in the classical style so close to the third president's heart. Nearby, three bridges carry traffic and Metrorail trains across the Potomac River between the city and neighboring state of Virginia, where the Washington National Airport is located.

Below: Brilliantly illuminated by natural daylight filtering through the huge skylight above, the marvelous collection of contemporary art exhibits in the superb East Building of the National Gallery of Art includes a giant hanging mobile by Alexander Calder. The 7-story building is an architectural masterpiece designed in 1978 by the internationally renowned architect I. M. Pei.

On the evening of April 14, 1865, President Abraham Lincoln was fatally shot as he sat in a box with his wife watching a play at Ford's Theater in downtown Washington. Restored to how it was on that fateful night, though still in use, the theater now contains a downstairs museum displaying items associated with Lincoln and his assassin, John Wilkes Booth.

river port of Georgetown. Now a fashionable residential district, bustling with shopping and night-life activity, Georgetown takes you back in time as you wander through its shady cobblestone streets lined with beautiful brick homes. Here you can visit Washington's oldest house, the Old Stone House, and Georgetown University, and ramble on the tow path along the historic Chesapeake and Ohio Canal. You can also browse among the fine shops on Wisconsin Avenue and M Street and in the well-known Georgetown Park Mall and Prospect Place shopping centers.

Across the Potomac, the 31 square miles of Virginia that were earmarked by George Washington for the District of Columbia were returned to the state in 1846. In this area is Arlington National Cemetery, where many of the nation's honored dead are buried, including John and Robert Kennedy. The cemetery also contains beautiful Arlington House, the home of Robert E. Lee before the Civil War. Nearby are the famous Iwo Jima Monument, which commemorates the World War II action, and the huge Pentagon, headquarters of the Department of Defense.

Many special places of interest are scattered throughout other areas of Washington. In the eastern parts of the city are the dramatic National Shrine of the Immaculate Conception, with its mosaic dome and tall bell tower, the largest Roman Catholic church in the country; Kenilworth aquatic gardens, by the Anacostia River; and the football fans' mecca, Robert F. Kennedy Stadium, home of the mighty Redskins.

In the surrounding districts of Virginia and Maryland are numerous spots that are worth a visit. As well as amusement parks like Kings Dominion in Virginia and Wild World in Maryland, the nearby area boast many historic sites, including the lovely old towns of Alexandria and Fredericksburg in Virginia. In this area, too, are former plantations like Woodlawn, adjacent to George Washington's own beloved mansion, Mount Vernon, the high point of any excursion out of the city he founded.

Index